THEOLOGICAL INVESTIGATIONS

Volume XXIII

THEOLOGICAL INVESTIGATIONS

VOLUME XXIII
FINAL WRITINGS

by

KARL RAHNER

Translated by

JOSEPH DONCEEL, S.J.
and **HUGH M. RILEY**

CROSSROAD • NEW YORK

1992

The Crossroad Publishing Company
370 Lexington Avenue, New York, NY 10017

Chapters 1 to 7 have been translated by Hugh M. Riley from
Schriften zur Theologie 15: Wissenschaft und christlicher Glaube
© Copyright 1983 by Benziger Verlag
Zürich, Einsiedeln, Köln

Chapters 8 to 19 have been translated by Joseph Donceel, S.J., from
Schriften zur Theologie 16: Humane Gesellschaft und Kirche von Morgen
© Copyright 1984 by Benziger Verlag
Zürich, Einsiedeln, Köln

This translation copyright © 1992 by The Crossroad Publishing Company

Printed in the United States of America

Library of Congress Catalog Card Number: 61-8189
ISBN 0-8245-1165-4

CONTENTS

PART ONE *Christian Life*

PART TWO *The Society of Jesus*

PART THREE *Piety*

v

PART FOUR *Sacraments*

PART ONE

Christian Life

1

ANXIETY AND CHRISTIAN TRUST IN THEOLOGICAL PERSPECTIVE

Our point of departure will be the customary distinction between fear and anxiety. Fear refers to a definite object that we know and that appears threatening to us. Thus fear is a relationship between the conscious subject and a specific, "categorical" object within consciousness.

THE THEOLOGICAL CONNECTION
BETWEEN ANXIETY AND FEAR

At this point, of course, the theologian might ask whether one can "fear" God, whether the expression "the fear of God" and similar ones are correct or whether they are used inaccurately. Since the word and the concept "God" occupy a definite, individual place within our consciousness and thus understandably provoke feelings of fear and awe, the expression "the fear of God" can of course be readily understood and its use is justified. However, if we proceed from the understanding that "God" does not really mean a particular object viewed individually which in the ordinary way is present alongside other individual contents of our consciousness and the objects presumed to be there, but rather that "God" means a reality that is totally unique, incommensurable, all-encompassing but itself never encompassable, already antecedent to every individual specification, a reality that implies an impenetrable mystery, it is understandable that the expressions "fear of God" and "awe of God" can be used only in a terminology that is highly inaccurate.

3

If we understand it in this way, this reality of God (despite the word *God*) is not a reality that comes to rest as an individual object within our conceptual systems. The subject's original relationship to God does not come about in the otherwise usual manner of knowing an object (Australia, for example), but rather it is present as spirit and freedom in the human being's original transcendentality which underlies all individual knowledge as the condition which makes this knowledge possible. So this relationship is one in respect to which the word and the concept "God" within our consciousness can only mean a subsequent secondary representation standing for what is originally meant. Only in a terminology that is highly inaccurate can one speak of "fear of God" or "awe of God." The expression "anxiety of God" would actually be more accurate, but this expression is not common and could be introduced only with difficulty.

But if theology has to treat of anxiety and fear, and when it does the two words have to be distinguished, and if theology treats of God and the human being's relationship to God, then strictly speaking it is obliged to speak of anxiety and not of fear. One could even go so far as to say that when the expression "fear of God" is used, and this expression is taken in a really strict sense rather than in a broad and imprecise sense, then we are talking about a God who does not even exist. In the strict sense of the word one can really fear only an idol which from the outset is viewed as a particular, albeit extremely threatening individual reality existing along with many others that are equally justified.

It is of course annoying and impractical that we cannot really use the expression "anxiety of God," since in the ordinary use of language anxiety is understood as something that has to do more or less with a nameless and bewildering terror of an interiorly destructive nature. But of course this should have nothing to do with anxiety before God (if we may use such an expression). Nor can we get around this linguistic difficulty by speaking merely of awe, adoration, a feeling of absolute dependence, submission, and so on. It is not as though words like these that characterize the relationship human beings are supposed to have to God were not justified or that they ought to be eliminated in favor of the word *anxiety*. All of them are justified and perhaps, too, in the ordinary way of speaking about human beings' relationship to God, they are more readily understood and more useful for proclamation. However, since the word *anxiety* does exist, and since the thing that is meant by this word and that has to be described more exactly also exists, the question whether and how this anxiety itself, properly understood, is relevant to those dimensions of the human being that are the concern of Christian faith and theology is an indispensable one.

Necessary Distinctions between Fear and Anxiety

But before delving deeper into this question we have to consider further what we said at the beginning. We have made a distinction between "categorical" fear and "objectless transcendental" anxiety. There are transcendental conditions for the possibility of knowledge (and of freedom), which are nonobjective and therefore conscious in a way that can be overlooked. The question can be raised as to whether and in what way this spiritual transcendentality of the human being, without its being actualized by being grasped as a particular object, can be conscious for itself alone in mystical states, in inward communion or in some other way; whether and how the empty, unlimited consciousness, oriented to being as such (or to "nothingness") can be present to itself alone. This question will not be dealt with here. But then we must presuppose and say — and we have every right to do this — that in the normal case of everyday consciousness transcendental anxiety exists in a synthesis with an individual conscious object of fear.

If for Kant concrete sense perception and the abstract concept always and of necessity belong together, if for Thomas Aquinas a particular intellectual concept cannot be known except in a *conversio ad phantasma*, then the same holds true for the relationship between anxiety and fear. Anxiety is experienced only in a synthesis with fear (at least in the ordinary case, and that is the only one we want to talk about here). In the individual case the relationship between the two realities is quite varied. A person can have fear without adverting in a really reflexive way to the fundamental condition of existence with its characteristic anxiety which this fear actually implies. Even when vegetables are being sold in a market, the transcendentally necessary logic is more or less present and operative even though the woman selling the vegetables does not "notice" it and has never even heard of such a thing. And conversely, in an experience of fear that exists without being reflected upon, the bottomless insecurity of existence as such can occupy the consciousness so completely and nameless anxiety can spread so far that one no longer even notices what the original source of the anxiety was. These variations of the more precise relationship between fear and anxiety in their differences and their unity are subjects of psychology and existential philosophy and not so much the tasks of theology.

Anxiety Concerning Salvation or the Ultimate Security of Existence before God?

If theologians are to speak of anxiety and have of course to put this in relationship to God, they are confronted with a difficult situation. To people today it seems obvious beyond dispute that one may not and need not have any anxiety before God. They think that anxiety before God is inherently an improper, foolishly pagan perversion of the human being's relationship to God. They perceive God (even though this perception is not necessarily justified) as the one who gives the ultimate guarantee that existential anxiety is unnecessary. On the other hand, religious people, relying on Scripture, find it a matter of course to speak of the holy fear of God, of working out their salvation in fear and trembling, of the fear of the Lord that is the beginning of wisdom. They view the overcoming of anxiety about salvation and of sinfulness and mortality as precisely the achievement of that faith which alone saves. And so they presume that this anxiety about salvation is always present in human beings who do not sinfully repress the truth of their existence.

Are we, then, threatened by God in such a way that we would have to have anxiety before him? The average, everyday Christian whose mental makeup is not overly complicated will be of the opinion that God can only be threatening if one sins. However, good-living Christians avoid sin and so they do not have to have any anxiety before God. In respect to definite individual sins, fear before God is, then, a specific matter that can actually be cleared up by the simple expedient of contrition and the avoidance of sin in the future. But this, then, is the peace with God that excludes anxiety and fear. Therefore spasms of fear and anxiety are to be struggled against; it is possible to overcome them over and over again by courageous trust in God and in one's own integrity and to dismiss them from one's consciousness. In this way the ordinary Christian could virtually arrive at that state of mind which is obvious from the outset to secular people today; namely, that before God, if he exists, there is no need to have any anxiety because God is, after all, by definition, the guarantee of the ultimate security of existence. How can we find a way out of this awkward terminology and the obscurity of the matter itself?

EXISTENTIELL INSECURITY AND
THE EXPERIENCE OF CONTINGENCY AS THE REASON
FOR THE EXISTENTIAL ANXIETY OF HUMAN BEINGS

We proceed on the assumption that human beings experience an ultimate insecurity of their reality, of their existence. This insecurity of existence as such need not necessarily be understood as something negative. It can initially be perceived as simply a fact that is so universal and inevitable that there is nothing particularly surprising about it. We do not originate from ourselves. We have had a beginning and we did not establish and decide this beginning ourselves. We are constantly thrown back upon and dependent upon realities, situations, and helps that are not our own and that are not ours to dispose of as we see fit. We are proceeding toward an end that we ourselves cannot determine (not even by suicide). As free agents we would like to take up this or that position toward everything in our lives. But this "everything" has not been chosen by us; rather, it is given to us and taken from us without our being consulted. We are people who have been put here without being consulted, dependent people who came from somewhere but who are not able to determine this origin and future ourselves. Even the ultimate free subjectivity is experienced as something that is not self-evident, something that is limited, that functions on the basis of elements outside ourselves, that cannot achieve pure reflection, that is condemned to itself. In brief, human beings experience themselves as those who are not secure in themselves alone, as beings who are not self-evident.

Human beings can repress this experience. People can forget this contingency in the face of the variety of things that make up their day-to-day life experience right up to their highest ideals, those, however, that they themselves have reflected upon. But the experience is there. It constantly thrusts itself forward. This experience of contingency can certainly be given different reflexive interpretations. It can be interpreted as the experience of createdness; atheistic philosophies can give it some other name. But it is there and it inexorably bears the character of what may be called anxiety in distinction to fear. This anxiety need not be a particular, physiologically and psychologically determinable individual event, and it cannot be such in its proper nature as distinct from its objectified reflection. As such it need not even be reflected upon or judged as something negative for reflection. It is entirely possible for human beings to flee into the routine of everyday life and to brush aside the desire of this anxiety to manifest itself as reprehensible depression, as a mental quirk. They are able to live with this anxiety in a happy-go-lucky way and it is possible that they will not even find a word for it.

In the light of a Christian anthropology of free subjects who as such are not only capable of performing this or that act in the objective order but also have free disposition over themselves in a radical way oriented to ultimate validity, we must say that this continuing condition of createdness, this origin of our existence from elements not at our disposal, and the anxiety that this implies, can exist either in the form of something merely given antecedently for freedom (for those who do not have the use of reason) or in the form of acceptance by freedom (usually without theoretical reflection) or in the form of rejection, of protest on the part of freedom. In the light of traditional ontology (which cannot be presented here) and Christian optimism motivated by the divine revelation of salvation, we may say that in general human beings accept themselves in this origin that is not at their disposal, despite all individual protests and despite the moral and objective shortcomings and individual contradictions to their nature (sins as distinct from "sin") which give these protests their concrete form, and that they freely accept the final existential anxiety that this also implies. And so we may say that they "are in agreement with themselves and satisfied."

But even then their existential anxiety is not simply removed. Even then their origin and their standpoint is not at their disposal. But their anxiety is in a state (difficult to describe because it is quite common) of release; it is a matter of course; it takes the form of an inner conviction, requiring no additional reflection, that we will not fall even though we are not holding on tightly. It is the conviction that the things that are not at our disposal and not reflected upon are ultimately more worthy of our trust than all of our clear calculations, that the obscure origin is more self-evident than what we think we can penetrate with our knowledge, that ultimately it is not better and more secure if we think that we alone should have free disposal of ourselves.

EXISTENCE IN ANXIETY AND
EXISTENTIAL FUNDAMENTALS OF CHRISTIAN TRUST

This is not the place to give a more detailed description of what has just been said and to transpose it into theological concepts with their numerous differentiations. We shall confine ourselves to the following statement. If our origin, which is not at our disposal, is the result of the creative act of the God who is and will always remains incomprehensible, who (both in fact and in freely given grace) sets us on a course whose goal is immediacy to himself (known as grace and the beatific vision), this fundamental redemptive acceptance of our existence in anxiety can develop into three fundamental Christian existential components: faith, hope, and love.

We cannot and need not occupy ourselves here with the question whether and how these three basic conditions are to be distinguished, or whether and how under different aspects they always mean one and the same totality of the redemptive acceptance of existence (as it is established by God in grace). If we consider the ordinary unity of these three basic acts within the single totality of the realization of existence, without thereby denying that a real distinction can be made among these three basic existential acts in the process of the realization of existence (the process of justification), we can also view this single totality under the aspect of hope; then we can describe this single totality as a final, comprehensive trust in this existence which is given anterior to freedom, which freedom cannot dispose of as it sees fit, and therefore which is an existence in anxiety.

This trust as understood here is not trust that we place in this or that individual element *in* our existence that might appear to us as something we can hold onto. Rather, it is a free acquiescence in existence in its totality and oneness in which the subject as such assumes the risk of self-abandonment. As we have already said, this single basic act of existence known as trust is not of course something that ordinarily happens in the isolation of mystical experience as such. Rather, it is accomplished by turning to the concrete tasks that are posed to freedom in dealing with individual material, social, and historical realities. These three aspects of our realities, as we have them in the world, for their part condition one another reciprocally, but this does not cause them to lose their individual identities. It follows obviously from this, by the way, that faith and love (despite their movement in the direction of the incomprehensible infinity of God as he is in himself) are realized in historical encounters which reach their unsurpassable culmination in the believing and loving human being's relationship to Jesus Christ.

TRUST AND DESPAIR AS ACTS OF HUMAN FREEDOM

The ("transcendental") trust that exists in union with an anxiety that is just as aprioristic must be described in further detail. As we have already said, traditional ontology (which views evil as a deficiency of being and not as another kind of being in a Manichaean duality, although this Manichaeism is a constant threat in the form of a latent reality that is not reflected upon) and Christian optimism (which proclaims the eschatological victory of God's love in the consummation of his kingdom and which in hope, and not in theoretical analysis, transcends all the limits that can be possibly be placed upon it) do not view human freedom as something that is confronted by two equally valid, albeit radically opposed possibilities. Furthermore, they do not view this freedom as something that would choose between two such radically opposed possibilities without its being for its part encompassed by the free sovereignty of God, who wills the good, a thing which in no way detracts from this freedom. Nor should one say that the sovereign and free God would necessarily require a hell so that both human freedom and the manifest character of God's justice might be upheld. But despite this, Christians must not be so presumptuous as to construct in theory or in fact a system for their existence which would absolutely exclude the possibility of saying a no to God which would mean eternal loss. Therefore, one must always allow for the possibility that the insecurity of existence over which we have no control and which implies anxiety might also lead to a free protest against this existence, and that the primordial trust as described, having been freely rejected, one might choose despair rather than trust.

What name we should give to this despair, the ways in which it appears, whether tacit or overt, unreflected or systematized, the wide variety of forms it assumes in its involvement with history which is necessary for it, too (forms that perhaps go by quite different names and only with great difficulty can be recognized as expressions of a final, free, culpable despair) — all of these things cannot be discussed here. We must leave this to a descriptive psychology that will have to try at least indirectly to detect this despair which can be the object of this psychology only to a limited degree because this despair as such is itself not an individual object within consciousness but rather an experience of the totality of existence as such.

The ultimate fundamental condition of existence (this primordial trust or this final despair) can be reflected upon to a certain degree; then it also becomes present in the consciousness as a particular quasi-categorical object, whereby, however, the really basic existentiell attitude and its quasi-categorical objective reality need not coincide, but rather they can contradict one another (all of which is the presupposition for the impossibility of our "judging" ourselves of which Scripture speaks). And so it is quite possible, for example, for people to construct a theoretical system of the absurdity of existence, while at the same time being in their real fundamental condition hoping and trusting persons who do not even notice the contradiction between their innermost realization of existence and their reflexive system of existence.

The converse is also possible. In their theoretical reflection and on the level of the objective reality of their actions, people think that they must have trust and that they do, in fact, have trust, while in truth their innermost fundamental condition is one of sheer despair, which of course can then assume the widest variety of forms. This implies that it is not possible for concrete individual human beings to have a reflexive certainty concerning the existence of this primordial trust.

In theological terms this means that human beings (according to the Council of Trent) cannot be absolutely certain whether they are in the state of grace. They do not even have the obligation and the right to entertain the desire to bring about, more or less by force, such an absolute certitude in itself. Just the mere hope that we have this trust, that we have this primordial hope as distinct from a certainty subject to our control and with which we could have sovereign disposal over our existence, is an intrinsic element of that confidence whereby in anxiety we may let go of ourselves in a way that is without anxiety and yet not fall (or fall into the hands of him and of him alone whom we call God and about whom to know in faith is granted to us only when this trust is realized).

This kind of trust that determines the whole of our existence cannot of its very nature be brought about by putting together individual contents of our consciousness either. We do this when we reflect on these contents, but in so doing we do not bring about real trust itself but only its reflexive representation within our consciousness. Real trust can be discerned only indirectly (in that we once again trust and are not compelled to make an explicit theoretical determination and analysis), and so this is why it is experienced as "grace."

Ultimately we come to a state of equanimity, despite the ever-present anxiety. Existential anxiety and anxiety about salvation mean ultimately one and the same thing, since "salvation" does not mean a particular event within existence; rather, it is the totality of an existence that has succeeded, an existence that as such and taken as a whole is a threatening one, and not a neutral terrain on which happy and unhappy events occur. Our equanimity comes from the conviction that when all is said and done nothing can really happen to us, and in this sense we are secure (despite the insecurity of existence which can become secure only when we accept its insecurity).

We examine our conscience whose individual contents and objects are always assessed as symptoms and manifestations of our actual free fundamental condition. We are at peace with our conscience; we reject what we disapprove of; and we have the conviction that while this contrition does not actually cause the forgiveness of our guilt, it is itself the sign that the forgiving grace of God, who alone can forgive real guilt that once freely incurred cannot otherwise be overcome by us, is reaching us. We experience in ourselves (despite all the anxiety) a lightheartedness, a feeling of relief and a cheerfulness (for no apparent reason), all of which gives us the right to hope that in the depth of our being that cannot be penetrated by the categorical judgments of our reflection everything is as it should be, that there is a peace which, as Scripture says, surpasses all understanding. We turn lovingly to our neighbor (without again subjecting this love to a test of truth) and in so doing we forget ourselves and are at peace. The apparently overwhelming anxiety that we shall never escape from ourselves and therefore that we shall be lost is a condition that for its part is imbedded in the truth that God is greater than our hearts, that he knows everything, and that even when our own strength fails, we are really forgiven and this failure is transformed from a burden into a relief.

All of the things that have been said here about a certain possibility of ascertaining this salvific primordial trust should not of course be looked upon as recipes with which the father confessor or psychotherapist can produce this primordial trust or demonstrate its existence with logical certainty. This is just as impossible as wanting to produce faith itself by having recourse to arguments for the trustworthiness of faith. All of these things can be nothing more than an appeal to the freedom that trusts, whereby, however, this act of freedom can and ultimately even must occur in such a way that for its part does not seek reassurance of itself, and its willingness to do without this reassurance is part of its own nature.

CLINICAL PSYCHOLOGY
AND THEOLOGICAL PASTORAL CARE

All that has been said has primarily nothing to do with a psychology geared to the therapeutic treatment of demonstrable psychic disorders. What has been said about an anxiety at the root of created being applies to the most ordinary of people who in a matter-of-fact way declare that they have no anxiety whatsoever and that they just take life as it comes and enjoy it. On the other hand, things that are the proper and praiseworthy concern of psychotherapy can have nothing to do with this fundamental anxiety, and so it is neither proper nor necessary for this psychotherapy to claim that it brings about in freedom the fundamental trust in existence that is supposed to extend to all the remaining fundamental anxiety. It is of course entirely possible that phenomena which fall under the scope and treatment of psychotherapy are ultimately rooted in a person's refusal of free primordial trust in existence as a whole. But this need not necessarily be the case.

An example might help to illustrate this more clearly. If someone suffers from insomnia after surreptitiously committing a "deliberate murder," and if this murder can be quite properly interpreted as the categorical objectification of a freely chosen despair concerning the meaning of existence, the insomnia that psychotherapy has to treat is certainly related to this actual origin of the phenomenon requiring clinical treatment. But it is altogether conceivable that a profound conversion to an innocent trust in existence will still not cure this insomnia; conversely, it is just as conceivable that this insomnia can be cured without overcoming the actual guilt. For while it is true that there is a connection between cause and effect, the effect can remain even though the original cause is no longer present, and under certain circumstances an effect can be overcome by means other than simply removing the first cause. This is the reason why psychotherapy and pastoral care are in the theological sense interdependent. However, they are not identical and one cannot replace the other.

It is obvious that in this brief essay we cannot go into further detail about the relationship between psychotherapy and pastoral care, even though this would be a highly rewarding task. However, we do want to bring out one point. All of psychotherapy can concern itself with all the psychic disorders that are accessible to it. It may even attempt to remove those disorders whose actual cause must be presumed to be in an area beyond its competence. On the other hand, it should not be the purpose of theological pastoral care to undertake a healing process in respect to phenomena that fall under the scope and analysis of psychotherapy, not even if it is justified in hoping that success in its own proper sphere of activity will produce results that will be psychotherapeutically beneficial. Since the goal of pastoral care (for example, in the sacrament of penance and in penitential sermons) is this salvific primordial trust, it is of its nature essentially different from the psychotherapeutic art of healing, even if it is able to avail itself of ordinary human, and hence psychotherapeutic means when they can be useful. Its proper means, however, are the word of proclamation and its culminations in the history of the individual, the sacraments. This word is not only the word of a human being, just like any other human word, but, strictly speaking, the word of God, since the human word exists (to some degree in a hypostatic union analogous to that in Christology) in union (not identity) with the grace of God in which God in his own reality offers himself to human freedom as the ground of this primordial trust, as its source and its goal.

This real offer, once accepted, is experienced (which does not mean that it is grasped with the certainty of reflection) in the experience of a human transcendentality accepted in hope free of anxiety, which does not tend toward nothingness but rather toward God's reality which cannot be encompassed and so will remain a mystery.

The refusal of trust in the face of and despite the insecurity of existence which is called despair finds expression in the widest variety of forms and shapes corresponding to the objective categorical reality within which and on the basis of which this refusal is actualized. These multiple forms of despair must be classified and described by psychology, depth psychology, and categorical moral theology. In doing this, one should bear in mind that an experience of the psychological and moral fathomlessness and impenetrability of existence which presses in upon a person intensely and floods the day-to-day consciousness — an experience that can be very much physiologically conditioned — is not yet despair in a theological sense, unless it were freely accepted by freely rejecting that ultimately divine security which for its part encompasses this experience of extreme insecurity. Whether this security is accepted in hope or whether it is really rejected, if only tacitly, is something which, as we have already said, cannot for its part be ascertained with reflexive certainty. (The Council of Trent was of the opinion that according to Luther's theology of faith this kind of reflexive certainty would have to be forced and could be forced, although Luther himself, of course, was aware of the constant challenge to faith, to trust in the fulfillment of salvation.)

In order to explain the radical nature of this lack of certitude ("the dark night of the senses and of the spirit"), one need not maintain that it implies a real and ultimate abandonment by God (a participation in such an abandonment by God as is attributed — quite wrongly, ultimately — to Jesus on the cross). One could readily say that given such a presupposition, this abandonment by God would be beyond the realm of experience. A particularly intense description of such phenomena belongs to the field of mystical theology (even if in their most proper essentials they are simply a part of human existence).

2

NUCLEAR WEAPONS
AND THE CHRISTIAN

W e shall now address ourselves to the problem of the moral justification of nuclear weapons as a political and military instrument. This limitation of the subject must not be misunderstood. The question of ethical responsibility raised by other kinds of armaments and methods of waging war confronts the human conscience with extremely difficult problems. For human beings are in conscience responsible for every kind of violence and suffering that they inflict on their fellow human beings.

However, we must first make the following objective observation. In conventional armaments we have possibilities ranging from collective self-defense, which in fact has always been permitted by the Church under the limitations of the just war teaching, right up to a holocaust which conventional weapons can cause and whose effects differ only in quantitative degree from a nuclear holocaust. But in the practical and concrete order there is a qualitative distinction (one that is still repressed in the consciousness of many Christians) in respect to the moral judgments of war today as opposed to earlier times because the threat of nuclear war as opposed to any previous war, due to its immediate and long-term consequences, affects not only the nations waging the war but also the entire human family and its future. However, that still does not mean that there has ever been a conventional war or that there can even be one today that really raises no problem for the Christian conscience.

16

JUST WAR TEACHING

Just war teaching — however much it intended to restrict war's murderous consequences and sought to uphold or restore justice as opposed to violence — has in the reality of history also served as a salve for the conscience which enabled Christian kings and emperors, Christian generals right on down to Christian foot soldiers to carry on their wars and colonial conquests without any noticeable scruples, to the extent that they recognized power politics at all as a profound moral problem. There have always been people who have equated the power to act in a particular way with the moral right to do so. For example, we need only call to mind the highly developed cultures that were sacrificed to the wars of colonial conquest in the age of Charles V or Philip II, the Christian generals who wore hair shirts and went on pilgrimages and yet at the same time waged wars; of them we must ask the question today how it was possible to wage wars like these while at the same time probably maintaining what is known as a "good" conscience, for the most part unchallenged. Consider the strange attitude that enabled even devout Christians to justify Hitler's war of aggression against the Soviet Union as a crusade against Bolshevism.

Therefore solicitude for the future of the human race demands today that we have the existentiell courage to pose anew the question concerning the forms and limits of our resistance when confronted with the problem of maintaining or restoring the right to life, justice, and freedom of thought, conscience, and religion. When reconsidering the question we must not simply proceed on the assumption that the conventional evaluation of the wars that have been waged in the history of the Christian West was absolutely correct. We must take the risk of departing from traditional paradigms for the interpretation of war since they are more an outgrowth of the political role played by Christianity beginning with the epoch of Constantine than a reflection of the Christian churches' basic truths of faith.

If people expect theological casuistry based on a conventional understanding of war to tell them under what circumstances, with what weapons, and within what limits even a *modern* war may be waged, they have not yet faced the gravity of the problem and the perilousness of the historical times in which they live. Traditional attitudes toward war are simply adopted as a point of departure for distinguishing between responsible and irresponsible actions without asking whether these traditional attitudes have been rendered obsolete, at least by the course of history even if they were supposed to have been justified in earlier times. People refuse to recognize the extreme danger that war in the modern world will result in an explosion of extreme and boundless violence — comparable to a nuclear chain reaction that has gone out of control — that will sweep all the sophisticated distinctions of casuistry onto the rubbish heap of history.

Furthermore, people are not sufficiently aware at the present moment of human history that ultimately every individual's decision of conscience is made alone and is answerable to the incomprehensible God; therefore, despite all of its obvious dependence on the historical circumstances in which it is made, it may not of itself always appeal to this dependence and let others make this decision for it. Human beings' dignity consists in a responsibility to God that they cannot delegate to others. But people who have experienced the loneliness entailed in this ultimate and direct responsibility to God and who have to fear their own capacity for error as well as their culpable self-deception will not consider it to be a presumptuous encroachment on their own freedom of decision if they are required to form their conscience in the community of the Church and as hearers of the word of God.

This formation of conscience on a question of such fundamental importance as has been indicated above really cannot consist in the unreflected adoption of, for example, the casuistry of a learned theological commission or in the adoption of reassuring declarations of individual ecclesiastical personalities or institutions, much less of political parties. It cannot consist in the opinion that the problem of present-day armaments is much too complicated for average Christians, that it is in fact beyond their responsibility and therefore must be left to the responsibility of experts. Rather, the formation of conscience must consist in guiding people to a fresh experience of the basic tenets of Christian faith.

REJECTION OF NUCLEAR ARMAMENT

After these preliminary observations we come to the presentation of our own position on nuclear weaponry. This position has two parts.

1. The acknowledgement of the theoretical uncertainty of *every* definite position on this question and the evaluation of the opponents of one's own position that this uncertainty implies.

2. The decision for a definite position. We reject unconditionally the use of nuclear weapons regardless of whether these weapons are to be used offensively or defensively.

As a consequence of this decision we reject nuclear armament and we opt for unilateral steps toward disarmament, without waiting for guarantees or reciprocal action from the other side. Our decision for this position arises ultimately from a Christian motivation since a decision must be made despite the theoretical uncertainty of a definite opinion, and this Christian decision can be made.

Epistemological Uncertainties

In our opinion, ways of securing peace and political freedom that are really effective and justifiable from a Christian viewpoint fall under the competence of human prudence and discretion, and such questions cannot really be clearly settled on a purely theoretical level. To maintain the opposite, in our opinion, amounts to overconfidence in the rational argumentation put forth in support of one or the other ways of securing peace. More will be said on this matter when the arguments are presented which the human conscience can appeal to in favor of nuclear disarmament, even that form of disarmament which commits us to taking "unilateral steps." Among Christians one should from the outset not attempt to conjure up the possibility of absolute theoretical certainty on questions such as these, and one should refrain from using such false certainties as a means of imputing ignorance, false pacifism, or (vice versa) bellicose desires to people who have a different opinion. This by no means implies that the definite position that we ourselves have chosen can be rejected as arbitrary and the Christian who opposes our position may not assert that this position cannot arise from a Christian motivation.

As a matter of fact, the epistemological situation that we are considering here in connection with nuclear armament is not unknown in Christian moral theology. In principle, Christian moral theologians have always been aware that both for the individual and for the churches there are ethical questions that cannot be resolved in a way that is really certain and beyond doubt, questions that are disputed even among Christians with a basic Christian attitude without their coming to a commonly accepted conviction, questions, however, which nonetheless ineluctably require a definite decision this way or that way on the part of those who have to take a course of action and so in a certain sense have to be decided *absolutely*.

For such a situation where a theoretical decision is impossible, moral theologians, and especially teachers of the spiritual life, have sought to develop norms and rules of conduct to assist individual Christians in arriving at a practical decision for which they can answer to God despite this theoretical uncertainty. Among Christians it has been the conviction, at least in general, that in cases where a theoretical decision is impossible individual Christians may not simply decide their course of action arbitrarily. Despite this theoretical uncertainty, they can and must make a definite, concrete decision in another way, one that is not simply left to their own individual fancy. In this context one relied on the gifts of prudence enlightened by grace, on the guidance of God's Holy Spirit, on inspiration. In any case, however, it is acknowledged that in such questions that cannot be theoretically resolved Christians in their concrete decisions can appeal to the ultimate sources of Christian motivation, to the actual decision of their conscience, and they may also attempt to explain this to others as far as this is possible.

The Second Vatican Council's pastoral constitution *Gaudium et Spes* (no. 43) states explicitly that parties involved in a dispute within the Church (therefore not one party or the other, but both parties) may appeal to a Christian motivation. The only thing that is forbidden in such disputes is for one party to claim official church approval for itself alone. A sober reserve is required of both sides in assessing their own competence in the area in question and their own motivation. In what follows it will become clear that we are not talking about an objectively impossible attempt to "harmonize" different decisions of conscience in respect to the concrete questions of nuclear armaments.

Preventing War

We must first point out that all reasonable people and all Christians are asking themselves *how a nuclear war can be prevented*. Christians, therefore, have no disagreement on the point that all possible measures must be taken to prevent such a war. The problem at issue is how to do this in a way that promises the greatest possible success. Given this presupposition, we say frankly and honestly that we do not impute bad faith or mere unreasonableness to those who endorse nuclear armaments under definite conditions as a way of securing peace, even though we cannot subscribe to the illusion that everyone involved in the process of nuclear armament really has an honest and upright conscience.

But as far as Christians are concerned, we further presume that they recognize the teaching of the churches condemning total war itself under any and all circumstances. We know that the Second Vatican Council (*Gaudium et Spes*, no. 80) calls *every* act of war aimed indiscriminately at destruction of entire cities or of extensive areas along with their populations a crime against God and humankind. A nuclear war essentially consisting of a chain of such actions, is, then, absolutely rejected. In the context of what is meant this holds true not only for the readiness and willingness to conduct a first nuclear strike in certain circumstances. In this condemnation it is obviously a question of the objective structure of such actions themselves which cannot be justified by any intention, therefore not even by the intention of defense. This unconditional rejection of such acts of war, which comprise the essence of a total war, must also be considered, each in itself, by those Christians and reasonable people who today consider further nuclear armament to be a meaningful way precisely of *avoiding* a total war. These people must, however, face the dilemma of how deterrence is to be maintained in a "credible" way against an adversary who also possesses nuclear armaments if, as has been presumed, they are not willing under any circumstances to engage in a nuclear war.

REASONS FOR A POSITION OF PACIFISM

In what follows we want to try to present the reasons for a "pacifist" position. Some of them are based on objective human considerations; others have their origin in ultimate Christian motivations. In our opinion these reasons have a right to serious consideration on the part of a really Christian conscience. Whether they move such a conscience to a concrete decision for this position or whether it decides on the basis of human and Christian motivation for the opposite course of action is something that can be decided only in the suprarational way that has been indicated above.

Rational-Humane Objection

It is our deliberate intention to present the rational-humane objection
to nuclear armament in question form because we do not want to convey
the impression that our argumentation is necessarily beyond all doubt.
The reader who here expects fully worked out theses and answers instead of questions should also be aware that problem areas are being
addressed on whose answer the survival of entire nations depends. We
should not like to conceal from ourselves or others by the use of clever
rhetoric the necessity of the utmost efforts of reflection or the fact that
answers supported by a consensus have not yet been found.

First of all, we consider the distinction between nuclear armament
and nuclear war as something that ultimately can seriously be called into
question as far as real life is concerned. Do those who consider this distinction to be viable in practice allow in a sufficiently realistic way, even
on their own side, for the malevolence, the craving for power, the mis-
interpretation of social realities as the Christian conviction of human
sinfulness compels us to do? Will such nuclear armament not lead to a
destruction of social equilibrium and of peace even among us, so that
there will be an ever-increasing temptation (as history teaches us) to
overcome the internal problems of society by waging external wars? Can
this armament really be justified except by attributing to political adversaries from the outset *only* the bad motives of an absolute addiction to
power and the will to assault their opponents? Why is it that in these
controversies the adversaries always depict one another in the most dia-
bolical light, unless this shabby and poor argumentation were necessary
to justify armament?

If from the bottom of their hearts people place their hope exclusively
on nuclear armament and summarily reject as unrealistic all attempts to
develop conceptions for securing peace in which the use of weapons of
mass destruction as an option for human action is rejected in principle,
they are tacitly presuming that on the other side, and not only on the
part of individuals but also of nations, at least among the power elites,
they would have to expect as a matter of principle that the basest in-
stincts, only the other side's aggressiveness and its urge to destroy, will
as a rule prevail. This is just the way to foster the mental climate in which
aggressiveness leading precisely to nuclear wars will thrive, a mentality
which does not really consider a nuclear war to be basically immoral
but endeavors to avoid it only as long as there is no chance of waging it
victoriously in its own interest. It is of course true that Christians may

not assume in guileless idealism that the others are not also sinners. This is why many Christians justify nuclear armament precisely with the argument that only in this way can adversaries be made to understand "that the effort required for an attack or a blackmail attempt does not correspond in any way to the advantages they might gain from it and therefore that it does not seem advisable."[1]

But if we are convinced that this legitimate right may be defended by a constant readiness for total war and that it can be defended in this way, do we not run the risk of claiming every right for ourselves while in fact ascribing total blame to the opposite side? Yet as Christians we ought to be far more afraid of the enticements and temptations to evil on our own side, a fear that is singularly absent in the current widespread mentality. It is precisely for this reason that we should also fear nuclear armament on our own side as a temptation to a nuclear war that threatens to annihilate the human race, even though it was originally intended only as a means of deterrence.

Does not nuclear armament tacitly foster the conviction that we have to advance the welfare of our own nation instead of considering from the outset the well-being of the whole family of nations? Does it make sense for us to say that we must continue to increase our nuclear armaments so that we can later bring about a situation in which we can seriously and successfully negotiate a really effective disarmament? Will this not result in a permanent postponement of such a situation, because the adversary will take immediate steps to catch up with us and the stalemate will remain, only this time worse, that we wanted to overcome in order to have more successful negotiations, and in which we are forever wrangling about the meaning of advance armament and subsequent armament?

Can anyone prove that nuclear armament really prevents the frightful chaos that we are all afraid of? Are those who are for nuclear armament for the purpose of preventing a nuclear war entirely sure that they really reject this war under any and all circumstances? To make this deterrence policy "credible," they at least have to pretend to the adversary that they are willing to embark on nuclear war, and this means that they have to dupe at least their own soldiers into believing that such a war is justified when they equip them with nuclear weapons, all the while taking pains to avoid any public discussion of the matter.

---

[1]See the position paper of the Central Committee of German Catholics, *Zur aktuellen Friedensdiskussion.*

Does this not inevitably produce a frame of mind that views geographically limited nuclear wars as a real option under certain circumstances and feels that it is possible to wage such wars? Are we fully aware that the development of new and more effective nuclear weapons can be a temptation for one side to take immediate advantage of its presumably superior position in order to forestall the adversary to whom we undoubtedly impute bellicose intentions? And in this process it is obvious that the possibilities afforded by the rapidly increasing development in the field of microelectronics increase the temptation to develop first-strike technologies and even to make use of them as soon as we think that a first-strike can be successfully carried out, even without our ascribing to the present-day political leadership of a country the intention of unleashing a first strike. With this kind of armament can we really have a guarantee that a nuclear war will not break out due to technical defects and miscalculation, even though it is not fully intended? Even if we could rely on technical fail-safe measures (experts doubt this possibility), has the adversaries' increasing fear of one another in an escalating arms race been assessed with sufficient realism, a fear that can lead to the outbreak of a total war even though neither side has actually entertained an aggressive intention?

We doubt that many of the proponents of further armament, who are convinced of their own sense of realism, are even sufficiently aware of their own fear and the fear of others. And we further doubt that this fear can be kept subject to political control in the long run. In addition to this the fixation that the tendency to this kind of armament gives rise to must necessarily lead to a neglect of the other tasks within the family of nations. Will not this preoccupation itself turn into a temptation to settle the unresolved conflicts within this family of nations by recourse to wars? In the long run, what effective means do we propose to prevent nuclear armament on the part of an ever-increasing number of countries? And finally, does not the continuation of nuclear armament lead to the loss of our possibility of preserving and developing those very values and goals whose defense we consider today to be the reason for nuclear deterrence?

The questions brought up here describe the magnitude of the danger with which nuclear armament is threatening us. Hence it is our wish that those who defend further nuclear armament under definite conditions would not present their arguments in such a way as to give the impression that they must appear as immediately evident to all persons of intelligence and good will.

When, for example, the Central Committee of German Catholics declares without a trace of scruple that the NATO double-track decision is an example of a policy that has as its aim the reduction of armaments, détente, and peace by providing a balance of military power, far be it from us to call into question the upright intentions of the Central Committee or of NATO. However, it would be advisable to temper this assertion with a bit of skepticism which would allow for a more open-minded evaluation of the different views current even on the side of the West concerning the criteria to be employed in judging the other side's willingness for détente and peace, and concerning the nature and the extent of the armaments that are required. In view of the way that the Central Committee formulates its case, can there be any room left to agree with Cardinal Höffner's declaration that Christians of equal conscientiousness can arrive at different decisions about how to secure peace?

When expressing judgments of our own about how peace is to be secured, our formulations should make it clear that we acknowledge equal conscientiousness on the part of Christians who have come to an opposite judgment. Beyond this it will hardly be possible to demonstrate which side possesses the greater intelligence and expertise, because an analysis of this kind and the results it yields will still encounter the same differences of opinion.

The Message of God's Kingdom

For those of us who are trying to be Christians there is a further horizon that impels us to oppose nuclear armament. It would be well both for our partners and our adversaries to pay close heed to the arguments that originate from this horizon too. The message of the cross, the resurrection, and the advent of God's kingdom moves on a level that is different from the level of ordinary moral activity. In their private as well as their public lives Christians have to deal not only with "commandments" and "norms" which they acknowledge as reasonable and justified and which they can make clear to a certain degree even to non-Christians. They are also aware of other criteria and motivations, "appeals" and "calls" through which God makes particularly urgent demands on them. This means that their decisions will be formed on a totally different horizon. What takes place on this level is described by Scripture with the words, "He that can take it, let him take it."

When called upon to make decisions involving the whole of their being, non-Christians also find themselves propelled by a force which likewise bursts the bonds of the reality that is subject to rational analysis. Even though the reasons they give for it are different, both Christians and non-Christians can come to the same decision of conscience, one for which neither they themselves nor others can give a completely adequate rational explanation. When this happens, Christians will rejoice in the knowledge that their own decision is being confirmed from another quarter. Just as they hope for themselves that God's grace is at work in their own decision, so, too, they quite naturally see this same grace at work in their non-Christian contemporaries drawing them, too, beyond the bounds of objective knowledge.

In their decisions Christians and non-Christians alike must adhere to their conscience. Both, however, must also be cautious in assessing their own motivation because the ultimate and real wellsprings of the motivation from which their decisions actually flow themselves defy transparent reflexive analysis. Christians are of the belief that they must leave it to God to pass judgment on what their real motivation is. In this world there is no final word about themselves or others.

The decision of Christians must ultimately be made before the cross of Christ. This is their salvation; this is where the true meaning of their existence shines forth in clear light. But, as Saint Paul says, it is in the cross that God is victorious through the powerlessness and folly of him who dies upon it, even though he was unshakably convinced that with him God's kingdom had come. Christians' decisions must conform to the proclamation of Jesus in the Sermon on the Mount. They must accept the folly of the cross which lays claim to Christians as their true wisdom. Saint Paul says that the foolishness of God is wiser than the wisdom of human beings, that what is lowly and rejected has been chosen by God that no flesh may glory in his sight and that the Scripture might be fulfilled which says that God's strength fulfills itself in weakness. This sentence sounds unworldly, indeed even pathetic and silly to those who wish to make God an immanent element of human history whose job it is to see to it that this history can always be understood and calculated and be brought to an outcome satisfactory to us. However, our reliance is not on a God who blesses weapons and guarantees success in this world. We try to believe in the incomprehensible God to whom we entrust ourselves precisely in view of the folly of the cross.

The horizon on which Christians have to make their decisions and which we have not described with anything even remotely approaching the full treatment it deserves is valid, of course, not only for the conduct of private life. The Sermon on the Mount has political significance too. It is also a touchstone for public activity. It may not simply be relegated to the private sphere because it is the constitution of God's kingdom, and this kingdom extends to the peoples of the earth and is striving to manifest itself in concrete history. To be sure, the particular, objective individual norms governing public life and politics are different from those of the personal and private sphere and those used to shape the lifestyle of individuals for the simple reason that the realities that these norms are meant to regulate are different. When the plain and simple business of living obviously requires a definite way of acting, no one will hesitate to agree that there is no need whatever to appeal to the Sermon on the Mount and one can refrain from invoking the folly of the cross.

Anyone who is considering the construction of a bridge even as a form of moral achievement certainly need not bother about a blueprint that contradicts the most elementary rules of statics. But when we are dealing with questions of what it means to be a human being in the fullest sense of the term, with questions of a complexity that is beyond measure and that defies total analysis, with questions that do not admit of a universally accepted solution through the application of immediately evident objective norms, Christians have the right and the duty to appeal to the Sermon on the Mount and to make their decisions under the cross, under its folly and its powerlessness. Christian politicians must also make their decisions on this horizon. They are not permitted to be merely representatives of a lifestyle which in its understandable bourgeois character is first and foremost *in possessione*. Christianity is, after all, not a preservative, to be used as sparingly as possible, for the purpose of safeguarding a humane, rational, bourgeois lifestyle from excesses that also threaten it. However much the bearers of political power in a democratic society depend on the voters for their mandate and have to submit their power to the controls of constitutionally established institutions and not least of all to the cross fire of public opinion, they nonetheless still may not pass off their personal responsibility to others for what they do or fail to do.

The question of a truly Christian moral theology, precisely how the ethos of the Sermon on the Mount is to be interpreted, how its "appeals" and "calls" can be validated in the political arena, has of course not been answered in a complete and precise way in the few indications we have given here. What concrete chances the Sermon on the Mount actually has of becoming an element that helps to determine history and politics

is of course also an open question. It is sufficient here to avow that for
Christians the Sermon on the Mount does have a part to play in political
decision-making. Even our secular and political life will go astray if we
fail to take into account the folly of the cross and the hope of eternal
life in God.

If we now put the question of nuclear armament in this framework of
the Christian horizon of decision and of specific Christian motivation,
our conviction is that we must say no to nuclear armament. If precisely
on the question of war and peace in the nuclear age, on such a radical
and comprehensive question, we disallow this horizon of decision, how
could we possibly continue to convince ourselves that the Sermon on the
Mount and the folly of the cross still have a really radical meaning in our
lives? If someone should reproach us with the fact that the principles of
the Sermon on the Mount and of the folly of the cross are not otherwise
tangibly evident in our lives either, we could still not accept this as a
reason for not letting them have an effect in the question of nuclear
armament.

Nuclear Disarmament

So from this standpoint we are for nuclear disarmament even if it means
committing ourselves to unilateral steps. Thereby we actually consider
the term "unilateral steps" to be one that discriminates against what
Christians are really deciding when they renounce armament. For this
term insinuates that it is a question of cunning calculation and of a trick
that is not to be taken with total seriousness because one expects the
other side to follow suit with "subsequent steps" and is resolved to rearm
as quickly as possible should the other side fail to follow suit, or in any
case does not follow quickly enough. What is meant here by the Christian decision is precisely that it is not part of a deal, but rather it moves
beyond the area of this kind of give and take. Christians motivated by
the appeal of the Sermon on the Mount, humanists basing their actions
on radical-human considerations and on a consciousness of their responsibility for the future of humankind and of the totality of life —
something for which there can be no completely adequate rational explanation — who decide to take this road must be aware of the danger
it involves. The possibility of losing political freedom is something that
cannot be excluded. It is part of their credibility to admit this danger.

But if they opt for disarmament even with unilateral steps — and if this option in some way succeeds in influencing the practical politics of their country — they may also have the hope and the expectation that this decision will be a blessing for the world. Why should this hope be denied them? Should it be a reason for writing them off as absolutely unrealistic dreamers? If large-scale disarmament were obviously taking place and the other side began to be convinced that it was meant seriously, can anyone say for sure that the adversary's response would only be continued armament or even war or some other kind of political aggression? And if this kind of power politics were the only response we received for our disarmament, can anyone really prove that this would cost us our political freedom in the long run, or that this loss would not be overcome by some other form of resistance (as we have seen in the example of Gandhi)[2] even against a foreign enemy. How can we maintain that this kind of disarmament in the form of unilateral steps would not bring about profound changes in the Warsaw Pact countries or that the people in power there would always be able to maintain their present course and cling to *those* intentions that many of the proponents of armament are accustomed to impute to them?

The demand for disarmament is necessarily and inseparably bound up with the demand for a change of attitude and a change in our political modes of thought in many respects. If this kind of change does not occur among the countries of the world, alternative conceptions of political security will not be able to exercise a historical influence. As long as this change does not reach the politically influential groups in the different societies, these alternative conceptions will be either ignored by the significant part of the political and military experts in East and West who opt for the current conception of the threat of "assured mutual destruction," or these alternative conceptions of political security will be rejected outright as unrealistic and dangerous. The proponents of assured mutual destruction will argue that their conception, while expensive, is at least something that in the long run could be managed by the experts. They will talk about the conceivable "military use of nuclear force," deploring as irrational and as a danger to peace all the fear that such talk engenders in people.

To be sure, this change must occur in both of the power blocks if a new order of peace, or at least initially a coexistence of the different social systems *without* the threat of mutual destruction, is to be a real

---

[2]For a treatment of this difficult question, see the document of the Evangelical Church in Germany, *Frieden wahren, fördern und erneuern.*

political possibility. Here, however, we are concentrating the discussion on a change of attitude on our side, because without this change it is useless to expect that appeals to the other side will bear any fruit. What we are dealing with here is a lifesaving task; it is the most difficult political challenge of modern times. Both to us and to many reasonable and responsible people it is painfully clear that given the present political reality, there is no comprehensive and clearly viable solution in sight. This is something that has to be worked out step by step. Nonetheless we are relying on the possibility that there is a way out of the peril of a nuclear holocaust, one that is justifiable from a Christian point of view and that can be translated into practical politics, and from this standpoint we consider it our right and our duty to point out some directions that we (together with many others) see as lifesaving.

Even in the democracies of the West there is an inherent unrest that has to be overcome, but it cannot be overcome by armaments but only by a change in people's attitude, a change which in our opinion cannot be seriously expected by those who in fact consider armament to be our only solution. Despite all the threatening signs of a worldwide crisis for whose scope history provides no relevant example, the West, even up to the present day, does not seem to be capable of presenting an ethically, economically, and ecologically convincing conception for the further development of peace and freedom for the entire family of nations or of seriously dealing with the notions that the Third World has in this regard. Without a conception of this kind how could peace and freedom be guaranteed even for the West alone? Without a conception of this kind, which would certainly also include profound changes that are now becoming necessary in the capitalistic way of life, how could there be a permanently peaceful solution to the North-South conflict? If, then, this kind of change has become an inescapable necessity today at all events, why should we overlook this when dealing with the question of armament and say instead that in these questions a change in our way of thinking that has moral, economic, and ecological consequences has nothing to do with the question of our chance for disarmament?

We are for disarmament in explicit conjunction with a change of consciousness among ourselves which will make us attach a higher priority to the misery of several hundred million people living in absolute poverty than to our own need of security. But a policy that really takes this misery seriously is impeded from the very outset if economic assets and human talent are increasingly tied up in armament. And the industrial nations must also acknowledge their share of the responsibility for the proliferation of armaments in the Third World. Not only do they bear part of the blame for many of the unresolved conflicts that have broken out in these countries, but they are also the chief exporters of munitions. And again, no one with two eyes in his or her head can be done with the matter by putting all the blame for this state of affairs on the Soviet striving for hegemony. Those who want to use the argument of legitimate security interests on the part of the receiver countries in individual cases should not close their eyes to the part played by the struggle of the superpowers on both sides for political and economic spheres of influence and by the desire to reap a profit from the sickness of deterrence, armament, and war that afflicts world society today.

THE BURDEN OF PROOF LIES ON THE POWERFUL

We now return to the point where our considerations began. In this peril our conscience points out two directional markers to us: the inescapable no to every use of nuclear weapons and, what for us is bound up with this, the demand for disarmament even with unilateral steps. First of all, we have to pause and become aware of the danger. So we support the appeal of the American peace movement calling for a freeze of nuclear weapons first of all in East and West — at least no further armament. This is still not enough, but halting is a presupposition for conversion. Markers are indispensable on a way that leads along dangerous precipices. Those who leave these markers out of fear and look for the way haphazardly are lost.

Others with a manifestly upright conscience are convinced that unilateral renunciation of nuclear armament, and especially large-scale unilateral disarmament, will only increase the danger of war. They consider the risks of nuclear armament even today to be smaller than the risks of a "pacifistic" position. We have given our reasons which show in an objective and in particular a Christian way what has led us to our position. We have also stated, and we repeat here, that we respect those who, even though they are working with us toward the goal of outlawing nuclear weapons unconditionally and toward the goal of total nuclear disarmament, and affirm the necessity of making a "constant and continuing effort" to abolish war in the atomic age, yet do not agree with us on the way to achieve this goal. People who claim for themselves the right and duty to form their own opinion in a situation of lethal danger would do well to call to mind Saint Thomas More's attitude in taking up his position. He claimed the right and the duty to sustain his conviction to the point of death, but he did not set himself up as moral judge of those who took up a contrary position.

At the conclusion of our considerations, we should like to present two additional thoughts. The first is addressed to Christian and non-Christian opponents of our position. We are not dealing here with questions of personal morality. In the question of nuclear armament nations must make historical decisions that cannot be postponed and these decisions have to be borne alone. The opponents of our position also make decisions involving the greatest risk for those who do not go along with them. Therefore they have no right to say that those who oppose nuclear armaments do indeed have praiseworthy motives, but they should keep these motives for themselves and may not elevate them into norms that help to determine the political life of others.

The second thought concerns the question of the justification of a definite position and is addressed to the people who have to make the decisions. The burden of justifying a definite way as being pleasing to God rests first of all on the powerful and not on the powerless, on the rich and not on the poor, on the successful and not on the unsuccessful, on the shrewd and not on the simple. Those who ponder this will not place on the powerless who support disarmament the entire burden of proving how their way can be realized in the clash of the political powers. Rather, it is the powerful themselves who have the constant burden of proving why they do not decisively take this way. Can we not say that in case of doubt the way that God is showing us is the way of disarmament and not the way of nuclear armament? However Christians decide, they must proceed from the conviction that what is acknowledged by them to be evil cannot be justified even if in the judgment of those involved in the action a lofty and noble goal is to be achieved.[3]

---

[3]See Karl Rahner, "The Catholic Church and the Peace Movement," in *Karl Rahner in Dialogue: Conversations and Interviews 1965-1982*, ed. Paul Imhof and Hubert Biallowons (New York: Crossroad, 1986), 359-61; and "The Theological Dimension of Peace," in *Theological Investigations 22*, trans. Joseph Donceel (New York: Crossroad, London: Darton, Longman & Todd, 1991), 38-42.

3

PLEA FOR A NAMELESS VIRTUE

All over the world people have explicitly recognized virtues, that is, ways of behaving that are morally good, and they have given these virtues names. It may be that they often did this only so as to be able to make demands on others. But still, nomenclatures and distinctions of this sort are unavoidable and they are useful. We see more clearly what we have to do. It makes it easier for us to check whether we are really living up to the moral demands placed upon us by our own nature and by our own life. Moral theologians and moral philosophers have worked out entire systems of virtues, subdividing them and showing their relationship to one another, and they have seen to it that there are no blank spaces on the map of our moral obligations.

The reason why ethics and moral theology today devote less attention to these catalogues of individual virtues may, perhaps, be due to the fact that they are concerned with questions antecedent to these descriptions and catalogues of individual modes of moral behavior. It may also be that we have the impression that this kind of greenhouse of individual virtues is not particularly useful for real life. But if in addition to knowing the things we are allowed to do as human beings and Christians, we also have to know how and why we are to act in face of the sheer variety of life and the multiplicity of its tasks, and if reflection also has its necessary and rightful place in the area of moral freedom, we must constantly inquire into the virtues, however we may choose to do it and whatever be the terminology we use in dealing with questions of this sort.

Are there virtues which have gone unnamed but which, even though practiced (we hope) in life, have received no explicit treatment in the reflection of moral theology and moral philosophy? Since all human tasks and modes of activity are interrelated, it is quite improbable that

33

a definite moral mode of behavior, even though it has not been given much reflection, could not be classified at all as belonging to an already known and explicitly named virtue, that is, that it has really remained nameless.

It is, however, possible that the theoretical reflection on the whole of morality has not grasped each and every individual element with equal clarity and explicitness with the result that one or other moral mode of behavior does remain nameless and is mostly lost sight of in a universal and abstract concept. The simple fact that the catalogues of virtues, ethical systems, and terminologies belonging to individual eras, civilizations, and styles of life were and are quite different and can hardly be brought into conformity with one another shows that something like this is quite conceivable. The lifestyle in one period of history unintentionally and unavoidably neglects this or that virtue which another lifestyle explicitly recognizes and cultivates. This cannot be explained solely by the fact that the extramoral and premoral conditions of human life vary and for this reason also require morally different ways of acting.

ANONYMOUS VIRTUE

Is it possible to give a concrete example that would substantiate the a priori expectation that there must be virtues that have remained anonymous? As has already been said, when something like this is attempted, one must always allow for the objection that what is meant has long since been known and that it has been named and is called this or that. But this is no problem, provided only that what is meant is now seen more clearly and is marked off from something else and something of a more universal nature under which it has been concealed until now. The remaining difficulty, of course, consists in whether or not a brief and understandable new name can also be suggested for what is meant. But even if a brief and clear baptismal name can still not be suggested for what is meant and has been discovered, the problem presented can still have a meaning and a solution. One simply draws attention with many words to a definite moral mode of behavior and leaves it to others to find an individual and understandable word for it.

We proceed from the distinction often or usually prevailing in moral activity between the problematic uncertainty of the rational-reflexive justification of a moral attitude and the absoluteness of a free decision as such. We always, or almost always (it is to be hoped), have good reasons for a moral decision, but these are rarely absolutely beyond doubt. There are usually serious reasons and justifications on the other side for an opposite decision, and yet the free act as such is itself unambiguous and absolute, and, if we examine it more closely, irreversible. It cannot be reached by that "on the one hand–on the other hand" consideration, by those reservations which are part of the nature of rational reflection. All of the traditional "moral systems" in Catholic moral theology presuppose this divergence between an ambiguous theory and practice that must be unambiguous, and they endeavor to provide principles that will enable a person to deal with this dichotomy. These principles are of no further interest to us here. What is important here is what all of these systems presuppose — namely, that quite often the moral reflection antecedent to the action itself cannot provide that unambiguousness and unquestionable certainty with which, whether we want it or not, we nonetheless perform the action itself.

SKEPTICAL RELATIVISM

In this situation that confronts us countless times in our lives a twofold (false) reaction is initially conceivable. In a *skeptical relativism* the significance of the moral reflection preceding the action can be devalued with the idea that this is not the important thing since it cannot provide the absolute unambiguousness which necessarily characterizes the action. This attitude of relativism is widespread, especially in respect to religious and ideological problems. We are aware of the problematic nature of all rational, fundamental-theological justification antecedent to an ideological decision of this kind, and so we consider it to be useless and superfluous. We feel justified in making the decision arbitrarily, according to whim, origin, and so on. On the theoretical level, we remain in an attitude of indecisiveness that refuses to be pinned down and think that in this way we have escaped making a decision. But that is not really the case at all since the refusal to make a decision is the very decision itself and quite assuredly not the best one. Or we refuse to accept the problematic nature of the moral reflections antecedent to a decision; we deny to ourselves and others that there is a problem; we declare that the rational reflexive justification of our own decision is in every respect absolutely obvious and that there are no serious grounds to the contrary that have not long since been convincingly refuted for every honest and intelligent person.

IDEOLOGICAL FANATICISM

Right up to our own day this kind of ideological fanaticism has been all too common among Christians in their confessional disputes. Even in the area of ideological, fundamental-theological and apologetic argumentation people on both sides acted all too often as though the justification for their own standpoint were completely clear and only ignorance and ill will could prevent people from recognizing this. Even the language of the First Vatican Council (DS 3009) proceeds somewhat naively on the assumption that the true religion must necessarily contain fundamental-theological arguments which must be immediately evident to every well-instructed person of goodwill. Catholic fundamental theology was not always and everywhere immune to the error that the certainty of fundamental-theological argumentation must more or less coincide with the absoluteness of the assent of faith itself.

In all areas (not only in the religious area) this kind of attitude, which wants to see the unavoidable absoluteness of the free decision as something already present in the antecedent examination of its objective and ethical justification, is precisely what constitutes the real nature of ideological fanaticism. Skeptical relativism which thinks that it can dispense itself from making a decision and ideological fanaticism which wants to derive the absoluteness of the free decision from an absoluteness of the rational consideration, an absoluteness which does not really exist, are the two false consequences that can very easily result from the insuperable difference between the problematic nature of reflection and the absoluteness of decision, between theory and practice.

THE MIDDLE WAY BETWEEN THE TWO EXTREMES

Between these two extremes there is a middle way. It is a virtue and it seems to me that this virtue is nameless. This middle way which takes seriously the antecedent reflection on the justification of a decision and which nonetheless does not demand more of the reflection than it can provide, which honestly admits its problematic nature and despite this does not stand in the way of the courage for a serene and brave decision, is the hallmark of the proper self-understanding of a person who is neither the god of an absolute and universal certainty and clarity nor the creature of a sterile arbitrariness which views everything as equally right and equally wrong, a person who has human qualities that command respect even if these qualities do not have the effulgence of the divine or the transparence of the obvious.

It is difficult to steer this middle course because there is no way of justifying its concrete application by referring back to an absolutely obvious and indisputable principle. It belongs to that area of life wisdom which intellectual acumen cannot alone provide. Ultimately it does not matter whether one along with Saint Thomas Aquinas calls this virtue an intellectual virtue or whether one calls it a moral virtue. It is the virtue that takes theoretical rationality seriously and yet does not turn practice into a merely secondary derivation of theory, but rather acknowledges an ultimate independence and underivability of freedom and of practice. It is the virtue of active respect for the mutual relationship of theory and practice, of knowledge and freedom, *and* at the same time for their disconsonance. It is the virtue of the unity and diversity of the two realities without which one would be sacrificed in favor of the other.

It seems to me that there is a behavior of this kind and therefore that a human virtue of this kind does exist. But what name are we to give it? That is difficult to say. If we were to call it the courage to make a decision that is meaningful and is still not simply the product of rationality, we would have chosen a too general and indefinite name because it would obviously contain more than is meant here. And so it would seem that this important virtue has no brief and generally understandable name. Presumably the ultimate reason for this is to be found in the fact that the relationship between theory and practice even today remains an obscure problem in philosophy. The virtue we are looking for can of course be subsumed under the virtue of prudence or perhaps that of wisdom. But if we subsume it in this way, something particular becomes lost in something that is general.

Whether or not this virtue's name is known is in the end not so important. But this virtue ought to be practiced. Today, especially, when one could get the impression that the majority of humankind is divided into weary relativists and obstinate fanatics.

4

INTELLECTUAL PATIENCE
WITH OURSELVES

The simplest things that wise people do spontaneously are often the things that can be talked about only in a cumbersome and tedious way. One of these simple things is, in my opinion, having patience with ourselves.

IS PATIENCE SOMETHING OBVIOUS?

It seems obvious to me that in general people need to have patience with themselves. But it is one of those obvious things that we do not really succeed at very well. There may be people who feel that they do not need to have patience with themselves because they are living in complete accord with themselves and what they are doing. But I hope we will not envy the good fortune of these simple souls. If we look at ourselves honestly, we shall see quite readily that we are not yet done with ourselves; we cannot produce a state of total accord with ourselves by a simple command, nor by a psychological trick or something of that sort. And so, in the absence of such complete accord with ourselves and in view of the fact that we are powerless to achieve this peace, we need to have patience with ourselves.

The person inside us that we really are greets painfully the person that we want to be. Here we are omitting the question whether we would be people who are still in a process of becoming and who have a future before us if this difference did not exist; the question whether this peace with ourselves would not be death; the question how one might conceive this peace so that it would be worth striving for as eternal life and eternal peace. In any event, however, we are now on the way; we are living between a past and a future, both of which, each in its own way, is concealed from us. We never have everything together that we have to live from. We are always conditioned historically, manipulated sociologically, and threatened biologically — and we know it. We can try to repress our knowledge of this situation; we can try to accept stoically what we cannot change; we can misuse the really good things of life as an anodyne for the mysterious disquietude of our existence and when this concealed disquietude manifests itself, we can interpret it as psychic depression that we have to weather or combat with a wide array of tranquilizers.

But if we have the courage to let this disquietude encounter us, if we do not turn from it but rather accept it without simply interpreting it as the stuff that forges heroes and without letting it reduce us to despair, then we have patience with ourselves; we are in agreement that we have not yet found pure harmony with ourselves. There are many people who think they have this patience and that it is the most obvious thing in the world. But if these people would take a closer look at themselves, they would see that they are not really accepting patiently the pain of their own disquietude, untransfigured and without animosity, but rather that they are seeking refuge in the routine of day-to-day existence, and in this way are claiming to be objective and sober. Or they would see that they are dominated by a despair that they do not admit or by a desperate resignation, and that they really feel that there is no sense in living. They would see that they are not practicing patience in the face of the questionableness of existence, but rather are practicing how to look the other way and get the substitute for patience with which they think life can also be lived.

THE PATIENT PERSON IS SERENE

People who are truly patient, however, really endure their disquietude. They accept it and do not turn away from the pain it brings. Truly patient people further endure the fact that they do not know for sure whether they are really accepting this disquietude in patience or whether they are not really rejecting it by erecting a cheap façade of patience. Patient people are patient with their own impatience and so serenely and almost cheerfully renounce any final accord with themselves. They do not really know the origin of this serenity in which they acquiesce; they hope that they have it. Indeed, in cheerful confidence they make no attempt to close themselves off from the anodynes of the impatient because they are precisely the ones who can handle them since they do not allow them to have any lasting effect. Patient people are serene and so they are free.

What we have become involved in when we acquiesce in this serene patience is a question that we cannot consider further here. In respect to this question there will be people who think that they have become involved in nothingness and so they could be the victors who from this standpoint overcome in themselves the dissonance of finite realities. There are other people who are convinced that nothingness, when understood in its true sense, is useless, that it has no power to produce peace. It is their conviction, rather, that when they really let go of themselves and accept the unrest, they have, whether they reflect on it or not, become involved with the one who is called God in the sense that this word is really understood in everyday existence, and that this involvement in God's silent incomprehensibility can succeed only because God in his grace accepts those who "let go of themselves."

Perhaps you yourselves have already grown impatient and feel that your impatience is justified. Your impatience may be justified in respect to my discourse on patience; however, it would not be justified if it were directed against the reality itself that I am attempting to indicate with my stammering words, if it were directed against that patient composure in the face of ambiguity, the composure that I presume exists among you and that is known as patience.

THE MENTAL CLIMATE OF OUR TIMES: BOUNDLESS KNOWLEDGE

If we are to speak further about intellectual patience or, better, about patience with the limitations and incalculability of our knowledge, we must first speak about an inescapable mental climate in which we find ourselves today as opposed to former times. Never before has humankind known as much as it knows today. People today have more than just a vague notion of how to keep body and soul together; they do more than just keep the memory of the past alive in myth, saga, and perhaps with a smattering of history; they work at more than just a bit of metaphysics with a lot of effort and a great many setbacks; they do not just practice religion and stammer about the divine in many tongues.

Today people work at science. They explore nature systematically; in psychology and psychoanalysis they see what makes them tick; in more recent times they have conquered new fields of knowledge like the social sciences. They develop a philosophy of their own sciences and then investigate the history of all these sciences. Even their everyday life experiences are erected into structures of systematic knowledge. They develop data processing systems and methods of storing their own knowledge.

Today all the countries in the world and the lives of everybody living in them have become part of this systematic process of science and they are involved in a continuous exchange. The number of books published is increasing at a dizzying pace; libraries are getting bigger and bigger; new methods of storing scientific data are being discovered; the progress of knowledge is no longer being left to chance or to arbitrary insight and inspiration but is being systematically calculated in advance, even though precisely in this way new elements are emerging that cannot be calculated, and the unity of all these sciences and the directions they are going to take are not things that can be planned in advance.

But if "people" know infinitely more than they used to, they at once become terribly embarrassed when asked who these "people" actually are that know so much and are increasing their knowledge as such a rate of speed. I am not one of these "people"; there can no longer be any one human being who can stand for these "people" who have such enormous knowledge. The desire to become a universal polymath is something we have had to forgo. The most intelligent are condemned to being narrow specialists (to use the current derogatory term) and to remaining such.

Of course even today we can strive for the broadest possible education; we can put a few encyclopedic reference works on our bookshelves which always contain a ludicrously small number of books; we can frequent reference libraries; in what are known as interdisciplinary dialogues we can listen to what others know and what they have to tell us and come away with the impression that we do not after all really understand what we are being told by one of the representatives of another science.

To a certain extent, of course, we can profit from the knowledge of others by turning on the radio or by using a computer that we would be incapable of constructing ourselves. We can master the necessary tricks that show us how to make an ostensible contribution to every discussion without at the same time betraying our ignorance, but in the end that is no help either.

Measured by the yardstick of the amount of knowledge available in principle at any given time, the individual person today is becoming progressively more ignorant. In former times people knew relatively little but an individual person could know almost all of what was then known. Today people know a great deal, but the individual can know only a tiny fragment of this. To be sure, this enormous amount of knowledge available in principle today can be stored in libraries and computers, and means can certainly be found to enable individuals quickly and conveniently to call up from this mass of knowledge just what they need right here and now or what they might be curious about. This, however, presupposes that these individuals are still capable of realizing that there is something of interest or use to them here and now that they do not yet know, a presupposition that is by no means obvious anymore.

But all this knowledge stored in books and computers is in itself alone only the material distillation of real knowledge and it will become real knowledge only when it is once again restored to the consciousness of real human beings. A human library on Mars would in fact no longer be a human library. But as opposed to former times, this knowledge that has taken on material form can no longer in its totality be translated back into the consciousness of the individual as such. So the fact remains: the individual as such, who alone can be the real repository of true knowledge, is becoming progressively more ignorant.

That might not be so bad because, as the saying goes, "What you don't know won't hurt you." In the case of individuals, however, this applies only when they are unaware of their lack of knowledge. Almost everyone knows today how enormously this ignorance can be repressed and how people can take an all-too-naive pleasure in the number of things really known to them. People who think that the really crucial knowledge the world needs is stored in their own little brains can actually fancy themselves to be educated people and they can even be pompous, narrow specialists. But today in a way never before possible, we can also become aware of the distance between what we do know and what we can know. Whether or not this dawning awareness of our ignorance may be called a *docta ignorantia*, a learned ignorance, is a question we can leave open. In any case, however, this ignorance is very painful for us and it is humiliating.

THE FUNDAMENTAL LACK
OF CONCEPTUAL CLARITY

Before proceeding any further we must point out another characteristic of our actual knowledge. This particular element has its origin in the enormous sphere of ignorance that surrounds our knowledge. To a degree heretofore unknown, this ignorance is relentlessly corroding the clarity of our concepts and the intrinsic consistency of our knowledge and threatening them. Conceptual precision and clarity, the delight of previous generations, is now diminishing rapidly. To be sure, in the past this clarity may to a great extent have been due to an ignorance that people were simply not aware of, and this made clear and simple thinking easy. It is easy to draw straight lines on a plane surface; in the past it was easy for people to define something if they were unaware of the obscure and problematic nature of the elements used in defining the concept.

For us today, however, each and every individual reality that we contemplate is related in many ways to countless other individual realities that would have to be taken into account if the first reality is to be rendered clear and distinct; and all the other individual realities, which would have to be understood in order to understand the first, begin to blur and disappear in a dense fog of the obscure and the unknown.

In the area of material realities who can still tell us what substance, time, space, and place mean? Can we still make a plain and simple statement about the human being today without being constantly tormented by the awareness that we have neglected or been ignorant of a thousand things that we really should have known and taken into consideration if we wanted to make an honest and responsible attempt to make such a statement? Is there anyone of us today who can use a concept of theology or philosophy without worrying about whether this concept has been used much too naively and superficially if we really do not know the whole complicated history of this concept? Do we not constantly have to ask ourselves whether we may use such concepts when we really know that their history has been treated somewhere or other in scholarly tomes that we have not had time to read in our brief lifetime? Are we not becoming increasingly unsure of what we are saying? Is it so easy to counter this by a reflexively produced naiveté?

In view of all this, the decline in the consistency of our knowledge is obvious. In former times we had at our disposal only a relatively limited amount of knowledge that could be kept in clear view and that was more or less — at least to our own satisfaction — structured in clear concepts, and for this reason its intrinsic coherence and its freedom from inconsistency was also obvious. However limited an individual's knowledge is when compared with the knowledge actually available today, it is, nonetheless, still enormous taken in itself and thus it is no longer possible for an individual to gain a full grasp of the mutual consistency of its individual elements. If an individual today should subject his or her knowledge to an honest and objective appraisal, he or she would have to say, "So much knowledge, so many opinions and views from every side have found their way into the storehouse of my consciousness that, try as I may, I really couldn't tell you anymore if and how it all fits together, and I couldn't even tell you how even in principle it could be synthesized into a consistent 'system.' "

All things considered, however, this has been the lot of human beings from time immemorial, since people have always been burdened with errors which were incompatible with other true insights that they had. But this situation of an insuperable inconsistency in the whole of our knowledge in itself has been exacerbated tremendously. Our knowledge is too vast for us to bring it even to some small degree of harmony. What we say today contradicts what we said yesterday and we do not even notice it. What can also happen, of course, is that given the lack of clarity in our concepts, we think we have discovered a contradiction between two statements and we challenge someone, even though these two statements might really be quite compatible if the concepts used and the limitations implied in both statements were clear.

In any event, the fragmentation of our consciousness has increased and we are aware of it. Indeed, we cannot refrain from considering others to be obtuse, naive, and primitive if they are not aware of this fragmentation and fail in their utterances to realize the lack of clarity in their concepts and the inconsistency in their knowledge.

That is the situation of our consciousness today. Overcoming this situation to the extent that it can be overcome is certainly a constant challenge and a task that we have to master. But we must also have the courage to see and to admit that this situation of increasing "stupidity," of an increasing lack of clarity in our concepts, and an inconsistency in our knowledge is ultimately insuperable, that it is the price that we constantly have to pay for the immense increase of our knowledge.

THE INTELLECTUAL VIRTUE OF PATIENCE

What are we to do in the face of this situation that holds inexorable sway over us? As we said at the beginning of our discourse: patience is necessary. We must have patience even in the face of our own ignorance. We have got to understand that this patience is anything but obvious, that it is no easy task. Those who are only ignorant are not even aware of their own ignorance and so they need no patience with their intellectual situation. But those who are wise in their ignorance — and I hope that we belong to this group — experience the bitter pain of their ignorance and must learn how to bear it in patience.

In this situation we must always ask ourselves whether we are avoiding the danger of letting ourselves sink impatiently into a skeptical resignation, whether we are not covertly attempting to rid ourselves of this task of patience in some other way, by repressing the situation or by taking naive pleasure in the knowledge we do have. We must ask ourselves whether we really do have this patience and are practicing it even when it seems to us to be obviously present among the virtues that we possess. If on this question we feel that we can quite readily set our conscience at ease, we would have to ask ourselves whether we have really faced the pain of our ignorance that today more than ever before is imposed upon us or whether we are wrongly allowing ourselves to be satisfied with our paltry knowledge, a satisfaction that is not permitted us.

I would now like to make a timorous attempt to show some of the implications of this patience that our situation requires of us. This might help us to understand a little better what is actually meant by this intellectual virtue of patience, this unknown virtue.

Patience as a Way to God

First of all, this patience is akin to that real *docta ignorantia* of which philosophers remotely speak and which mystics in East and West strive to attain. If we experience that an infinite ocean of nameless mystery spreads out beyond the pitifully small island of our knowledge, and if we interpret this experience in the light of the experience that we have previously been speaking about, perhaps the unity of this twofold experience can bring us a little closer to the enormous courage of the saints and mystics who submerged their soul in its source, and awaken this courage in us too. For they experience this ocean of holy mystery bounding "the tiny island of their knowledge" no longer as a boundary that confines them; they dare to set out on this ocean; they are not afraid that its silent immensity will swallow them up; they entrust themselves to this "unknown that is known," seeing in it the blessed mystery that shelters them. They dare to enter the void of their consciousness. The individual elements of knowledge cease to exist, and in the ensuing "nothingness" they experience the real and comprehensive truth that can no longer be divided up into a number of individual propositions.

We may proceed no further here in our discussion of this ineffable mystery which transforms the pain of ignorance and of our own obtuseness into the blessedness of the light which to our everyday consciousness appears as a dark night. Nor need we spend much time here warning of the dangers that at least Christians are aware of who know that the patient endurance of our earthly multiplicity and inconsistency is ultimately the only way that leads through the reality of death with Jesus, the crucified, to the blessed incomprehensibility of the true God; who know that true mystics must always be ready to leave their sublime contemplation, their mystical silence, and divide their bread with the needy; and that the solemn festival of blessed union with the incomprehensible mystery can be celebrated only when they have plodded through the drudgery of everyday existence and its duties. Here we only wanted to suggest briefly the notion that the patience we have undertaken to praise might also be the entrance gate to that *docta ignorantia* that brings all human knowledge in its distracting details into the light which we Christians even today do not hesitate to call God.

Patience and Tolerance

But this patience with our intellectual situation contains still other implications. Let us consider tolerance first. On the one hand, we say that people should be tolerant of one another, but that truth is inexorably intolerant of error. That is assuredly a maxim that we can and must subscribe to. It is really not our intention here to talk about a convenient relativism. Nor are we denying the fact that the legitimate freedom to make concrete decisions necessarily involves a certain unyielding intolerance toward those who want to decide differently, even if we might wish this to be otherwise. Not everything in the world can always be settled by a compromise that suits everybody.

Nevertheless, if the reasons we have given for intellectual patience are correct, we can see that the truth which is our human truth and not God's divine truth involves in and of itself a dimension of tolerance. For our statements and concepts, however correct and true they may be, and hence certainly not willing to accept a contrary statement as equally justified, point of their very nature to unknown elements which, had they been known and taken into consideration, would also cause these statements and concepts to appear in a different light, inasmuch as these are always statements and concepts that point beyond themselves. The unknown elements would require us to be more cautious in interpreting these statements in their approximate truth. They would make it understandable that these finite and historical statements of ours, even if their validity remains intact, would have much less need of rejecting as error the things that someone else is attempting to assert as truth.

It was an axiom of scholastic philosophy that an abstraction did not necessarily imply an error: *Abstrahentium non est mendacium*. This axiom is correct, but it is also a dangerous axiom which those with excessive zeal for their own convictions pervert over and over again. Not only in God's heaven are there many rooms, but also in the house of the one, all-embracing truth.

Those who experience the pain of their own ignorance and endure it with patience can be more tolerant, and genuinely tolerant, in the area of ideology than those who view this tolerance as nothing more than a convenience for people who have to live with one another but are divided in their views. To anyone who has the impression that the legitimate and inexorable claim of truth over all the facile forms of relativism hardly leaves room for the tolerance which we have just tried to show as an intrinsic characteristic of our human truth, then, prior to the quite necessary and altogether possible attempts to reconcile this apparent contradiction, I would say that an admittedly temporary lack of compatibility between the adamant stand on behalf of the truth on the one hand and tolerance on the other has to be endured with the patience we are talking about. It is quite possible that this reconciliation of tolerance with inexorable conviction is also a task that has to be mastered anew as is true in thousands of other cases where we adhere to two truths and convictions without clearly seeing that they are inherently compatible even though they are apparently contradictory. Those who really manage to have intellectual patience with themselves will also be tolerant toward their neighbors and will not behave as though they were absolute truth in person.

Knowledge and Freedom

We are all called upon to exercise this patience in yet another way. There is always a radical tension between our knowledge and our freedom. In a certain sense our free acts are irrevocable and hence absolute, while the knowledge leading to these decisions cannot fully justify their irrevocability. There are always reasons for deciding one way or another, even though this does not mean that the reasons are equally valid. Choosing among these reasons, freedom makes its decision for one course of action and translates this into reality, leaving the other course perpetually unrealized. For us today, the ever-present condition of incalculability between insight and freedom which then turns freedom into something more than the mere executor of reason has become more acute as a result of the situation now calling upon our patience.

More than ever before, the insight that forms the basis of our decisions is fragmentary and vague. We have to make our decisions knowing that we are ignorant of many things which, if they were known to us, would actually render our free decisions transparent and innocuous. Today, more than ever before, we know that all our decisions are hazardous ventures into the unknown. Of course we do have to decide because usually the attempt to abstain from making an unambiguous decision would itself amount to a decision, one that would usually be the worst possible decision and the one least capable of being justified. But these decisions that must be made and so in principle have a moral right to stand despite their lack of lucidity must still be made on the basis of a rational justification which is always strained beyond its limits, and this tension causes us pain. But this is why patience, the endurance of the present-day tension between rational insight and free decision, is especially difficult and yet at the same time more necessary than ever.

Today our intellect, when called upon to make a free decision possible and to justify this decision, is harassed by countless contradictory reasons; yet it still may not permit us to cast aside our rational responsibility and make things easier for ourselves by making our decisions in a purely arbitrary way. How difficult it is today to steer between the extremes of succumbing, on the one hand, to a weary skepticism and relativism that see everything as equally right and equally wrong, and boast of a detachment and wisdom capable of dissolving everything into a void, and of paying homage, on the other hand, to a fanaticism that sees no need of a rational justification that requires us to bridle the vehemence of our emotions and subject its concepts and arguments to an objective examination if we are going to use it as a basis for acting. Our times and our generation would, however, probably not seek refuge in a voluntaristic irrationalism because the rationality that we are capable of having sees more clearly today how fragmentary and arduous everything is, provided that it does not overestimate itself and that it has patience with its own inadequacy that it has realized and suffered through.

IN WINTRY TIMES: PATIENCE

Presumably we could expand our considerations into a treatise on one of the dianoetic virtues as they used to be called. It was a conviction in former times that the dimension of knowledge viewed in itself contained not only technically developed skills, but that this cognitive dimension itself was also composed of elements that called for a moral qualification, that is, virtues, as paradoxical as this statement might appear at first glance. The times we live in are to a great extent blind and can see no virtue in cognition and knowledge but only a proficiency that is ultimately not subject to value-judgment, and hence is more or less free of responsibility. The potential for catastrophe present in this cognition that is blind to values is therefore usually not noticed until it is too late. But this cannot be treated in greater detail here.

I shall speak no further of the patience that we must have today in view of our cognitive limitations. I hope that I have not overtaxed your patience. It seems to me that as a result of the progress we are experiencing today in all the dimensions of knowledge, individuals have the growing feeling that they know very little and are not able to overcome the inadequacy of their knowledge; that the intoxicating pleasure of former times that accompanied the acquisition of ever new knowledge is denied them, without their being allowed for these reasons to commit mental suicide; that therefore they must have patience with themselves as in wintry times.

5

A BASIC THEOLOGICAL
AND ANTHROPOLOGICAL
UNDERSTANDING OF OLD AGE

You could say that I must be the right person for this job. I am a theologian and I shall soon be eighty years old. But things are not quite as simple as that. After all, in traditional theology aging and old age are not subjects that have been explicitly treated in any great detail. Hence any theology of old age would have to begin with research in other anthropological disciplines to ascertain what they know about old age. It would then have to ask whether and how this knowledge has theological significance and whether theology can bring this knowledge to a deeper level.

But an investigation of this kind also presumes a competence that I do not possess and at my age am no longer capable of attaining — not even for a contribution to a theological gerontology. For example, when I delve into Simone de Beauvoir's huge tome on old age and am confronted with the enormous amount of information contained in this book (information which, however, has not always been effectively synthesized), the task I am expected to perform could discourage a person of my age.[1] But I have the feeling (and this itself is a tiny contribution to this theology of old age) that a touch of timidity is permitted because honest patience with one's own weakness and pusillanimity is both a prerogative of old age as well as a challenge to it.

Nor can I simply collate and assemble the explicit theological statements that Scripture and tradition have made on the subject of old age.

---

[1]Simone de Beauvoir, *La vieillesse* (Paris, 1970).

50

Scripture itself has perhaps said a great many important and wonderful things on this subject, but it assuredly does not contain an explicit and consistently structured theology of old age. Hence any attempt to construct a systematic teaching from the statements of Scripture would, properly speaking, yield only the system of the particular theologian making this attempt, but not really that of Scripture itself. Recourse to the Church's tradition would quite quickly find it necessary to move beyond this tradition into the immeasurable breadth and multiplicity of the most diverse styles characteristic of aging and old age and their interpretation in human history because human life experience and life experience that is explicitly Christian cannot be completely distinguished from one another.

OLD AGE AS A HISTORICAL AND SOCIAL PHENOMENON

The human process of aging and old age that we ourselves experience is a union of nature and history, physiology and social situation (or however one wants to describe this indissoluble unity in duality that determines the total existence of human beings throughout all of their dimensions) that defies total analysis. Human beings have a "nature" about which the natural sciences today, from physics to biology, from paleontology to modern medicine, can tell us an enormous number of things that can be used in a scientific gerontology. This gerontology tells us how this biological creature, the human being, grows old and how this aging process affects all the dimensions of human beings reaching right up to the very tip of their highest mental and spiritual faculties.

These natural sciences (along with a psychology of old age that is also based on natural science) can also describe how this aging proceeds, even though they perhaps do not ultimately know why this complex biological reality known as a human being inevitably grows old and dies. But even though all these natural sciences together have developed their gerontology, human aging and old age have not been completely described, and so it is not possible to say that individuals understand their own old age and know how to deal with it properly on the basis of scientific information alone. Rather, aging and old age, despite their ultimately inseparable union with their biological side, are phenomena of a social, historical, and cultural kind.

One can say (from the standpoint of natural science) that human beings always grow old and die in the same way. (For example, in the mummies of the most ancient times physicians can discover the same illnesses that we still have today.) One can also say (from the social and historical standpoint) that aging, old age, and dying in every historical period and social situation (both of which are constantly changing) are completely different. The second statement is also true.

In primitive tribes old age and dying are experienced differently from the way we experience them today in a home for the aged. The way society views old age, the power or lack of power that old people have, the number of old people and their average life expectancy, economic and medical possibilities of dealing with the situation of old age, and so on in different cultures, different economic systems and social orders reveal an enormous variety of forms, so that one might almost say that in the different historical periods and cultures almost the only point of agreement in respect to old age is that it ends in death.

Moreover, the explicit interpretation of old age and death in different cultures, religions, and worldviews itself works retroactively in helping to determine how aging and dying will be experienced in the concrete, so that from this standpoint as well the most diverse styles characteristic of the way old people live and die can be found. And finally, human beings for their part in their unity and incalculable quality are not merely random specimens of a genus or of a collective entity but also unique individuals who help to shape their own lives in inalienable freedom. So in this light, too, old age is not merely a social and cultural-historical phenomenon in a socio-cultural context but also a part of the ever unique individual that every human being is.

If, then, old age is both a union of nature and history that cannot ultimately be completely dissolved and an existence that is ever unique, for us old people this has a simple, yet strange consequence, and dealing with this is also part of the burden and the challenge of our old age. We are nature; that is, we have to accept ourselves as people who are growing old biologically together with everything that this inexorably implies in regard to the waning of our vitality and of our intellectual powers as well, without making a senseless protest against God and the nature willed by him. Our old age is also a historical and social phenomenon. We do indeed have the right and the duty to attempt to influence present history and our society and to change them so that they will become more humane and more just, but this historical and social situation which our old age helps to determine and which itself is a part of our old age is for the most part practically unalterable in the time still remaining to us. And so this situation must be accepted with serenity and patience, and this acceptance is something that is part of our old age if we live it successfully.

OLD AGE AND THE PAST

Old age also inexorably means that, as a matter of fact, we have most of our life behind us. This is a truism, but we have to consider this statement closely in order to understand what it really means. If we are talking about "a matter of fact," this term is just the right one. Our past (at least at first glance — we shall also have to take a second look) is an objective "matter" which came to be through the "way" in which we exercised our freedom, and in a true sense this past has become definitive. But the person who thinks more exactly and profoundly, particularly if he or she is a Christian, must be taken aback by our remark that we have our life "behind us." For we should really have to say that in old age we now have our life present "before us." Out of countless possibilities, as though out of a dark ground, which lies behind us as something "given" and not subject to our disposal, the free history of our life, by means of our free actions, brought the concrete shape of our life forth and brought it before us. And this concrete shape of our life is something that *is* and it stands before the critical gaze of our memory and what we have stored up there. Whatever may be the case in regard to the events of mere natural history once they have happened and are past, the human being's past with its history of actual freedom is not just something that once was and has now simply fallen down into the nothingness of what has ceased to exist, something that is dissolved and is nothing anymore.

Precisely because in freedom it once became the way it is, our life *is*, not gone, but rather it has gone forth from the dark ground of the merely possible as something eternally real. However one may explain this fact of the eternally abiding character of the history of freedom, and it is certainly not easy, the fact remains. To understand it better one may have recourse to the idea of the "Book of Life," the heavenly book in which God has inscribed all of our deeds according to which he will judge us. Or one may prefer to understand it in terms of the soul. The substantial and abiding ground of our spiritual soul receives from the actions of our lives permanent impressions which no longer pass away, even though we forget them and other waters of time flow over this ground. Or perhaps we can succeed in making present to ourselves the

permanence of our free history, which only seems to be past, in contrast
to our dangerous "forgetfulness." Whatever explanation we choose, it
is ultimately secondary. The inescapable fact remains that now in old
age we are the persons that we have become throughout the whole of
our lives.

We can try to forget this or to repress it. In old age our brain un-
dergoes physiological changes that can make it impossible for us to
recollect many things from our past or can cause us to remember events
long past more clearly than things that have recently happened. Our
remembrance of our own past can be colored in a way that does not
correspond to its reality; we see things in a kindlier or more terrifying
light than is really warranted. None of these things alter the fact that in
old age we are *the* persons that we have become throughout the whole
of our lives. Herein lies an immense challenge for us in our old age. It is
not the only one, not entirely, since we are still living our lives and we do
still have some future that we have to shape. When we old people think
frequently and intensely about our past life, this is not an idle exercise
nor need it make us sad. Old age still has a great deal of work to do on
the history of its past life. The shape that we have given to our lives and
that we now are is not yet complete.

Under certain circumstances this shape can be changed quite radically and improved. If we were now to proceed under the catchword
"contrition," our considerations would be too limited. Christians are
certainly aware that when they turn to God in repentance and conversion, to God who is also Lord of their own past, the God of forgiveness,
they can give their past life an entirely new interpretation, they can give
it another shape, a radically new meaning. But as true as it is that we cannot forgive ourselves the evil of our past life, but rather must and can
let ourselves be forgiven by God in humble love, still the notion of contrition and forgiveness can easily lead to the misunderstanding that the
evil past is only blotted out and thus simply sinks into the abyss of what
is merely past. If we consider the matter more exactly, however, contrition and conversion do not erase the past but transform it by God's
action in our lives. The past, even the evil past, receives a new meaning.
But this gives old age a great and positive task in respect to life past,
and it makes it possible to accomplish this task.

There is a lot of talk today about "overcoming the past." This is mostly
idle chatter that does not even understand itself. But the person who is
old has a really blessed task and one that can be accomplished. Perhaps
it would be better to call this a new shaping of the past rather than over-

coming the past. Old people can still learn; they can learn things from the past that help to interpret this past anew. They can eliminate the bitterness that has accumulated in them like sediment. They can acquire a better understanding of their lives than they have had before. They can become wiser and more serene. By turning to God and together with him they themselves may once again with the forgiving God judge the shortcomings and dark elements of their lives mercifully and grant pardon; with the Church's liturgy they may interpret all this as *felix culpa*, "happy fault."

Looking at our own past life can make us more tolerant of others. We can try to reduce the lifetime accumulation of aggression and prejudices against ourselves, against others, and against the outward circumstances of our lives. (In an hour of peace and quiet we need but attempt such a "revision of life" to see how much has to be done in this area and how much could be done.) In a word, old age has not only the eventual task of repentance, in the narrower sense of the word, in respect to guilt incurred in past life, a guilt which has not ceased to exist merely because it is part of the temporal past; over and above this, old age has also an almost boundless task in respect to what we have become in the past and now still are.

We old people are not finished with our lives yet. In a true sense everything is still open; only the future will reveal the outcome of life's drama. And everything that is inexorable in the light of the past is subject to the verdict of the God of a love that can transform everything, and who can also change our past life into blessed freedom without having to wipe it out. In his eternity all our time can remain valid and yet be so transformed that our time has been preserved and can then be accepted without regret. To be sure, our hope of this has its source in a faith that is credible only in the light of Jesus Christ and his message. That faith must be proclaimed in the Church over and over again.

At this point perhaps another remark is called for by way of afterthought. From the standpoint of our biological and physiological life, which in the highest degree helps to determine even our mental and spiritual life, it is quite possible for us in our old age to be beset by a physical and mental condition which makes it more or less or even completely impossible for us to accomplish all of these beautiful tasks of old age that we have spoken about or propose to speak about. Let us be honest and let us face up to the harsh realities that can strike even us. We can become piteously senile. A softening of the brain can occur. No moral theologian, much less any other reasonable human being, will deny that in our old age we can be assailed by excruciating physical pain and deep, physiologically conditioned depression and mental confusion of such a kind that one can no longer seriously say that we are really morally accountable for the things we do in states such as these. We can admire saints in their martyrdom and Indians at the stake for the unrelenting clarity of their mind even unto death. In the end, however, it is not within our power or the power of our freedom, but it is within God's to say whether a similar state of mind will be possible for us in our old age and when we are dying.

We can hope that in death our mind will be tranquil, lucid, and composed. We must do everything in our power to cope, in courage and resignation to God's will, with the pain and depression that assail us in old age. But we are not obliged to do more than lies within our power, and Christian teaching does not expect the impossible of us. If physical pain and psychic depression plunge us into a state in which we can no longer do what we are, presumably, obliged to do, then we have come to the point where the eternal God in his love gently relieves us of all responsibility for our life. What "happens" after that is, humanly speaking, irrelevant and does not matter in God's eyes. If a person in this state seems to be desperately cursing God, this must be viewed as a physiological occurrence and not as a human act, just as in the case of a dying person whose mind begins to wander. We can pray for a cheerful old age and a "happy" death, but the shape in which old age and death will come to us is something that lies in God's hands. It is one of the tasks of old age to prepare ourselves to accept this situation of old age and death that is approaching us in a way we cannot foresee, and to know that everything can be grace, even when there is nothing more left to us but the helplessness of the vanquished.

OLD AGE AS A BRIDGE BETWEEN GENERATIONS

We shall now speak of a special task that old age can perform. Old people can often try to be a bridge between generations. We should not harbor illusions or promote utopian ideas in this matter. The elderly poor reduced to living in a crowded home for the aged, more or less forgotten by their own kin, have practically no way of taking on the task we are about to describe, and as human beings and Christians they must find other ways of coping with their old age. But many old people do have the opportunity to perform this task. But they have to be willing to see what it is and seize the opportunity of doing it.

The role played by "grandpa" and "grandma" in many families is well-known and prized. For the two generations with whom they live the youngsters love to have them as go-betweens and the grown-ups cherish them for this. In former times old people had an almost institutionalized function of giving counsel, handing on traditions, and serving as a stabilizing force. This intermediary function of old people need not be restricted to family and clan in the narrower sense. It can be expanded far beyond these. Just because the leaders who have the decision-making power in the various organizations of society do not let old people have "the last word" is no reason for them to withdraw in a huff from these organizations, condemn themselves to the limbo of old age, and feel that they have been put on the shelf. They should demand a little bit of modesty and self-effacement of themselves and not hesitate to continue in these organizations in a cheerful and matter-of-fact way, even though now they might perhaps not always be given a seat in the front row. Continuing to make an appearance at the customary social get-togethers with friends and acquaintances, even if one is a little bit hard of hearing and does not catch everything that is said and so is now forced to play second fiddle, can really be a Christian task of old age. One must want to be present here and there, even though sometimes it can be a little bit boring for the elderly person. Just going to a lecture can be a task of old age in mediating between the generations. The elderly man need not try to look and behave like a young fellow and the elderly lady need not feel obliged to turn up at every party. But old people should not be afraid to stay with the rest of humankind without feeling inhibited and self-conscious about it. Their life experience is capital that can yield interest for coming generations.

The same can also be said about continuing to work in church organizations and parish societies. In these, elderly people can still perform any number of functions which might appear too lowly to others and yet are still important for church life, even though it might be nothing more than collecting used postage stamps and getting them ready for shipment to the missions. Old people have to act as intermediaries between the generations. They just have to be willing to see this intermediary function and perform it, even though it might seem to be only a modest one.

FAITH IN ETERNAL LIFE

In all the phases of our lives all of us live on the border of God's eternity. Younger and middle-aged people can be victims of heart attacks, traffic accidents, and other fatalities. But we old people are living in a situation in which, both from within and from without, we receive special signals warning us of our closer proximity to this end allotted to all human beings, warning us that death is approaching inescapably. We are still living, but we are looking toward the end.

Our Christian belief in eternal life accompanies this. This eternal life should evoke something more in us than the grumbling admission that we have no objection to it since, after all, we cannot go on living here forever, and so almost with a kind of resignation whose lack of faith is scarcely concealed we let them give us the message of eternal life. We must look toward this eternal life in loving hope. And so we old people live in a strange and unique state of tension between the courage to live here and now and the hope of eternal life. We are still living and so we must strive to go on living. To be sure, the candle of our earthly life is burning lower now and its flame casts a dimmer light and often flickers anxiously. To be sure, this limits our possibilities and we have no need of talking ourselves into the illusion that it is just a matter of willpower to keep up our former stride. There are a lot of shallow slogans for this ("You're as old as you feel," etc.) that we should not goad ourselves with, but rather honestly and objectively admit the fact that our vitality is ebbing in all the dimensions of our life (including the intellectual one). Nonetheless, the fact remains that we are still living and we should have the desire really to live the life still remaining to us and live it to completion.

Some old people let themselves go. They neglect the rules of physical hygiene and do not otherwise keep themselves up even though they are perfectly capable of doing this. That is stupid and cowardly. The elderly lady who takes care to make a well-groomed appearance without trying to imitate young girls is doing just the right thing. People quite advanced in years can have all sorts of interests; they can keep up their personal acquaintanceships, take up new hobbies, and so on. To be sure, we know that the time is coming when we will be lying on our deathbed and will not be able to do these things anymore. But what we still can do, we really should do, instead of letting ourselves get cranky, and with false resignation and cowardice wish to thrust ourselves prematurely into that darkness into which God will one day lead us; but he will do it gently and softly and not in the way we do it to ourselves. In old age we can talk about something other than our illnesses and our aches and pains. As long as we still have ourselves under control — and we should not try to convince ourselves prematurely of the opposite — we can forbid ourselves this kind of talk which is useless to ourselves and a burden to others.

In a word, as long as we live we should also want to live. But for Christians, life here on earth is seen in the perspective of eternal life. This hope of eternal life is not a cheap consolation when we have nothing else left; it is a sacred task. Is there any reason why old people should pray less than in their earlier years? It is stupid and mean to consider every form of religious devotion practiced by ourselves or others in old age as suspect, and to want to expose it as the cowardly grovelling of a person in the last decrepit stages of life who now wants to become "religious" quickly. Without doubt, there are forms of religious devotion in old age that are bogus and cowardly. But these are not the only ones. Might a person not become more mature, wiser, and therefore more devout as well in old age? Why should a person's religious development have to be arrested at an earlier, perhaps quite infantile stage? Just to avoid having to admit that one has learned a little more and is forced to abandon a number of things formerly considered to be right? If we now perhaps take a critical look at many of the things we have done in the past, this can no longer change these things externally, but that is still no reason for us to persist in our old standpoint, since even the things that can no longer be changed by us can still be transformed by God's incomprehensible goodness and power. In old age we should not hesitate to have the courage to become more devout.

It is true, of course, that the expectation of eternal life that is implied in this, and that has to be shaped more intensively, can have very different shapes and forms. So we are not obliged to demand of ourselves a particular shape such as is customarily described in the lives of the saints. "Till we meet again in heaven, you dumbbell,"[2] the sister of one of my deaf brethren said to him, and died. This kind of lighthearted trust is not bestowed upon everyone. Saint Theresa of the Child Jesus died in a quite different way in the throes of her consumption, assailed by the indescribable darkness by which she was engulfed. And yet she trusted and hoped.

[2]The word play here is not apparent in English. The expression *taube Nuss*, here rendered "dumbbell," literally "empty nut," is a colloquialism like our "old coot." However, the word *taub* also means "deaf." — Editor.

The hope of eternal life takes on different forms in death, and to die in the way that God has disposed is also a part of true hope itself. With Jesus we must pray, "Father, into thy hands I commend my spirit," but in death one may also pray with Jesus the words of the psalm, "My God, my God, why hast thou forsaken me?" because God will answer this prayer, too, by giving us his eternal life. And so the forms of the hopeful expectation of eternal life that we have while living our old age vary considerably. The hope of eternal life can fill the hearts of some as a wonderfully consoling light and thus they can draw nigh to the final hour in joy. To others it is given (this is ultimately the same grace) to live in the steadfastness of a prosaic faith without desiring to paint heaven in their own colors: "I believe in life everlasting." People such as these will say to themselves, "My own heart is weak and narrow. I am almost afraid to look for a place where there is still room for this faith alongside the weariness and barrenness of my old age. But God is greater than my heart and does not demand more of me than I am honestly capable of doing." Old people are placed on the borderline between time and eternity. And there is where they have their most sacred task. This can be a heavy burden. But God bears it with us and takes it from us when we can really bear it no longer.

6

AUTHORITY

AUTHORITY IN GENERAL

We are presupposing that the etymology of the word *authority* provides very little help for an inquiry into the intrinsic nature of authority.

Preliminary Remarks on Conceptual Methodology
and Limitation of the Inquiry

Auctoritas in the sense of "authorship" obviously implies that the thing caused is dependent on its cause and thus in certain circumstances that the cause can continue to exercise a determining influence on the thing caused. However, in the various human societies the idea of authority is commonly understood as a relationship between the person holding the authority and the person determined by the authority in which relationship a causal and total origination of the person determined from the person determining is not implied or at least need not be implied.

At the beginning of our considerations it is of course not really certain that the different realities characterized as authority can really be subsumed under a more or less univocal concept. Nevertheless, the attempt may be made to elucidate the one and the same concept that more or less fits all "authorities." If this attempt is successful, it will enable us at least to draw a few general lines of demarcation and to set up a few general norms which from the outset are valid in their application to all "authorities." It must, however, be understood that the general concept of authority being sought here can only be a very "analogous" one.

Furthermore, it remains beyond doubt that concrete "authorities" are necessarily and to a very great degree different from one another despite the unity of this general concept. Therefore this must always be kept clearly in mind if lines of demarcation and norms are to be predicated about individual "authorities."

It would no doubt be methodologically wrong, even in an ultimately theological treatment, to begin here with the "authority of God" as the point of departure. For in the presumed origin from God (and if one will, from his authority) of any and all legitimate authority, it is clear from the start that God's authority (if one wants to apply this concept to him) is of an absolutely unique kind. A Christian theology and a sober rational philosophy can always and everywhere "ascend" to God, but they cannot proceed from him as that which is first known. Even when making this ascent they must use a large number of a posteriori empirical concepts, one of which is of course the concept "authority." And finally, God's authority is not part of the sphere of social relationships in which we are quite rightly seeking our concept of authority.

Possible "Frictions" among Free Subjects as a Starting Point for a General Concept of Authority

We proceed from general and very elementary phenomena which can be observed in human life, quite rightly acknowledging in them, without going into detailed analysis, an ontological dignity and a transcendental necessity. Both things and persons make up the environment in which human beings exist in this world. There is a plurality of individual realities which (quite apart from a reciprocal dependence on one another) cannot simply be understood as mere determinations of one and the same reality. Rather, they are really different from one another, demarcated from one another, each standing in itself, each a "substantial" reality. This "substantial" difference of the individual realities comprising the things and persons of the human being's environment may for its own part be a very variable concept. And even the relationship between independence and relativity to other things may also for its part be quite different in individual cases (even to the point of plural determinations which can be conceived of one and the same reality).

There is no doubt, however, that at least human beings as subjects, who are aware of themselves and have a free history, each with a responsibility of his or her own, are not simply mere determinations of the world or of a higher collective entity to which individuals are simply subordinate, but rather that they really have in themselves a specific independence that cannot be derived from anything else. At the same time, however, these nonderivable individuals are determined from outside: they stem from their parents; they are physically and biologically dependent on others for their existence; they are involved in intellectual and personal exchange (with other cultures) without which not even the physical-biological existence of human beings could in fact continue.

In their actual realization the free independence of human beings and their mutual interdependence condition each other reciprocally. The interdependence and determination from outside necessary for the existence of human beings in all their dimensions would not attain their goal of securing human existence if the free subject, instead of choosing to affirm them, simply wanted to close itself off to them. The free subject, even as free subject, is not absolutely self-sufficient. Rather, its condition is necessarily one of reaction to determination from outside, without which it could not as such exist. Conversely, however, even the determining element from outside is itself often the product of the free action of the subject, which product is then retroactively operative on the subject itself and on other subjects.

The plurality and diversity of the realities existing in the world, and especially among human beings, and the reciprocally conditioned relationship of independence and determination from outside are not, at least in fact, present in such a way that the individual entities fit together in a way that is "frictionless." "Frictionless" may be a very unphilosophical word. It refers to all sorts of realities. Two bodies cannot simply be present simultaneously in one and the same place, at least according to our empirical observations in the macrocosm; the biological realm is dominated by a "struggle for existence" concomitant with death and annihilation, and this assessment from the standpoint of the individual living organism is not without justification; the physical and changing environment of the biological realm is not always and to the same degree favorable to the individual living organisms; at least from the outset, harmony and peace in the area of the freedoms that cannot be derived from one another do not prevail in such a way that the exercise of freedom on the part of one person is likewise always positively the goal and the presupposition of the freedom of another. But all of these very different realities taken together — and these are what we mean when we say that they are not "frictionless" — do reach a common point of agreement in that they are resistant to one another, do not simply fit together smoothly, tend to contradict one another when making claim to a common space where they can exist.

Authority as the Mandatory Power to Regulate "Frictions"

Thus the question arises as to how these "frictions" are to be eliminated. They cannot mean simply that there is an absolute "struggle for existence" in which one entity considers the other as an enemy pure and simple whose existence is simply to be ruled out due to this threatening friction.

Thus the "regulation" that is required varies quite considerably according to the concrete cases and the different levels of being. In certain circumstances it is even quite possible for it to be identical with the right of the stronger, or with what are known as physical and biological laws. In our search for regulations of this kind we are restricting our reflections here exclusively to the relations of personal, free subjects among one another. Material and biological dimensions are also obviously included in these human free subjects. Thus, in this regulation being sought, such regulations as are part of the human being's subhuman dimensions must not be omitted (or just simply excluded by an ethical idealism). We must insist on this, even though the "frictions" that this implies and the subhuman regulations of these frictions, being susceptible to the influence of free, human decisions, themselves raise a problem and constitute an object requiring regulations which derive from the dimension of the free subject as such.

One could stop here and ask whether an approach beginning with the possible "friction" among free subjects might not be too narrow to provide an understanding of authority from the outset, or whether it might not lead in a false direction. One might also ask whether this approach does not from the outset conceal the real nature of authority in its majesty and dignity. However, if authority means the mandatory power to regulate human beings' social relations on the one hand, and if one acknowledges on the other that the free subject has a dignity and legitimacy that takes precedence over the regulations imposed upon it by other natural instances (something that could be demonstrated in an ontology and a theology of the free subject, and would have to be demonstrated, and this is of course impossible here), this approach cannot be summarily dismissed as inadequate or misleading. Overcoming frictions can quite properly be understood positively as providing a free subject with the possibility of self-realizations which are inconceivable apart from the overcoming of such frictions. But in this way authority as the mandatory power to remove these frictions can quite properly be vested with a dignity and importance which, at first glance, one might think is ignored in an approach of this kind.

Human Freedom Presupposes the Necessity of Social Regulations

The kind of regulations that we are seeking can serve to eliminate frictions arising in the interpersonal relations of individuals as such without their having to be part of the actual social sphere. Or they can be regulations that serve to eliminate actual social tensions. This distinction is to be expected because we are presupposing here that the relationship between the human being as an individual and an individual free subject on the one hand and the human being as a member of a society on the other is not one of absolute identity, in virtue of which one aspect of the human being could be completely transferred to the other. With this presupposition it is our intention here to inquire only about regulations pertinent to frictions in the social sphere. Therefore we are prescinding here from a consideration of regulations that can be sought, for example, in the area of personal love and the possible cases of conflict there, however important and necessary for human beings these regulations may be.

No one will deny that in the social sphere there can in fact be disharmony and contradictions arising from the needs of individuals and of particular groups in a society, and that frictions like these — or whatever else you want to call them — do actually exist in all societies. There will of course be social systems and theories which implicitly or explicitly proceed on the assumption that there really is an ideal social order capable of being grasped and put into practice, and that once this order is realized it will necessarily and permanently exclude these frictions among this society's concrete members, and this will mean that everyone can live in perfect harmony, peace, and happiness with everyone else. Given this presupposition, the regulations to be sought would consist of structures and norms which would have to be realized once and for all in this society along with instructions on how to bring about this not yet existing society.

Here, however, we are proceeding on the conviction that a society of this kind is impossible. The course of the world in general, which is one of the factors conditioning this society, cannot be foreseen in its ultimate concrete form and so it certainly cannot be manipulated in a completely effective way. And human freedom, after all, in its own history is constantly creating new and unforeseeable situations, tendencies, desires, and so on, which for their part are not just secondary material for the social order, but rather themselves help to change it and to call it into question.

So if this presupposition is the starting point, the rules being sought for the elimination of social frictions can also contain some sort of ideal conceptions about a desirable social structure or one that is desirable for the immediate future. But these rules cannot simply correspond identically to this social structure. Rather, they must of necessity also contain elements that are always merely provisional; they must be rules of temporary assistance and of improvisation; they must be capable of being implemented in such a way that the regulation governing one case here and now may and must be different for another case. The necessity of having the kind of regulations (and people responsible for them) which admit of improvised temporary assistance is simply a consequence of the impossibility of having a definitively ideal social order in which the necessity of regulations on a case-by-case basis would have abolished itself. This necessity is also a consequence of the nature of human freedom (here it does not matter whether and how this second reason is identical with the first). Freedom does not mean that we simply do what is commanded by general laws which would only have to be known precisely enough and their purpose comprehended for them to transform freedom into the peace which makes us happy in the knowledge that we have done what is necessary. If freedom really creates something new that cannot be completely and positively known and deduced from its presuppositions (at least by us), the regulations which such new realities require are not already present in the general constitutive structures of the realities alone, but they themselves must be set up anew.

At this point it still does not matter whether this new regulation required by a definite act of freedom is itself one that must be derived in a (morally) unambiguous and compulsory way from the situation at hand or whether it is itself, rather, a (morally legitimate) free regulation which could justifiably be different. In very many instances the second is certainly the case. But at the moment that is not the point at issue. Despite the necessity of a balanced regulation of conflicts in a society, that is, of "frictions" which are present in a society due to the plurality of realities that have not yet been harmonized a priori, such regulations are obviously not always present in advance. They have to be decided upon first and constantly be set up anew, and for this reason they require concrete agents who are themselves present in history. When eliminating these frictions in a pluralistic society, these agents have the task of respecting the demands arising from the objective circumstances. Thus they have to be "just" and respect the legitimate claims of all the competing and conflicting realities, and when making these regulations they may not lose sight of the unity of the social system. But it is a necessary and unavoidable part of their legitimate duties and rights to make a decision that does not and cannot completely arise from the objective claims of the matters at hand. There are various reasons why this is true, but they cannot be enumerated exhaustively here.

First of all, the reality to which this regulation is supposed to react has either come to be through an exercise of freedom or such exercises of freedom have helped to determine it. Even apart from the fact that no reality involving ourselves can be known by us completely and therefore does not present all the persons involved in the action the same aspects determining their decision to act, at least those established realities to which the regulation is supposed to respond are realities that cannot ultimately be derived or foreseen, so that in this light the indeterminability which is already peculiar to every reality becomes essentially more acute. It is precisely the ambiguity of the reality that makes it impossible to respond to it with only one single legitimate reaction.

Furthermore, it is part of the nature of the freedom claimed by the agent of such a regulation, a freedom also claimed to make this regulation (at least until the opposite is proved), that in the case of categorical decisions it can choose among *several* possibilities, all of which are morally permissible. For it is senseless to assume that freedom means only the choice between two alternatives, one morally good and the other morally reprehensible, that there is no freedom when freedom's choice is limited only to what is morally good, that real freedom exists only when it has to take into account what is morally reprehensible as well as what is morally good. But if this regulation is a *free* one, if and because it cannot be made in any way other than an act of freedom, it necessarily contains, partially at least, the nonderivability, the "arbitrariness" characteristic of an act of freedom. It must of course be "objectively sound"; that is, it must take into account as far as possible the nature, the independence, and the freedom of the realities which have to be balanced in making this regulation. But this regulation will not labor under the opinion that there can only be *one* objectively sound regulation and that this may not contain an element of the free, non-derivable decision.

THE INTRINSIC NATURE OF AUTHORITY

We have seen the necessity and the reality of a phenomenon that we call "authority."

The General Concept and the Concrete Manifestation of Authority

The word *authority* is known to us from the everyday use of language, and time and again we have experienced a reality that we call by this name. And now we declare that what we have just seen in the preceding reflection is to be called "authority." The justification for making these two terms identical is found in the fact that there are no demonstrable phenomena which would not perforce have to be called "authority" in the ordinary use of language that would not be identical with what we have come upon in our preparatory consideration. It is of course conceivable, as a matter of fact it is to be expected from the outset, that those realities which we encounter concretely and which in day-to-day life we usually call "authority" also manifest peculiarities which were not discovered in our previous consideration. Even presuming that this were the case, without citing examples for it at the moment, this still need not be evidence in refutation of our making "authority" identical with the phenomenon that we have in mind. For it is conceivable that the concrete reality of a definite authority possesses peculiarities which really are a part of the correct concept of this authority already envisaged by us, even though our correct conceptual approach has not yet worked out distinctly this peculiarity of this definite authority. That is quite possible.

It is also conceivable that the concrete phenomenon of authority that is our point of reference is amalgamated with realities from which it is not clearly distinguished, realities which in principle are not part of its essence and which have to be eliminated from the really essential concept of authority as such. For example, for authority to be recognized and to function in a seventeenth- or eighteenth-century society a particular style was required that is not necessarily bound up with the actual essence of authority. The manner of recognizing papal primacy still customary at the end of the twentieth century does not necessarily derive from the essence of the pope's primacy in the Church. If we allow for both of these possibilities, there is no reason why we cannot say that we have indeed envisaged in a general way the real essence of authority in our preparatory considerations. One must bear in mind that the essence of authority described here in a general way will be considerably modified according to the concrete nature of the society in question. Therefore we must dismiss the objection that this or that concrete authority in a definite society manifests peculiarities which cannot be positively deduced or understood from our concept of authority.

An Attempt to Describe Briefly the Reality of Authority

For a reality such as authority it cannot be expected that an actual definition or a succinct description can be found. Those realities which refer to being as such or to a subject that is open to absolute being in an unlimited way occupy no position that would permit one to "define" them from outside. If we keep this in mind, we need not be upset by the expected objection that such definitions work with tautologies.

In a brief description that still has to be explained, we "define" authority as "the morally justified capacity of a human being to regulate and determine social relations among members of society in a way that is binding on these members." According to this description, the holder of authority is a human being. Whether and how such a concept can be applied to God to denote a relationship of God to creatures, ultimately, of course, unique and nontransferable, need not for the moment concern us here, as we have already indicated in our introduction. As a creaturely reality, authority falls in any event under those statements which characterize all finite realities as creatures of God. It comes from God, is constantly sustained by him, is directed to him, is responsible to him, is finite and conditioned, and its establishment in a way that is absolute is forbidden. There is a danger that it can be corrupted and turned into an idol. It always exists in a historical process whose future outcome cannot be foreseen. It can be a means of redemption as well as a vehicle of guilt.

Individual and Collective Bearers of Authority

If the bearers of authority thus described are human beings, it is understood that they are in full possession of their essential being in a way
that can be actualized directly. Human beings in any other condition
(as embryos, as legally incapacitated persons, etc.) can receive authority potentially, but they cannot have it in act. It has been pointed
out above that there must be authority in societies. The necessity of
socialization arises from the nature of human beings, and so there
are societies which, without prejudice to their mutability in individual detail, participate as such in the necessity of socialization. And
then there are certainly societies which stem from free establishment
on the part of human beings or as such have only a remote and ten-
uous connection with a participation in the social nature of human
beings. But if both necessary and freely established societies are presumed to exist, the necessity of having authority and those who bear
authority holds true for both. *How* exactly these bearers of human
authority are constituted concretely is at this point an entirely open
question. The fact that the bearers of authority might really be identical with the totality of the members of the society in question does
not in principle preclude the necessity of authority. The only presupposition for this is that these collective bearers who are really identical
with the society (or with a definite group in it) are capable of freely
making a regulation because of which there must be such an authority. Whether or in what more concrete forms such collective bearers of
authority can be conceived is a question that we can for the moment
leave open.

Of course it also conceivable that the possibility of a regulatory activity on the part of collective bearers of authority will increase or
decrease in stages which are difficult to determine and recognize, and
for this reason a conflict can even arise as to whether or not this
possibility still exists. In our previous considerations what we had in
mind was rather an individual bearer of authority because the regulation that he or she must make has a margin of freedom and must
be made freely. In the ordinary case it seems to us that the bearer
of authority is the individual human being. In saying this, however, it
is still an open question how this individual bearer will be found and
appointed.

Basic Elements concerning the Appointment
of Bearers of Authority

The agent responsible for this appointment can of course be a collective body. One can object that this collective body (a town or city council, a parliament, a senate of cardinals, a meeting of members of an association) which appoints a bearer of authority exercises thereby a function of social regulation and so it must itself have authority. Therefore this authority must be conceived as something more original than that borne by a collective body. The following must be said in regard to this objection. First, it is not an a priori fact that all legitimate bearers of authority must be appointed by a collective bearer of authority. The history of human socializations obviously contains examples of bearers of authority who do not derive from collective appointments. (How the college of cardinals is a bearer of authority will be an obscure problem in church law.)

The moral dignity of personal subjects certainly means that a society consisting of such subjects has both the right and obligation to live in an orderly fashion. It follows from this that it also has the right and the obligation to appoint someone to regulate social relations if (in the abstract or due to concrete historical circumstances) such a person does not yet exist. But, apart from the fact that a larger society, if it is to undertake such an appointment, must be conceived as one already ordered and constituted in some way or other, indeed even as one already provided with bearers of authority, the question remains whether one should even call this right and obligation of a society "authority," if it is actually directed by all to all at the same time and does not yet possess the peculiar element of a one-way claim on an individual by society through the medium of a concrete bearer of authority. A community's right to make such an appointment is, after all, not being called into question just because one does not want to call the community's possibility of making this appointment "authority." In democratic societies we are accustomed to trace back the authority of the individual functionaries to an appointment by this society itself, thereby quite understandably ascribing "authority" to the collective body, the society itself. But the problem that then arises is whether one is to conceive the appointment of the functionary as creation, as communication of authority itself, or as mere designation of its bearer to whom his or her authority then comes from some other source (from God, from the natural law, etc.).

But does the capacity for appointing a bearer of authority always and necessarily presuppose actual authority on the part of those who make the appointment? Or is this capacity (where it must be conceived as present in a collective body as such) actually rather a consequence of the fact that no authority is as yet present? Is it not rather an expression of the obligation to see to it that there is a bearer of authority and thus to ensure the concrete existence of authority? The usual contrary notion is presumably based on a feudal conception which views bearers of authority as persons who authoritatively through themselves directly create moral obligations in their "subjects," and who are endowed with a sovereignty ultimately emanating from God that bestows on them a special dignity over and above all other members of the society in question.

This of course gives rise to the following questions. What is the source of an authority so conceived? Does not the society bestowing the authority have to possess this kind of authority from the outset? Or is this authority bestowed directly by God as soon as the bearer is designated? If one leaves aside these notions of a special dignity on the part of the bearer of authority, there is nothing preventing the society — if and to the extent that it may be conceived as not being in advance possession of an agent for regulating social relations (something that is not obvious) — from providing itself with a bearer of authority of this kind, even though it does not antecedently possess real authority in the sense in which we understand it. In this light, then, it is always individual persons who are the bearers of real authority, as is, in fact, the case in democratic forms of government. The fact that a small group is the bearer of one and the same authority may be viewed as a marginal case as far as this fundamental principle is concerned, because even in this case there must be a very small, manageable group, and even though equality of the members is the goal sought by this group, it still must have a *primus inter pares*, a first among equals. And so here, too, we see that the principle ultimately prevails according to which the bearer of authority is fundamentally an individual person.

The Theory of Delegation and the Theory of Designation

Scholastic social teaching treats the question that we have just come upon as the problem of what it calls "the theory of designation" and "the theory of delegation," and asks which of the two theories is the correct one. Both theories presuppose a social reality in which the concrete bearers of authority together with their authority come from a society.

The *delegation theory* presupposes that the society in question itself possesses the authority and transmits it to concrete and legally competent bearers of authority. As far as the authority of the state is concerned, the presupposition here is that this authority cannot be retained by the society as a whole, but for its really concrete exercise must be delegated to concrete bearers of authority, no matter whether the bearer of authority is a democratic parliament and a democratic government or a monarch. This view of course raises the question whether one can speak of authority in the proper sense if it cannot be exercised by its own bearer but must unavoidably be transferred.

According to the *designation theory*, the social entity from which the concrete bearer of authority comes does not itself initially possess this authority. It only constitutes or designates the concrete bearer of authority to whom this authority itself then comes from elsewhere (from the objective necessity of having an ordered society, from God, etc.). This theory is certainly applicable in very definite cases (for example, when the college of cardinals elects a pope during a vacancy of the papal see, and must elect one, although this college without a pope cannot be said to be in possession of the papal powers). However, the question still remains whether this designation theory applies in the case of constituting the authority of the *state*, or whether the people of the state are themselves originally in possession of the state's authority and transfer it in this way to a government (in the sense that all the power of the state "comes from the people"). In this designation theory this legitimate *capacity* for designating marks off its bearer from others who might eventually lay claim to this designation, and a mandatory power, a right, is ascribed to this bearer in regard to which the question may be asked whether this right might not also be called authority.

Thus on closer inspection it would seem that the two theories differ only in their terminology but not in fact. The delegation theory cannot deny that the "delegated" authority in the concrete is vastly different from the authority residing in the social entity that makes the delegation. The designation theory, on the other hand, must presuppose that something resembling a mandatory power, or authority, is present in the entity that makes the designation. It is no longer possible to discern a really objective difference in the legitimacy that those social entities have to constitute a concrete social authority. Of course one can imagine cases where in view of concrete circumstances a social entity (for example, the totality of the male members of a small tribe, etc.) holds full and total social ("state") authority and then in particular instances delegates this authority as such (for practical reasons). Such cases, however, are marginal; they are due to concrete circumstances and do not by and large stem from the necessity of the general nature of authority.

The Dignity of Authority and the Order of Precedence among its Bearers

The moral necessity for the existence of a bearer of authority, the moral demand that the exercise of this authority makes in respect to the observance of a social regulation are not identical with authority itself. They are extremely variable and correlate to the nature of the society in question and to its necessity or nonnecessity. One can say that authority in any society derives as such from that society's necessity of having functionaries. There is a moral obligation to respect both those who bear these functions and the necessary functions they perform, even in cases where their individual decisions unavoidably involve an element of the "subjective" freedom of the bearer of authority. One can say that this authority also has a certain dignity due to the fact that it also makes a moral demand on the society's members. But this dignity does not actually elevate the bearers of authority to the highest position in the society in question. Judged from the standpoint of a society's nature and meaning, this highest position (if one chooses to view a society as structured on a vertical axis from above to below and the converse) is occupied by those whose activity contributes the most to the realization of this nature and meaning. In principle, however, it is not necessarily the functionaries who do this, "those who govern," but rather, in a secular society constituted in form of a state, for example, either those who are indispensable for its continued existence or those who make the greatest cultural contributions. In the Church it is not the bishops and popes as such, but rather the saints (both those who are known and those who remain hidden).

The Relationship between Authority and Coercive Power

The opposite impression (the notion that bearers of authority have a particular rank that places them on a level above others) is probably due to the fact that in the societies actually existing the bearers of authority do in fact have a position of power as a presupposition or a consequence of their authority as such, through which they compel a particular respect for themselves. But this power, which can extend to the actual use of physical force, is not identical with actual authority. This more or less demythologizing view of authority as a function of society, an authority that on the one hand is necessary but on the other hand secondary vis-à-vis the actual nature of a society and its task and its life, does not, however, deny that in view of the great and often essential diversity among societies there is also a great, and under certain circumstances essential, diversity among the authorities and their dignity.

If a distinction must be made between authority and an actual power to coerce, because the former in its regulations in themselves appeals to the free moral consent of the members of the society in question while the latter means that the area in which a subject (in itself) can exercise its freedom can be changed without the subject's prior consent, this distinction still does not tell us very much in advance about the more precise relationship of these two entities to each other. Fundamentally one will have to say that authority can be quite real even if it is not linked with "coercive power" (even with coercive power that is morally beyond reproach). There is no cogent reason for thinking that the possibility of establishing even a moral obligation would always and of necessity have to be conjoined with the possibility of using physical force. The mutual moral obligations arising from a personal love do not possess a power of coercion for their realization either.

Conversely, authority does not necessarily exclude in its bearer every capacity for the application of physical force. The only presupposition is that one does not consider the use of force to be always and inherently immoral, and that in a definite society for definite regulations of social relations the application of this force can be shown to be indispensable for the efficient functioning of these regulations. In this case, of course, a concrete authority in a concrete society is of its nature and in a morally legitimate way equipped with the capacity for using force. It is obvious that the concrete use of the force necessary in certain circumstances for the exercise of authority must be proportional to the greater or lesser importance of the social regulation that has to be undertaken by the authority, and that one does not overstep the boundaries imposed by the situation.

If and to the extent that the regulation intends an order that includes a morally absolute value, this power to coerce connatural to authority has more or less the character of punitive justice. Here, however, one must bear in mind that a social authority together with the coercive power connatural to it is not properly and directly the guardian of the God-given moral order as such, but is only tangential to it in an indirect way to the extent that it is required to establish and protect a social order. When and if moral values and transgressions against these values have no (grave) consequences for the social order as far as can be judged (and this assessment is historically quite variable), a secular authority should not presume any punitive power either. Whether or not this is different in the ecclesial society is a question that will be treated later and depends on the question whether or not an ecclesial authority is equipped with a power to coerce vis-à-vis the members of the Church.

SUMMARY AND CONCLUSIONS

Authority is necessary for a society's existence and therefore it partic-ipates in the (graduated) necessity of a definite society, the necessity of which can in its turn be absolute or hypothetical. Therefore a dis-tinct bestowal of authority is not necessary. The only thing necessary is to determine in an objective and morally irreproachable way who in a concrete society the bearer of this authority is, an authority that must of necessity be present in this society. The interrelationship be-tween a particular individual and this individual's function of being bearer of authority can vary considerably. This interrelationship can even be conceived in such a way that a particular individual actually and beyond challenge exercises this function and that if this function were to be wrested from the society, great damage would in fact be inflicted on the society and its well-being. It cannot be said that the democratic claim that every member of the society must be involved in the appointment of a bearer of authority is an inalienable and abid-ingly subsisting valid right of every human being. A democratic right of this kind does not issue simply from the abstract nature of any so-ciety nor does it emanate from the fundamental rights of every human being. This right, however, can exist in a derived way if without it the society in question would itself incur great damage in its nature and its activity.

AUTHORITY IN THE CHURCH

If one wants to discuss authority in the Church in a context of philosophical reflection, a fundamental difficulty arises right from the outset.

The Necessity of Church Authority as a Result of the Socialization of a Common Faith

A Christian church, and especially the Roman Catholic Church, certainly considers itself to be a society. In so doing it simply cannot avoid having its self-interpretation confronted by concepts and insights that come from a secular sphere of human experience and social theory. Otherwise ecclesiology would have to avoid using the word *society*, and the churches would not be permitted to manifest empirical realities whereby they obviously occupy a prominent place in earthly societies. How the individual churches more precisely determine the relationship of their social realities to their actual proper nature according to their different denominational self-interpretations is a matter of indifference. This proper, intrinsic nature of the Church may be conceived in a variety of ways in the different Christian denominations; such individual Christian socializations may or may not merit the name "church," (and if they do not, then they are called "sects"); a Christian conviction or mentality may even exist in an individual instance without there being a real socialization. But a common Christian mentality, a common faith, and a common way of life are inconceivable apart from some form or other of socialization. But if Christianity at all times and in all places does factually manifest a socialization, a society, that is, a Church, then an authority is also present everywhere that lays claim to making binding regulations for the relations of the members in this Christian social reality, relations which of course even here are not simply and permanently regulated already. In the different Christian churches and churchlike societies the authority that is always and unavoidably present will be interpreted and exercised differently (according to the total self-understanding that each of these societies has of itself). Since, despite all the diversity of their self-understanding, all these Christian churches still derive their nature and their justification for existence from Jesus Christ, albeit in very different ways (indirectly or directly, exclusively or otherwise), in all of them it is actually unavoidable that the authority be conceived, whether explicitly or not, as coming from Jesus Christ.

Because of the limited space available to us here, we must restrict our observations to the question of authority in the Roman Catholic Church. Since this Church has the most stringent understanding of authority, the authority present in it is not something that has validity for the other churches. Still, as an extreme instance of something that has ultimately one and the same nature, the Roman Catholic Church's understanding of authority can be instructive for the self-understanding of the other churches and their understanding of authority. It is obvious that we cannot present here a Catholic ecclesiology in the proper sense, that is, a doctrine of the concrete constitution of the Catholic Church, for the purpose of developing from it a concrete understanding of authority in this Church. Rather, it is our intention to present only a few disparate observations on this matter in a way that is not entirely systematic and by no means exhaustive.

THE ORIGIN OF AUTHORITY IN THE CHURCH

The nature of authority in this Church is conditioned by its origination. Initially this matter seems to be simple in Catholic ecclesiology.

Church Authority and the Problem of the Church's Foundation

Whatever the case may be in respect to the question of the origin of authority in the Church as seen in the ecclesiologies of the other churches, Catholic ecclesiology at least has taught for centuries that the following is part of the dogmatic, absolutely binding self-understanding of the Church. Authority in the Church does not come from below, from a mandate given by the Church's people, but from Jesus Christ, the founder of the Church. It has been handed on by "apostolic succession" beginning with Jesus Christ through the officeholders themselves and in this way it has come to the present-day bearers of this authority.

If we prescind at first from other questions of this doctrine's precise interpretation which is concerned with the problems of the more concrete and historically variable appointment of officeholders in the Church, we find not only in Protestant, but today even in Catholic ecclesiology and fundamental theology, a problem in regard to the origin of church authority that was not clearly discerned in former times. Beginning with the twentieth century the general and comprehensive problem of the Church's foundation by the historical Jesus has been one of the acute problems among the questions raised by what is known as modernism. Today the response to this problem must be more differentiated than was possible or necessary in the past.

In earlier times one proceeded on the assumption that the historical Jesus in his earthly life, partly after his resurrection (at the time no real difference was seen between Jesus' life before and after his resurrection as far as the question of the foundation of the Church was concerned), founded the Church by explicit and formally expressed words of institution, that through Peter and the Twelve he appointed in an unambiguously juridical sense a college of officeholders for this Church with the explicitly expressed intention that this college of officeholders should continue to propagate itself in a Church which was explicitly assigned a task even for a distant future. In connection with this the problem of the imminent expectation of the eschatological end, even in the consciousness of Jesus, was passed over completely. While it is true that even the ecclesiology of the Second Vatican Council does not teach this conception with a definitively binding force, it is still more or less tacitly presupposed as obvious. But what this conception basically means of course is that the Church really comes from Jesus, crucified and risen, as the eschatologically unsurpassable self-promise of God grasped in the faith of a community, wherein definite social realities of the pre-Easter life and activity of Jesus can and indeed must also be conceived as being a constitutive part of the post-Easter community of faith (the circle of disciples, the position of Peter, the institution of the Last Supper, etc.).

If Jesus crucified and risen is to be God's unsurpassable, historical self-promise for the whole world, there must exist for all times a community of faith that accepts this self-promise of God in faith and bears witness to it before the world. Such a community of faith, if it is to be the historically abiding presence of God's eschatological self-promise to the world in Jesus, must necessarily be a socially constituted entity, and thus it must also come in a legitimate way from the historical Jesus and his circle of disciples. Conversely, however, one will not have to ascribe to the consciousness of Jesus that ecclesiology which is a description of the local churches and the one Church in apostolic times, much less the completely structured Church from the second century to the First Vatican Council. Here, of course, we cannot go into further detail on the problem of the Church's foundation by Jesus. Here we are simply presupposing that the Church can and does come from Jesus in a way that is binding even though we cannot adhere to an act of church institution on the part of Jesus in exactly the same way as this act was formerly conceived.

The Historical Margin of Freedom for Shaping Church Office and Its Authority

Presuming what has been said above, authority in the Church can indeed be understood as coming from Jesus (the pre-Easter Jesus and the risen Jesus) without having to have unambiguous recourse to a verbal and juridical mandate and to the institution of a juridical form of succession for this mandate. This means that the concrete modalities governing the exercise of this church authority (even as Jesus' authority) can be ascribed to a development of the post-Easter Church to a greater extent than has been previously conceived according to the old model of institution. This thesis need not mean, at least not in every case, that concrete structures of this church authority, the specific characteristics and requirements on the part of its bearers, the mode of handing on the authority, and so on, would have to be liable to change for all future times just because they are historical forms that emerged in the apostolic Church and cannot simply make claim to explicit verbal instructions of Jesus, particularly because such instructions cannot be demonstrated historically and it is senseless to postulate them simply for the purpose of maintaining the old model of institution.

I have explained elsewhere[1] that a constitutional structure in the concrete Church can be conceived as being *juris divini*, (of divine, irreversible command) and is to be expected even though it did not take on historical form until the time of the apostolic Church, and that it nonetheless belongs to the irreversible decisions of the Church's history, and that this is a history that the historical subject "Church" can no longer go back beyond. Those who consider this to be absolutely inconceivable would have the burden of explaining how the canon is part of the Church's normative faith for all times, even though it did not take shape and was not constituted as such, albeit relatively early, until after the "death of the apostles." On the other hand, as has already been said, this conception implies that for its historical development, even

---

[1]See *Concern for the Church: Theological Investigations 20*, translated by Edward Quinn (New York: Crossroad, London: Darton, Longman & Todd, 1981).

in what pertains to the shaping of office and its authority, the Church has been given a wide margin of freedom. This margin of freedom must not be prematurely narrowed by a constitutional doctrine that retrojects present-day church structures into the earlier times in a way that is too unhistorical so as to exclude other possibilities with dogmatic absoluteness.

The authority of the Church originates from Jesus and for this very reason it is historically quite flexible. It need not deny itself as though it were nothing other than a mere human construct; at the same time it need not simply identify itself with historical shapes and forms of its constitution and its authority under which it has appeared in the course of history if these shapes and forms can themselves be recognized as things that have developed historically. It is entirely possible in a dogmatically binding way to define particular church structures and the authority contained in them as things that are permanently normative, for example, the primacy of the pope. In so doing, however, one should not overlook the fact that a definition of this kind unavoidably occurs according to a concrete conceptual model (indeed, that it cannot be abstracted from this model in an absolutely perfect way) which is not, after all, a part of the abiding essence of the thing itself.

The origin of church authority from Jesus and the origin of the Church as God's irreversible self-promise to the world in Jesus crucified and risen are for us, therefore, not two things that cancel each other out. In order to understand this, the Church, from whose nature and reality its authority derives, should not be understood as an abstract idea from whose speculatively conceived nature its authority can be postulated. From the very beginning the Church is the concrete community of faith, and it is this as the historical permanence of God's promise of himself in Jesus. And since it is and always has been socially constituted in a concrete way, albeit originally in a very modest form, it lays claim to possessing authority. There is no necessity of deducing speculatively from the Church's abstract nature the concreteness of its authority together with the bearers of this authority. It is quite sufficient to grasp that the concrete Church makes its legitimate claim to concrete authority on the basis of its theological-metaphysical nature. To put it more concretely: one cannot deduce speculatively that there would *have* to be a *Peter*. One can, however, experience that the concrete reality of this entity "Church" is present in this post-Easter community of faith and that otherwise it is not present, and that it claims its authority on the basis of its nature.

For the origination of church authority from Jesus in later times, it is sufficient to demonstrate how and where the later Church in the clearest possible way can trace itself back to the earlier Church without a revolutionary rupture between the earlier and the later historical form of the Church. Even prescinding here from the question whether and in what sense other Christian churches and societies can rightfully lay claim to some of the authority of Jesus (something that cannot be denied and in fact has never really been totally denied by the Catholic Church because the Catholic Church has never denied the existence of valid sacraments in other Christian churches), in any case it is the conviction of the Roman Catholic Church that it stems from the first Church in a continuity that is historically unassailable and most complete, and therefore that it possesses from Jesus the authority which comes to the concrete, eschatologically permanent faith community of Jesus.

ON THE RELATIONSHIP OF AUTHORITY
AND COERCIVE POWER IN THE CHURCH

We have already pointed out that authority in a society and the legitimate possession of the power of physical coercion need not necessarily exist together in every case. Naturally the concrete exercise of authority always implies a change in the freedom possessed by a member of this society prior to his or her consent. To this extent one may say that authority necessarily includes an element of coercive power. But undoubtedly there are societies in which this authority is legitimately equipped with the possibility of exercising coercive power that goes beyond what is already necessarily implied in authority as such. If this is true, then there is a real question whether the Church's authority according to the dogmatically certain self-understanding of the Church is equipped with a legitimate coercive power which goes beyond what is already necessarily implied in the exercise of authority (and which in concrete cases can have a very considerable impact, as, for example, when the bearers of church authority withdraw a person's ecclesiastical teaching license). As has been stated already, traditional canon law teaching has given an affirmative answer to this question right up to most recent times. This teaching proceeded on the assumption that while the Church had no right to use force in respect to non-Christians, a baptized person, by the very fact of his or her being baptized, belonged irrevocably to the Church, and that the Church has in regard to such a person a power of coercion which as a matter of course was conceived as something going beyond the exercise of its authority.

If we make bold to answer this question in the negative, both for today and tomorrow, it does not mean that we are passing a negative judgment on former times in the Church. It is entirely possible to conceive of social situations, a symbiosis of Church and secular society and so on, in which the exercise of such a power of coercion was legitimate. If today one denies both the possibility and the meaningfulness of a papal church-state and says that this cannot be derived from the permanent nature of the Church, this is not tantamount to asserting that the church-state of the tenth or of the sixteenth century stood in absolute contradiction to the nature of the Church.

If today we not only take into account the sacramental nature of baptism and its permanent sacramental character in regard to the question of church membership in a concrete social sense, but also take seriously the teachings of the Second Vatican Council concerning the freedom of religion in which the argumentation proceeds from the nature of faith as a free personal act and hence must have validity for the baptized as well; furthermore, if we take into consideration the Church's understanding of itself as a free community of like-minded persons in contrast to societies existing from a natural necessity, we will be permitted to say that the Church in the light of its intrinsic nature does not have to be conceived of as being equipped with a power of social coercion. According to this kind of understanding, then, attempts to exercise such coercive power are either part of the remnants of an earlier social situation of the Church and its consequences which perhaps might *still* be legitimate here and there. Or, on the other hand, they should be assessed as attempts to claim for the Church a power which it does not possess either on the basis of its own nature or its present-day situation in a pluralistic society. Therefore the Church should nowhere respond to a conflict between itself and one of its members with civil and material consequences. In this connection, it should not be denied that the blunt reaction of bearers of authority can in particular cases unavoidably involve unpleasant consequences even in the material and civil sphere. But fundamentally authority in the Church pertains to the regulations of those relations in it which are implied in the *nature* of the Church.

TEACHING AUTHORITY IN THE CHURCH

It is beyond doubt that according to the Catholic Church's understanding of itself there is a teaching authority, a teaching office in the Church. Yet the question about the nature of this teaching office is more obscure than is commonly supposed. That the Church is a community with a common faith and creed oriented to the unsurpassable salvific significance of Jesus Christ, and thus that the Church has something to do with teaching, is something that requires no further explanation. It should also remain clear that the teaching authority, however it is to be conceived in a more precise analysis, derives its sustenance and its life from the "authority" of the truth to which the Church bears witness. A mere appeal to formal teaching authority on the part of the ecclesial teaching office, if it is not combined with an ongoing, intensive effort to elucidate the meaning of what is proclaimed and taught, would ultimately result in a destruction of faith itself because faith implies an existentiell, practical, and theoretical relationship to the truth of faith itself; hence faith may not be reduced to mere obedience to the formal teaching authority of the Church. Furthermore, the existence and the claim of an ecclesial teaching instance is itself an object, and a secondary one at that, of that faith which, antecedent to this recognition of a teaching authority, lives from the compelling power of the truth contained in God's revelation of himself in Jesus Christ.

The recognition of the ecclesial teaching authority is dependent on the "authority" of revelation which ultimately (despite all the *reciprocally* conditioned relationships that the concrete realization of faith involves) sustains the teaching authority and is not sustained by it. This is an obvious teaching of Catholic fundamental theology which forbids us to see in this teaching authority an absolutely primary datum. The question concerning the actual nature of the ecclesial teaching authority focuses on whether this authority itself implies a completely theoretical instance of truth instituted as such by the omniscient and self-revealing God, or whether it must be deduced from the nature of the Church as an eschatologically permanent and socially constituted creedal community. This question is not a theoretical quibble because there are some important consequences involved regarding the more precise exercise of this teaching authority depending on how we answer it. In our opinion, the second answer to the question is the right one. The teaching authority is a necessary element of sociopolitical authority in the Church, but only if the nature of the Church as a socially constituted creedal community that receives God's historical promise of himself to the world in an eschatologically permanent way is taken into proper account. But it is not more than this.

There is a teaching authority in the Church not because the truth of revelation as such must be guaranteed for itself but because there must be an eschatologically permanent presence of Christ's word in the history of the last days. If this were not the case, one would have to expect that God's salvific truth of revelation, which has always been present, would everywhere and at all times be furnished with an authority of this kind. This limitation of the teaching authority in the Church does not mean that we are denying the theoretical character of the truth of revelation itself which, after all, is not simply and absolutely coterminous materially and logically with the object of the Church's teaching authority. Therefore one could say that it is the task of the teaching authority in the Church to see to it that in the Church the truth of revelation is given proper witness and proclamation. Only to this degree and extent does this teaching authority extend as well to the correct belief of the individual who, so to speak, has to take it upon himself or herself to see to it that his or her faith corresponds to this social presence of Christ's truth in the Church and through the Church in the world. The Church's teaching office can provide this pure presence of the truth of revelation in the Church, but it is not in a position to supervise the conformity of the individual's specific faith with the Church's doctrine.

In respect to the individual's faith, when this faith takes on tangible form in society, the teaching office can only ascertain that this particular expression of faith does not contradict the universal faith of the Church. The teaching office cannot actually go beyond this negative form of certification, a kind of *nihil obstat* that this expression of an individual's faith is not open to objection on grounds of orthodoxy. The more concrete norms governing the practical activity of the ecclesial teaching office that result from this interpretation of its authority cannot be considered further here. What has been said can of course also be applied to the concrete exercise of church authority in regard to the other dimensions of the Church (the practice of Christian life, the administration of the sacraments, etc.), which are part of the nature of this community of faith.

PART TWO

The Society of Jesus

7

THE SITUATION
OF THE SOCIETY OF JESUS
SINCE ITS DIFFICULTIES
WITH THE VATICAN

I am dividing my presentation into three parts. In the first section I would like to present some general and fundamental considerations that in some way or other have a bearing on all the events that have occurred and the declarations that have been made since the pope appointed a personal delegate.[1] In the second section I would like to present some reflections on a paper of Father Dezza in which he treats of our relationship to the ecclesial teaching office. In the third part of my considerations I make reference to a further paper of Father Dezza that discusses our apostolate and the norms for this apostolate set up by the thirty-second General Congregation of the Society of Jesus.[2] It is obvious that the remarks I intend to make will not be able to deal with every aspect of the subject. So it is naturally to be expected that relatively unimportant matters will be dealt with in detail and much more important things will only be touched upon briefly or not even mentioned at all. I shall certainly try not to speak in a disrespectful way. However, in a case of conflict between honesty and respect I am for honesty. It is likewise obvious that many questions will be treated for which there is

[1]On 5 October 1981 Pope John Paul II appointed Father Paolo Dezza, S.J., as papal delegate entrusted with the leadership of the Society of Jesus.

[2]In connection with this, see the recent *Letter of Father Dezza to the whole Society of Jesus* (2 March 1982), esp. the appendix, "Guidelines (direct norms) for putting into practice the wishes of the Holy Father" (nos. 1–9). On 8 December 1982 the convocation of a General Congregation was announced.

either no unambiguous and generally accepted answer at all or for which the answer will at least have to remain outstanding on my part. I do not intend to develop a fully balanced casuistry concerning obedience in a religious order.

I also want to admit in advance that while my remarks concerning our relationship to the ecclesial teaching office will indicate the difficult and problematical nature of this relationship, they will not really provide any simple rules that can be neatly applied to specific cases involving possible conflict between the teaching office and the individual theologian or the truthful conscience of a Jesuit. Many of my brethren will certainly regret this.

THE CONDITIONS OF OUR TIMES AS A CAUSE
OF THE DIFFICULTIES OF THE SOCIETY OF JESUS

First, I would like to present a fundamental and general consideration. It goes without saying that our order has its difficulties and that there are some things that are not as they should be. In times past this was also the case, and it is quite legitimate to ask whether the difficulties we are having today are greater than those we had in the eighteenth century. Specific abuses which can be remedied by a little bit of effort and clear thinking should be remedied.[3] But the difficulties we are having today, taken as a whole, are conditioned by the general situation of the Church and the world. If we look at the matter closely, we shall see that it is the intellectual, spiritual, cultural, and social situation of today's world that is at the root of the difficulties and problems that we are experiencing and suffering in our day-to-day life in the order. Every period in world history has to some degree or other labored under the impression that it was standing at a precarious turning point between two worlds and that it was threatened by enormous dangers; so caution is certainly called for when analyzing such situations and Cassandralike cries should be uttered sparingly. The fact remains, however, that today we are really living in a time of violent upheavals and cataclysmic dangers the likes of which have simply never been known before.

Never before has the world population numbered six billion and there has never before been a time when this population could increase to

---

[3]In connection with this, see V. Seibel, "Die Gesellschaft Jesu auf dem Prüfstand," *Geist und Leben* 3 (1982): 213–23.

ten billion within the space of a few decades. Rational technology has never before existed, as we know it today, nor has the secularization on a global level that we are experiencing today. There has never before been such an interlocking of individual societies and countries on this earth. There has never before been a religion which, as an organized social entity, set out to be a world religion, to move out beyond its own limited cultural roots and to inculturate itself in many historical periods and civilizations, even though it has a historically and regionally limited origin, an origin which cannot simply be discarded.

This then, briefly indicated, is the general situation of our historical era and of the Church in which we live today even in our religious order. If this radical situation, which has never before existed, had no determining influence on our order, the order would be dead. However, if the order is a living reality, it is necessarily involved in an intensive communication with the total situation on the intellectual, spiritual, and social level. Is it any wonder, then, that we share in the sufferings brought on by the problems, the insecurities, and the uncertainties? Should our question not rather be whether we are bearing too little of the burden of this totality of the world's fate? Should our first question not rather be whether we really want to perpetuate too anxiously and conservatively that mentality and manner of living characteristic of the religious ghetto into which the Church maneuvered itself during the epoch of the pian popes, even though it should actually be clear to us that genuine conservatism consists in having the courage to do something new?

What I want to say is simply this. We really ought to view all of our difficulties, honestly admitting them, ultimately as a matter of course, and in the final analysis we should rather be amazed that these difficulties are not greater, since it is by no means certain and obvious that the absence of such difficulties is a sign of health. It is only the dead or those groups ossified in their conservatism who have no difficulties.

There is no use in considering reforms in our course of studies or training unless we put them in the framework of this kind of analysis of our spiritual and intellectual situation. When reflecting upon our external lifestyle, we must take into account realistically that the difference between our own present-day lifestyle and that of our contemporaries must not and cannot be essentially greater than the difference between an eighteenth-century Jesuit's lifestyle and that of the other people of that time; in other words, that the practical norms for this lifestyle cannot be derived from that of the eighteenth century. This is of course a truism. However, if one calls to mind that a few decades ago the installation of an elevator in the Biblical Institute in Rome was still a problem requiring a solution on the part of the superior general of the order, or if one recalls Father General Janssen's regulation determining the transportation of typewriters from one house to another or his attempts to make us wear a cassock, then one sees that such truisms are apparently not always grasped.

Recollections such as these are not intended as a reproach for the past but only to draw attention to the fact that the dangers of such mischievous conservatism has not yet been completely eliminated even today. I am not talking about laxity or worldliness in our lifestyle, but I would like to express my concern about possible renewed attempts to impose a lifestyle on us which perhaps in Poland or in Rome does not yet manifest that difference from the lifestyle of the rest of the world as it does here among us. In our theology, in our training, and in our lifestyle there can obviously be defects even today which perhaps can be more clearly seen and corrected by looking at the past. But in a falsely understood fidelity to its history, an order should not create difficulties for itself or let such difficulties be created by restoration attempts which would make sense and have durability only if we could reverse conditions that are simply beyond our control, on the assumption that only the old days were shaped according to God's will.

Honestly and objectively speaking, I have the impression that from this standpoint all these fundamental considerations are not being given sufficient weight in the declarations of our curia. Obviously the Constitutions of Saint Ignatius should be heard in these Roman declarations. Obviously these decrees will always refer to declarations of previous General Congregations and generals. But if a present-day dogmatic theology cannot be simply put together from texts of Holy Scripture, even despite the permanent immutability of divine revelation, then it is even less appropriate for such Roman decrees to give rise to the impression that they are doing nothing more than reiterating the old norms and that everything beyond this is only a reluctant and peevishly granted concession to what even Rome itself sees as something that can no longer be reversed. Should not the declarations from Rome also have the courage and clarity to give expression to the difficulties which, after all, do exist and which cannot be gotten rid of simply by adhering to a few naively formulated principles?

When recently one of our brethren, no doubt with polemical exaggeration, wrote to Rome saying that many of the statements coming from the curia of our order sounded like a Soviet declaration on the occasion of an armed intervention in a foreign country interpreting the action as one of brotherly assistance and friendship, that was surely an exaggeration. But it would certainly do us no harm if the people in Rome exercised more consideration of the way in which we perceive style, a way that is more honest and open. I shall come back to this point later.

Obedience

However, when "total obedience to the Holy See" is being spoken about, given the necessary distinctions, one can certainly recognize elements that are quite important and correct, but in our part of the world we do in fact have the impression that there is in reality no total obedience (and that Ignatius did not really demand this), that a "total obedience" of this kind cannot be achieved so easily because it is not exactly known what this obedience really commands us to do and what in definite circumstances it does not command, that one indeed hears from Ignatius that obedience reaches its limits when confronted with a conscience that protests against sin. Roman declarations are stylistically formulated in such a way as to lead one to think that such limits can never seriously occur in real life, something that is just not true even if one attributes to the Roman offices at least as much moral capacity for judgment as to oneself.

The Notion of Church

A further problem that constantly comes up when one reads the Roman declarations is the following. It seems to me that these declarations are undergirded by a notion of Church, a notion that cannot be readily grasped and is certainly not explicitly formulated, which I consider to be false from a dogmatic, human, and realistic standpoint. One has the impression that it is presupposed that all true and legitimate activities in the Church, all new initiatives and ideas, proceed from the highest powers in Rome or at least that they cannot be legitimate unless they have the explicit or at least tacit approbation of Rome. This notion of Church, which in the secular sphere would be called totalitarianism, is, however, wrong.

Certainly everything that occurs in the name of Jesus must ultimately occur fundamentally within the Church and its unity, and everything that factually occurs outside of this Church under the inspiration of the gospel contains an internal dynamism oriented to the one Church of Jesus Christ. But even if this is true and even if the Holy See bears ultimate responsibility for the unity of this Church to the extent that it is tangibly present in society, a responsibility that has no higher earthly power beyond it, this does not mean that there can be no legitimate pluralism of initiatives and ways of shaping Christian life.

Historically there is always this kind of pluralism which from the outset is not positively inaugurated and shaped by Rome, even if one on formal grounds chooses to see in the existence of this pluralism without contradiction on Rome's part a tacitly granted approbation. This pluralism is legitimate. The first desert fathers went out into the desert without a positive approbation that would have been obligatory for them. The poor man of Assisi gave his clothes back to his father without having positive approbation for this from the official Church. The veneration of the Most Sacred Heart of Jesus arose and was propagated when those in Rome did not want to hear about it. The new exegesis arose in the face of opposition from the Biblical Commission under Pius X. Saint Teresa of Avila established her convents only in the face of massive difficulties with Rome. In the quarrel between the Catholic workers' associations and the Christian labor unions under Pius X, the German Jesuits were certainly not the ones who fulfilled the wishes and intentions of the pope, but they were right nonetheless. Saint Ignatius might not have been seized by a fit of trembling when Paul IV was elected pope if no tendencies had been permitted to exist in the Church which the Holy See had not given its positive blessing to from the outset.

I certainly do not maintain that things as obvious as these would be challenged in Rome if thematically presented in a clear-cut way. But one should not pretend either that things were different from the way they really were, or simply cover over decisions with a cloak of silence when afterwards they have proved to be wrong and have been revised. Such measures should also be revoked explicitly. (The prior censorship imposed on me before the council was never revoked either by the Holy Office or by our curia; therefore it would actually still be in force.)

What I want to say is this. In our relationship with Rome we should never act as if this legitimate pluralism did not exist in the Church, as if we were nothing other than executors of the Holy See's commands and wishes. We stand in the true and Catholic relationship to Rome precisely when we serve the pope gladly and with genuine self-effacement, but not only when we do this. The Holy Spirit does not grant his initiatives to the Church solely and exclusively through the pope. Therefore there are no principles that can be facilely applied to the Church's life whereby, if we only adhere to them exactly, every conflict between Christians and the Church's officeholders right up to the pope would be absolutely excluded. Somebody once told me that the biggest obstacle to the beatification of Vincent Palotti was the fact that he once said that Pius IX was obtuse. Was this an unecclesial utterance or is it quite permissible in an honest, down-to-earth, and thus Christian and Catholic mentality? In any event, difficulties in all these things cannot be eliminated by paying covert obeisance to an ecclesiastical totalitarianism.

THE JESUIT ORDER AND THE TEACHING OFFICE

It is obvious that Father Dezza's statements contain a number of elements that are quite correct and important for Jesuits. Papal teaching, even if it does not contain a dogmatic definition, must in principle be accorded the proper respect due to it, corresponding, of course, in its turn to the degree of binding force that this teaching itself intends, and which in the nature of things can be quite minimal. (For example, if the pope speaks of the Yahwist in one of his Wednesday audiences, Old Testament exegetes will be happy at the recognition thus accorded to their teaching which from Pius X on had been proscribed for decades. It is, however, obvious that they can ascribe no real theological importance to a remark of this kind.) It is also obvious that criticism of papal statements must be made in a manner that manifests a basic respect for the ecclesial teaching office. It is obvious that criticism of this kind has no place in sermons or in catechetical instruction, as, for example, has been emphasized by the 1967 instruction of the German bishops, "even if the faithful under certain circumstances are to be instructed concerning the nature and restricted scope of such a provisional doctrinal decision," as the bishops remark.[4] To put it briefly: "A serious effort to evaluate positively and to appropriate even a provisional doctrinal statement of the Church is part of the proper attitude of faith on the part of a Catholic," and this is especially true of a Jesuit.

But, as the German bishops emphasize, there is no denying that there can be cases in which the well-informed conscience of a Christian and

---

[4] J. Neuner and H. Roos, eds., *Der Glaube der Kirche in den Urkunden der Lehrerkündigung*, 10th ed., no. 469.

of a Jesuit can disagree with such an authoritatively proposed teaching, withhold assent to it, and also give expression to this with the required respect because the ecclesial teaching office can err and has erred in making such merely authoritative doctrinal declarations. "The Church has always been aware of this possibility and has also admitted it in its theology and has developed rules of conduct for such a situation." This fact, which no one seriously doubts, does not really emerge clearly in Father Dezza's paper; it is more or less covered up and repressed. There are conclusions resulting from this that are really unacceptable even to the most ecclesial of Jesuit theologians, and if, despite this, they should be insisted upon, they would do great harm to an objective and responsible theology, would make Jesuit theology unworthy of trust in the eyes of the public, and would even engender a climate of dishonesty. We shall now treat this in detail.

On the Theology of the Jesuits

The following contains eight points.

1. First of all, Father Dezza's paper is extremely imprecise, since it does not tell us clearly whether the rules of conduct developed in it are valid only for us Jesuits or for all theologians who think with the Church. This lack of clarity has nothing to do with the question whether the Jesuits have a proper and special obligation to respect the ecclesial teaching office that non-Jesuits do not have. An additional moral obligation, which one need not hesitate to admit, does not answer the question whether other and additional norms apply to Jesuit theologians or not. In the first case Jesuit theology would lose its public credibility; it would be perceived as a mere mouthpiece for an authoritarian teaching power.

The question then arises as to how to justify this kind of difference of Jesuit theology in doctrinal matters as opposed to any other theology. There can be no such justification. From the spirit of their order the Jesuits can be obligated to special fidelity to the ecclesial teaching office, but this fidelity can only manifest itself in the exact observation of the rules that apply to all theologians. In the following, then, we presume a negative answer to the question just asked.

2. Father Dezza's observations concerning our attitude toward declarations of the ecclesial teaching office that contain an ultimate dogmatic

binding force need not be challenged. These observations may be taken for granted. But they are too simple to provide much help for a theologian. There is no doubt that under certain circumstances, even in the case of those definitions proclaimed by the Church, theologians present very different interpretations, even though the theologians recognize the absolutely binding force of these definitions as a matter of course. In such a case, it may well be that the official magisterium inclines to one definite interpretation rather than to another, even though this does not mean that this preference has itself the force of a definition. What is to be done in a case like this? At this point Father Dezza abandons the theologian, failing to take into account that even today the obligation in regard to a dogma almost necessarily leads to the question of the theologian's attitude toward the merely authoritative teaching office of the Church. According to the teaching of Vatican I, it is certainly correct that further explanation of a dogma may not alter its original sense.

But things are not as simple as Father Dezza makes them out to be when he makes a distinction between the content of the statement and the way the statement is expressed. Father Dezza employs a massive oversimplification that is no help for the theologian. For it is undeniable that even perpetually binding dogmas can be bound up with conceptions, patterns of thought, and so on, that have to be eliminated, so that the question arises as to where the boundary lies between those conceptions that can be amalgamated with the dogmas and the actual dogma itself and what criteria must be found to enable one to draw this boundary. (For example, does the doctrine of original sin, which was certainly formulated under the presupposition of monogenism, imply an absolute obligation to this monogenism, or can monogenism be given up as was permitted by a commission directed by Dhanis in Rome under Paul VI, although a scheme of Vatican II and *Humani Generis* were of another opinion?)

3. What Father Dezza says about the Catholic theologian's relationship to nondefined but authoritative doctrinal statements of the ecclesial teaching office is, to say the least, so imprecise and one-sided that if these rules were to be proclaimed, one could fear that they would cause conflicts of a most profound nature. According to Father Dezza, a critical position toward such official teaching on the part of a Jesuit theologian can be presented only privately to the Roman teaching office. Father Dezza does not even allow for the publication of critical positions in scientific journals. But to forbid or to suppress this would mean

the death of theology. How can we seriously be expected to make the progress absolutely necessary for the efficaciousness of the gospel and the faith of the Church if every advance should first be required to have the positive blessing of the Roman doctrinal office which, at least up to now, has in many cases taken up a position that is objectively wrong? At the time of Pius X, how could one have taken those positions that are accepted today by the whole of Catholic Old and New Testament exegesis if a prior approbation for them had been required by the Biblical Commission? How would the teaching of the biological link between the human being and the animal kingdom have become possible — a teaching that was even permitted by Pius XII in 1950 — if all the theologians and biologists between Darwin and the middle of our century would have had to get previous approval from Rome?

The fact of the matter is that the ecclesial teaching office can err and has erred quite often, even in our own century, and that in the concrete such errors that are detrimental to the Christian message can be overcome only if public criticism of these errors is possible, no matter how cautious and respectful such criticism may be. This criticism must be possible at least in scientific journals and books. In unpublished theses circulating in the Congregation for the Doctrine of the Faith, which I happened to see, the legitimacy of this kind of scientific criticism on the part of theologians is fully recognized for journals and scientific works. Father Dezza does not say anything about this; as a matter of fact, he rules this out for Jesuits. He does not really even mention the possibility that the teaching office can err and has erred, something, for example, that the German bishops explicitly admit. Or is this something that still has to be proved? Do we have to point to doctrinal statements of a very authoritative kind under Pius X which no exegete today any longer accepts and which have been retracted by Rome only partially and half-heartedly? Do we have to make a point of referring to numerous declarations in the struggle against modernism which emanated from the teaching office at the time and which are hardly accepted today by any theologian trained in the history of dogma in the form in which they were presented at that time? Shall we point to the development of Christian social and economic teaching which contains a large number of official declarations that objectively contradict one another? Are we to understand official declarations on the liturgy containing differences that verge on contradiction merely as declarations that have nothing at all to do with the actual teaching office?

Such errors do in fact exist and we might have expected from Father

Dezza practical and down-to-earth advice on what to do in such cases. The concession of an "internal difference of opinion" will not suffice. This internal difference of opinion alone is not enough to keep scientific research "open," to use Father Dezza's term. The possibility of bringing one's objection only before the "teaching authorities of the Church" is simply not enough. If the possibility of airing an objection in the "social media of communication" is excluded, then it seems that critical positions on the scientific level as well are also excluded by Father Dezza. But that would be the death of theology in the way it is required to function for the salvation of souls. However, if Father Dezza does not want to exclude criticism on the scientific level, why does he not say so explicitly, since this is of the utmost importance for the work of the theologian?

If the teaching office can make errors in its teaching, how can one go along with Father Dezza's demand that our teaching "must be in complete agreement with that of the magisterium," always and absolutely. If we really take this word *complete* with total seriousness, we would be required to teach, defend, and propagate errors even when we recognize them to be such; we would have to vouch for these errors until the teaching office revokes them explicitly. Or perhaps the word *complete* does not really mean complete at all. If this is the case, then one might warmly recommend a use of language that is more in keeping with our ordinary German usage that esteems sobriety and honesty. Father Dezza's statement that teachings which in the sense expounded above are not in agreement with the magisterium must "not be disseminated in publications by Jesuits" is at the very least so undifferentiated that it can be used as an instrument for suppressing any free theological research that is also required to be critical.

4. We must also draw attention to the following difficulty. It is obviously correct that theologians must keep in mind the people they are talking to, and so not every theological statement is suitable for everybody. But one must honestly and realistically admit that modern communications media make it very difficult to keep theological reflections locked up in the *camera caritatis* of the theological sciences. No matter how esoteric the language of theological criticism may be or how obscure the place of its publication, we may be sure that journalists will bring it to the attention of a broad public. While it is true that the customary distinction, and the one also made in the previously mentioned theses of the Congregation for the Doctrine of the Faith, between scientific and

nonscientific publications even today is not devoid of all meaning, still it is not really helpful for the activities of theologians and contributes little to the ecclesial teaching office's legitimate attempt to direct theological work into proper channels. Father Dezza does not give us any really helpful rules for dealing with this problem.

Father Dezza does admit that there can be "difficulties" and that "it seems important that they be made public." But what does that mean? Does it mean then that we really may publish these "difficulties," or could an exegete even as early as 1930 state that the traditional way of making Genesis dependent on the historical Moses is not only "difficult" but also wrong? What does a Jesuit theologian do when an educated lay Catholic asks him for information on a theological question concerning which the Jesuit's conscience in all honesty forbids him to do nothing more than just repeat and positively defend the magisterium's authoritative, but nondefined teaching? When it is a question of his own conscience and the salvation of the questioner's soul, can he communicate his own conviction when it diverges from Rome's authoritative teaching? Would he have been allowed to do this, for example, as early as 1930 in regard to the biological origin of the human being, even though Rome did not explicitly permit him to do this until 1950? How is a Jesuit supposed to conceal his opinion which he might perhaps share with the overwhelming majority of Catholic moral theologians in Germany who are not in total agreement with the teaching of *Humanae Vitae*? If the curia of our order is going to provide helpful instructions for Jesuit theologians, it will have to address itself to questions such as these.

5. Father Dezza's instruction does not contain a fully realistic understanding of the task of theology. If we should take Father Dezza's remarks at their face value, we would be forced to come to the conclusion that theology's only task is to accept, explain, and defend the explicit teaching of the teaching office. This, however, is a view of theology that does not correspond, for example, to the view propounded by John Paul II in Germany (in Altötting). It is simply not true that the teaching office "is based" only on the direct "assistance of the Holy Spirit" and not on the work of theologians as well. Naturally the teaching office has a function different from that of theology, and this function cannot be reduced to scientific theology alone. If, however, the teaching office does not receive any new revelations and if besides this the Holy Spirit's assistance is an *assistentia per se negativa*, then it is sim-

ply impossible for the teaching office to manage without the work of the theologian, even though perhaps in former times theologians and official teachers were one and the same persons.

Have there ever been formulations or advances on the part of the teaching office that were not first to be found among "theologians"? One could cite any number of examples showing that the teaching office at first mistrusted theological work and tried to slow it down, then finally accepted it and perhaps even acted as if these findings had always been clear and obvious to the ecclesial teaching office. Are not many of the present pope's pronouncements in regard to human rights, religious freedom, and the interpretation of Christian marriage drawn from these findings of theological science which the official Church first looked upon with deep suspicion.

6. Does not Father Dezza even elevate a papal encyclical practically to the level of a solemn definition, even though an encyclical does not intend to be such and is not such? Why does Father Dezza declare that the sole duty of the servants of the Church is to "communicate" the teaching of an encyclical to the faithful "and to help them to live it"? How are we to argue against Hans Küng's objectively false criticism of papal infallibility when Küng says that *Humanae Vitae* lays practical claim to infallibility while at the same time containing a teaching that large segments of the Church are justifiably opposed to? What are we supposed to say when Father Dezza practically forbids each and every objection to a papal encyclical?

7. In view of all these considerations it seems to me justifiable, with all due respect to the papal delegate Father Paolo Dezza, to express the urgent desire that before the general publication of the guidelines being discussed here, he should once again in a detailed and open way avail himself of the counsel of really competent theologians who really understand all the particulars and difficulties contained in the questions under discussion and who themselves possess experience in their own field of work.

8. What has been presented here had to be composed very hastily and makes no claim to being perfectly systematized. It is the pope's desire that we Jesuits be required to uphold the Second Vatican Council. If this is done by means of a detailed and precise study of the entire teaching of the council, many other important things bearing on the questions

under discussion could be found. What about the *consensus fidelium* if it is brought to bear on our question? Would it not be possible in the council's sense to understand even the theologian's mission as a charism and the theologian as one who in a peculiar way receives the promise of the Holy Spirit's assistance? Could not insights be gained from the teaching of this council that would open perspectives for a legitimate pluralism even in theology, insights that cannot be attained by mere conformity to the Roman teaching office alone? If the council's teaching contains insights on freedom of religion which were previously not recognized by the official ecclesial teaching office in the nineteenth century, could not this fact lead to further insights which are important for our question? If statements in the council were deliberately avoided that were previously put forth by the Church's official teaching office and that had also found their way into preconciliar schemata (statements, for example, concerning monogenism, the relationship between Scripture and tradition, the nature of inspiration, etc.), could insights not be deduced from these statements concerning a legitimate distance even from authoritative doctrinal statements, if such previous statements under certain circumstances were also tacitly abandoned even in the council?

THE APOSTOLATE OF THE SOCIETY OF JESUS

In the third and final section of my talk, I want to deal with Father Dezza's third paper of 26 February 1982 which takes up the question of our apostolate.

Faith and Justice

It must first of all be stated that Pope John Paul II in his address to the fathers provincial, and Father Dezza as well, appropriated the fourth decree of the thirty-second General Congregation which says that our mission today consists in the service of faith and the advancement of justice, just as the Synod of Bishops recognized in 1971 that the advancement of justice is an integral part of evangelization.

This of course, does not answer all the questions concerning the more exact relationship of these two tasks and their unity. But perhaps one might put it in the following simple terms. Just as Christians are commanded to love God and their neighbor, just as these two tasks condition each other, and while one cannot be simply reduced to the other, still they form an indissoluble unity, so too is the case with the twofold task which our order has set for itself in the thirty-second General Congregation. Both the popes and Father Dezza as well make it obvious to me that the attacks voiced in some quarters among us against the twofold nature of our task as established in the thirty-second General Congregation are certainly not justified.

Excesses which assuredly occur here and there in our work for justice in the world cannot be avoided or combatted by rejecting the position of the thirty-second General Congregation itself. One might even go so far as to say that it is by no means obvious that the Society of Jesus is everywhere shouldering sufficient responsibility for this second task (the efforts to promote justice). It goes without saying that we must reject any attempt to reduce our total task in the wrong sense to the horizontal plane of a mere struggle for social justice in the world. A genuinely serious political theology will share this opinion. As always in life, the difficulties of course lie in managing the details. The emphasis will differ according to the different countries, social situations, the possibilities that the different provinces have at their disposal and also the capabilities and talents of individual Jesuits. The dangers of a false or excessive emphasis will likewise be different.

In this connection, Father Dezza's remark also seems to me to be noteworthy when he says that the social apostolate has not only a fundamental place in the planning of our apostolate but that in all other forms of our apostolate the social dimension must also be taken into account. If we really take this statement of Father Dezza seriously, we could deduce from it the legitimacy of what is known as "political theology," for all that this theology really wants to do is to introduce into all the dimensions of theology an explicit reflection on the social aspect of all the realities that come under theology's scope and give this social aspect its proper due. When Father Dezza says that the advancement of justice is to be understood "as necessary in the light of the service of faith," that can certainly be understood correctly, provided that "faith" is understood as the absolute totality of the Christian life and the Christian task. It may, however, be feared that someone might take this as the occasion of once again trying to reduce the advancement of justice to the proclamation of faith, which was the exclusive understanding of the concrete advancement of justice in former times. Assuredly one can speak of a "primary goal of our religious and priestly apostolate which consists in the proclamation of the gospel and in the communication of faith in the grace of Christ," and naturally at all times and in all places human beings, and so, too, priests who proclaim faith, have a relationship to God in faith, hope, and love that infinitely transcends all immanent and interpersonal values.

But when using the word *primary* we must bear in mind that even in an order of priests love of neighbor together with all the challenges and possibilities this involves cannot ultimately be simply made equivalent to this transcendent love of God and be dissolved in it, since God has created a real world which is truly different from him, and in addition to this he has himself become a man, divinizing the world unto himself in such a way that he has communicated to it that it is precisely only in the world that he can be reached, but that it is indeed he himself, and therefore the first commandment of love of God and the second commandment of love of neighbor can no longer be separated from one another.

An Order of Priests

In human life and its socializations and so, too, in the Church it happens that individuals have different functions and tasks. Our order, at least according to its status under church law up to now, happens to be an order of priests. And so we who have taken upon ourselves this priestly task and function in the Church and in society can expect to be just that, priests, and that we want to be priests. Whatever more precise theological interpretation this priesthood may undergo (and in this respect theology even today faces momentous tasks particularly because the priest, too, in a historically changing world cannot simply remain exactly the way he was in former times), in any event the fact remains that we have taken on a particular task with our religious priesthood. Therefore a Jesuit cannot occupy himself with anything and everything that is good and even necessary in our own day and age. And so when popes Paul VI, John Paul I, and John Paul II insist that in principle we are to keep within the limits of our priestly task given by the nature of the priesthood and established by canon law, this is something that may actually be taken for granted. We Jesuits need not feel called to do anything and everything.

Both the history of our order and our present-day activity show that our radius of action is really quite broad. It should not be our desire to take upon ourselves anything and everything in the world just because it is good and perhaps absolutely necessary. Mother Teresa is doing wonderful things in Calcutta. In Central America I have no difficulty imagining a mission under Christian inspiration that is accomplished with a rifle. But this is a far cry from saying that things like these must also be a part of our tasks and even that they must be a normal part of our tasks. In the ordinary case it is quite right for the priest to leave to lay Christians tasks which are not his but which belong to lay persons. It is the part of reasonable human beings and Christians to limit themselves soberly to a particular task in the human race and in society.

Those who feel called to the Carthusian life of contemplative solitude should not become Jesuits. And those who have the entirely conceivable Christian vocation to become social revolutionaries should likewise not become Jesuits either. We have the right not to want everything. Only those who are able to affirm this limitation of the order's tasks should become and remain members of the order. For when we accept this limitation, and it is, after all, not really a straitjacket, we serve the whole of the Church and humankind better than if we wanted to carry the whole world on our shoulders.

True, the popes and Father Dezza as well admit that there can also be "extraordinary cases" in which a Jesuit may move beyond the limits actually imposed on him in principle by his priestly task, that he might indeed even be required to do this. When Father Dezza says that this might be conceivable only in "really extraordinary cases," this restriction cannot reasonably be construed to mean that there can be no such cases like these at all. When Father Dezza says that such cases require the "consent of the bishops and of father general" one will be permitted to take the liberty of adding that a consent of this kind coming from the other side is in certain circumstances even demanded and is not something that merely lies within the discretion of these superiors. One may ask which bishops are meant since it is a well-known fact that the bishops have considerable differences of opinions concerning critical social questions. In all realism one will also make allowance for the case that someone who knows with certainty that he is called to this kind of direct political mission will depart from the Society of Jesus in peace as Hermann Muckermann did in a similar case a few decades ago. Naturally our efforts to promote justice must be in "accordance with the directives of the local hierarchy." But it must also be honestly admitted that in the concrete situations of life this norm cannot be the only principle governing our action. Particularly in this area conflicts can arise similar to those that can arise with the teaching office in the theoretical area of theology. So, too, in the advancement of justice obedience cannot simply be blind obedience, nor can it be the sole norm. In the final analysis, abstract norms alone will prove insufficient for overcoming conflicts in this area too.

PART THREE

Piety

8

DIMENSIONS OF MARTYRDOM

I would like to make a plea here for a certain widening of the traditional concept of martyrdom.

The traditional concept as used in the Church is well known. We are not inquiring here how it developed during the history of the Church, or how it is related to the biblical concept of martyrdom, or how this New Testament concept itself is further connected with such notions as preaching, prophecy, confession, death, and so on.

Here we start with the traditional concept of martyrdom. As used in dogmatic and fundamental theology, this concept means the freely endured (not actively fighting, like a soldier) acceptance of death for the sake of faith. "Faith" includes Christian morality, as clearly shown by the fact that Saint Maria Goretti, who was killed in 1902 by a youth from the neighborhood because she strenuously resisted his importunities, is honored by the Church as a martyr. "Faith" may mean the whole of the Christian confession, or one single truth of the Christian doctrine of faith or morals. Of course, in such a case, this single truth is viewed within the totality of the Christian message. Death *in odium fidei* (because of hatred for the faith) must be consciously accepted; therefore, martyrdom and "baptism by blood" must be distinguished.

What is peculiar is that the Church currently excludes from the concept of martyrdom a death suffered in active combat. So our question is whether death suffered in active combat in behalf of the Christian faith and its moral demands (including social ones) must necessarily remain excluded from the concept of martyrdom. This question is very important for Christian life in the Church, because granting the title of martyr to a fighting Christian would amount to a strong recommendation by the official Church of such active combat as something to be imitated by other Christians.

First it is evident that such concepts as those of which we are speaking have a history and may legitimately vary in meaning. The only question here is whether in this case the passive endurance of death for the sake of the faith and suffering death in active combat for the faith, or some of its demands, might not be brought together under the one concept of martyrdom. Although they are different, these two kinds of death have many features in common, and putting both of them under *one* concept does not deny the lasting distinction between them. There are many concepts that put two realities together because of their resemblance, without thereby denying or necessarily obscuring their differences. For example, the concept of "sin" is used by the Church both for original sin and for freely committed personal sins, without denying the radical differences between these two conditions.

Of course, it is certainly true that the *endured* suffering of death for the sake of faith has a special relation to the death of Jesus, who became *the* faithful and reliable witness precisely through the death that he suffered. But this undeniable difference between the two kinds of death does not prevent us from bringing them together under the one concept and using the same word, martyrdom.

In order to see this and in order to make clear the inner and essential similarity between these two ways of dying, despite their differences, we must consider many things. First, the "passively undergone" death of Jesus is the consequence of his fight against the religious and political authorities of his time. He died because he fought; his death may not be seen apart from his life. On the other hand, those who die in active combat for the demands of their Christian conviction (at times, of course, also for social causes) also "endure" their death. Even such a death is not directly intended; it includes a passive element just as the death of martyrs in the traditional sense also includes an active element because, through their active witness and life, they too brought about the situation in which they could have escaped death only by denying their faith.

The question is, of course, how to describe the active struggle more precisely and how to distinguish it from similar events, so that this death could be called martyrdom. Not everyone who dies in a religious war on the Christian side should be called a martyr. In religious wars too many worldly motives intervene. The question remains open whether every combatant in such wars confronts the possibility of dying and really accepts death. But why wouldn't Archbishop Oscar Romero, for instance, who fell in the struggle for social justice, a struggle that he carried on because of his deeply Christian conviction, be a martyr? He certainly considered the possibility of dying.

We must not imagine the passive endurance of death solely in the way in which we habitually picture the first Christian martyrs standing before the tribunal and being condemned. The passive endurance of death, accepted in a voluntary decision, may happen quite differently. The modern "persecutors of Christians" will not give today's Christians any chance at all to confess their faith in the way in which it was done in the first Christian centuries and to accept the death which the tribunal decrees for them. Yet death in the more anonymous forms of modern persecution may be foreseen and accepted as it was by the ancient martyrs. And this death can be a consequence of an active struggle for justice and other Christian values. It is strange that the Church canonizes Maximilian Kolbe as a confessor and not a martyr. Rather than focus on his earlier life, an unprejudiced understanding of Maximilian Kolbe will consider his behavior in the concentration camp and at the moment of death, and understand him as a martyr of unselfish Christian love.

The difference between a death in active combat for the sake of faith and death passively endured for the sake of faith is too subtle and too difficult to determine to make it worthwhile to separate them conceptually or verbally. Ultimately, both express the same resolute acceptance of death prompted by the same Christian motivation; in both cases death means acceptance of the death of Christ, which, as the highest act of love and courage, puts humanity unreservedly at God's disposal. It is a radical unity of active love and endurance of the painful being-snatched-away-from-oneself, while facing the incomprehensible but powerful no of men and women to the love of God revealing itself. In both cases death appears as the complete and public manifestation of the true nature of Christian death. Where death is suffered in a struggle for Christian conviction, it also bears witness to an unshakable faith that, inspired by God's grace, is ready to go all the way up to and including death, and all this is patiently endured in an experience of the deepest inner and outer powerlessness. That applies also to death in combat, because, like the martyr who suffers in the traditional sense, the combatant experiences in his apparent failure the power of evil and his own impotence.

In this plea for a certain widening of the traditional concept of martyrdom, we may also appeal to Thomas Aquinas. He says that, through a death that has a clear relation to Christ, one is a martyr when one defends the commonwealth (*res publica*) against the assaults of its foes, who would try to destroy the Christian faith, and in doing so suffers death.[1] The destruction of the faith in Christ, against which such a defender fights, may also refer to a single dimension of the Christian faith. If it did not we could not call martyrdom the passive enduring of death for the sake of a single Christian moral demand. Thus Thomas proposes in his *Commentary on the Sentences* a broad concept of martyrdom, such as the one we are suggesting here.

A legitimate "political theology" and a theology of liberation should take up this conceptual widening. It has a very concrete practical meaning for a Christianity and a Church that wish to become aware of their responsibility for justice and peace.

---

[1]IV *Sent*. dist. 49 q. 5 a. 3 qc. 2 ad 11.

9

EUCHARISTIC WORSHIP

The Church has a history that is still far from over, that is difficult to foresee, and that time and again surprises us. This applies also to piety, both that of individuals in the Church and that of the Church herself and of large groups in the Church. So there exists a *history* of piety. Such a history always brings about changes that provide novelties wrought by the Spirit of God. But unavoidably it also contains its dangers.

Throughout the changes in her history in general and in her piety in particular, the Church of Jesus Christ, because it is assisted by the Spirit of God and of Jesus Christ, can and will not lose her identity. Hence in this history the nature of the Church remains the same through all change. Moreover, the past never disappears in such a way that it would have nothing more to say to the future. As history goes on, something ancient can again become new, can instruct and inspire later history. That is why, if we wish to create a new future, we may have to return to the sources. The ancient customs that are continually revived in this way do not come into later times as something lifeless and dead, or as a respectfully preserved museum piece; they stay alive by insinuating themselves actively into the future. They change while keeping their ancient nature.

What has been said in general about the Church, her history, and the history of piety applies also to eucharistic piety, to the piety with which the institution of the Lord's Supper must always be celebrated. The purpose of this short essay is to say a few words about the possibility of reviving ancient customs in the history of eucharistic piety, of not indifferently giving them up as out-dated, but of viewing them as a new possibility and task for the future.

113

When we honestly consider the present life of the Church, we cannot deny that eucharistic piety has experienced a certain decline. Is adoration before the tabernacle, with the sanctuary lamp burning, still practiced as it used to be in the past? How many monasteries continue to have "perpetual adoration"? Has the Corpus Christi procession in many places not been given up or at least considerably reduced? In how many churches is the monstrance still used today? Genuflecting before the Blessed Sacrament is frequently omitted. Most people who come to Mass sit down in the pews right away and wait impatiently for the service to begin. That it would be possible to kneel down for a few moments and to adore the Lord present in the Eucharist never seems to occur to most of them. Receiving communion as one attends Mass has, more than formerly, become almost a natural Sunday practice, but possibly too often only a routine. Giving thanks privately after communion and at the end of the Mass used to be almost taken for granted. Nowadays it seems to be more or less forgotten. Certainly there exists no necessary connection between the sacrament of "confession" and the reception of the Eucharist, although only a few decades ago, many Christians considered it obligatory. But are average Christians today sufficiently aware of the obligation of going to confession before receiving communion when they have committed a serious sin? More examples might be mentioned of a decline in eucharistic piety. What should we say about it?

It is, of course, not possible here and now to consider all the manifestations of eucharistic piety that were customary during past centuries and to wonder whether they might be revived. Many of these practices will certainly not have any promise for the future, although they may have been very pious and we may regret their loss, if we used them in our own lives. I do not know whether a beautiful monstrance will always remain part of the usual furnishings of a church. But undoubtedly in the eucharistic piety of the past there were many things that should be kept, that make sense even for the future, and that should not perish. They belong to that past which the future must recover, if it is to be great. Today I will mention only one of them and say a few words about it: quiet individual prayer before the tabernacle.

To be sure, we may adore God everywhere in spirit and in truth. God hears the prayer that we say alone in our room. It is true that Christians should learn to find God everywhere and in all things, thus making their daily life into a religious service. But if we are honest, we will have to admit that only those who are always and everywhere united with God in love will really value the liturgy, public prayer in the Church with their brothers and sisters, and the explicit and bodily expressions of their nearness to God. Those who wish to be united to God will value the explicit and bodily manifestations of their piety as lovingly performed high points of their union with God. They know of no opposition between the permanent devotion of their daily life and the hours that are expressly consecrated to God.

This applies especially to eucharistic piety. It is part of the Catholic faith that Jesus Christ is truly present with his divinity and his humanity under the eucharistic species. It is true that this presence under symbols of human food points to the reception and enjoyment of this eucharistic nourishment. Nevertheless, in this nourishment Jesus Christ is present with his divinity and his humanity not only when received but also before that, so that he may be received in a bodily way. That is why Catholics may, under the eucharistic signs, adore Jesus, the divine pledge of their salvation. True, compared with the real reception of the heavenly bread, such adoration is not the highest point of the sacramental happening. But it is a practice that follows legitimately from the Catholic belief in the true presence of the Lord in the sacrament.

Therefore this worshipping of Jesus in the sacrament must not disappear. Its history may have started from almost unnoticeable beginnings. However, in salvation history and in the history of the Church something cannot disappear simply because it started almost without being noticed. No, as Catholics we wish, individually and together, to look to the sign of the presence of the one who has loved us and has offered himself up for us. It should not be unusual for us to kneel at times in private prayer before the Lord who have saved us.

Forty years ago in Vienna I still saw people in the trolley car make the sign of the cross or tip their hat when the car passed a church. Such a custom may have become strange for us, and not without reason, so that we should not try to revive such expressions of piety. However, real worship of the sacrament of the altar, both in private and in common, even apart from Holy Communion, must not disappear. We should examine ourselves and ask whether this holy tradition of eucharistic piety still appeals to us. Do we not want to carry it on? This ancient custom contains a blessing for the future, a blessing we should not miss.

It seems to me that in the Church of the future as well as of the past, and not only on exceptional occasions, we should see Christians kneeling in church, alone and in silence, before the tabernacle in which the bread of life is kept, so that it may be received. These Christians know that God is everywhere, that he carries everything with his power and his love, and is incredibly near to everything; they know that the whole world is the cathedral where he is eternally adored. But these Christians also know that their own adoring love is not always near the God who is always near them. They know that they themselves must continue to try to be near God. And they know that the God who is everywhere present in power and in love has, because we are not always near him, created a few places and realities that make it easier for us, prisoners of space and time, to reach his presence.

Now Jesus is *the* event in which God has granted his salvific presence to finite human beings in an unsurpassable and irrevocably way. And it is before this Jesus, present in the body although hidden under sacramental signs, that these Christians are kneeling. In Jesus God has, in an unsurpassable and definitive way, become world. In this sacrament we discover how he leads this world back into the splendor of God. Christians kneel before him. They look at the one who has been pierced. They are in the bodily presence of the one in whom God has assumed the world as his own reality. These Christians pray silently, they allow the quiet peace of this sacrament to fill them, they can tell this sacramentally present Lord of their life about their concerns. But ultimately they only desire to be introduced by this sacramentally present Jesus into the truth and love of God, which radiate silently from this sacramental sign.

It seems to me that even today and in the future we must not forget what our Christian forebears practiced. The sanctuary lamp of our Catholic churches continues to invite us to a silent lingering before the mystery of our redemption.

10

DEVOTION TO
THE SACRED HEART TODAY

D
evotion to the Sacred Heart is going through a crisis. Yet it has a long history, it has been strongly supported by recent popes, even until Paul VI, and it occupies a very high rank in the liturgy.

In Western Europe at least the heart of Jesus is hardly ever mentioned in a sermon. Writings about this devotion have clearly become scarcer during the last few decades, the Messengers of the Sacred Heart are obsolete. Even Rome's official utterances are less numerous and more reserved. And in the religious orders that have made this devotion their special task the members seem to have lost courage, to have been intimidated by a modern trend in spirituality that seems to be almost unable to do anything at all with a devotion to the Sacred Heart.

I intend to defend the position that, even today, the worship of the divine heart of Jesus Christ can and should be meaningful and significant. Although I will try to explain who might be expected to promote this exercise of Catholic piety of the last few centuries and who may continue to find it useful, my conviction does not derive from a pessimistic evaluation of the present situation of the Church and of modern spirituality in general.

THE CHURCH IS SUBJECT TO CHANGE

The Church and her piety are part of history. Therefore not only in the past but in the present and the future as well, they are legitimately subject to change. The same God-given realities do not always occupy the foreground of Christian faith, although that one and selfsame faith always centers around the eternal God, Jesus Christ, and the irrevocable self-communication of the incomprehensible God in Jesus Christ. That is why it is natural that in an age of universal atheism and of a secularization that is more than the legitimate acknowledgment of the autonomy of earthly realities, in an age that knows less and less about the central message of Christianity, in an age of deadly danger for the whole world and of hitherto unknown and arduous challenges in organizing social life and the international community, in such a time the theme of an explicit verbalized devotion to the Sacred Heart cannot have, in the general awareness of the Church or in the ordinary awareness of the faithful in the world, the same "central position" that it supposedly occupied for the two past centuries, up to the middle of our own.

In the darkness of our times, which are threatened by the death of both spirit and body, we cry to the incomprehensible God of our history; we announce, with the last power of the faith, that we have kept the crucified one as our own fate; we hope that this fate hanging over us individually and socially will end up in salvation.

It is not surprising then that, in the presence of these ultimate questions and of the answers to them which we grasp with all the courage of our existence, devotion to the Sacred Heart no longer attracts us. It sounds too bland, too individualistic, too merely "introspective." We no longer see why we should translate, even if it were possible, the ultimate answers to the ultimate questions, which are forced upon us and expected from us, into the language of a devotion to the Sacred Heart. We have the impression that this devotion is slowly entering the domain of ways of acting and speaking that belong to a Christian past. These ways existed once, they were lively and good, but they no longer appeal to us. It is like the special veneration of Jesus' Five Wounds, the Infant of Prague, the Precious Blood, and many other practices of Christian piety, which once captivated and delighted the spirit and heart of Christians.

As we recall from history how important indulgences once were in the Church (fifty years ago we ourselves may still have had high esteem for them), and as we consider that even a pope who cared as much for tradition as Paul VI did, while maintaining the traditional doctrine of indulgences, admitted without hesitation that Christians were free with regard to indulgences, and as we notice that they continue in use only in small religious subcultures, playing no more role in the life of the universal Church, we can naturally wonder whether devotion to the Sacred Heart will not meet the same fate.

THE CHURCH NEEDS PEOPLE
WITH MYSTICAL-CHARISMATIC EXPERIENCE

However, I am convinced that the opposite is true. I have pointed this out previously, and I intend to submit here a few considerations in defense of this conviction. This conviction does not include the opinion that devotion to the Sacred Heart should in the future loom as large in the awareness of large numbers of people in the Church as it still did under Pius XI and Pius XII. If in the Church's consciousness, as constituted by all Christians, this devotion should not in the future be as natural and as intense as it was formerly, I would not protest against this or try to oppose this trend.

However, there is also in the Church, and there ought to be, a somewhat esoteric elite, which is not made up of specially trained people, such as theologians and officeholders, but is an elite to which may belong the poor and those who are socially weak. I mean here the elite of the saints, of those who, on account of their mystical-charismatic experience, are always for the Church a source of new life and a witness to God's grace in the world. Such a secret elite must exist even in the more democratic Church of the People of God. It stands to reason that this elite should contain as many priests as possible. Although they have a social function in the Church, these representatives of the Church should, as much as possible, combine letter and spirit, law and freedom, rite and grace, official function and free charism. I am convinced that in such a properly understood humble and unselfish elite, including priests, devotion to the Sacred Heart should and will have a future. This devotion must have a distinct character, even though it may differ considerably in its style and way of speaking from what used to be. It will differ less explicitly than before from ordinary Christian and priestly spirituality. Such a conviction is not to be understood as a prophecy, but rather as an invitation to shape priestly piety, a shaping that is not only grace but also an act of our freedom.

With this conviction in mind I can offer only a few short considerations on behalf of devotion to the Sacred Heart. We cannot appeal here to the Gospel of Saint John to defend devotion to the heart of Jesus. It is impossible to bring up the great history of this devotion, in order to ask whether we, the Church's present-day philistines, intend to betray this wonderful history of piety. We cannot survey every dimension of this devotion which Pius XI did not hesitate to declare the sum of the Christian religion. It is impossible to explain the dogmatic and theological meaning of worship of the Sacred Heart, which should be known before one ventures to present one's own opinion about it. It is impossible to say anything here about the archetypes in the depths of human existence of such perennial and universal words as *heart*, even though we know more about the physiological cardiac muscle and are capable of replacing it in heart transplants.

Here and now I would like to call attention to two ideas. The first one belongs to the history of theology. The other one considers the very unusual historical situation in which the Church exists today. Taken together, both considerations may at least make us wonder whether it would not be theologically imprudent, and even foolish, to expect a disappearance of devotion to the Sacred Heart, even though in the Church we can never simply passively await the future or predict it by means of rationalistic computations, since the future remains entrusted to our freedom, responsibility, and action.

THE CHURCH —
A UNITY THAT KEEPS ITS IDENTITY IN HISTORY

The first consideration refers to the irreversibility of the history of the Church's consciousness. The Church is one. Despite all great, often terrible, and absolutely unforeseeable changes she does not lose her identity. This implies that new events may occur in her, events that are really important, that determine her future destiny, that truly cannot be rationally deduced from what came before. They are new, surprising interventions of God's Spirit in the Church. It does not follow, and it is even excluded, that important events which shape the whole Christian Church fade away without leaving a lasting trace simply because they occurred after the time of the primitive Church.

Possibly there exists a true history of *jus divinum* in the Church. This divine law is not simply transmitted all the way from Jesus to the present without any changes. Rather it attains its reality only through later historical decisions. The binding decisions of the councils cannot be rejected later on. They cannot even be totally forgotten. The history of the liturgy is not only a series of changes, but it is also one unified history.

In that history the inner nature of Christian public worship not only remains the same; in its new forms it realizes itself in such a way that the basic nature of former historical forms is maintained and becomes manifest.

Many things in the Church's life, in her piety, her relation to the secular world, her interpretation of nature and of humankind, and the organization of ordinary life, may at first sight seem to disappear and be replaced by something quite different. However, as this history is the history of the one Church, the history of the one body of the one Christ, it is more than an external succession of single events, even if these events are considered to be grounded in a reality and a doctrine that remains rigidly the same. The Church grows while remaining the same. That is why she cannot simply lay aside and forget her former history. She is always the one that she has become. She always acts according to the experiences gathered in her history. She is always young, but this youth, with its possibilities of the surprisingly new, is the youth in which her past history resides. This is something like the case of the adult who, as Paul says, lays aside what is childish, without thus becoming a new child who simply starts over. The Church always brings her history with her into the present and in this way carries it on.

The memory of the past, a memory that keeps things alive and out of which the present emerges in ever new ways, thus preserving the past, is a basic category of ecclesiology. Without it the history of the Church cannot be understood and lived. Of course, that which remains of the past in the present and the future of the Church varies according to the relationship between an historical event and the basic nature of the Church, a relationship that, naturally, can vary much in the single events that occur in the Church.

Today there may be no hermits living atop a column. They have become an oddity of historical curiosity. But the real spirit of the fathers of the desert and the experience of that time may nevertheless have a meaning for us today. We would not belong in the Church today, if we left all this behind us as wholly unimportant, if we did not keep it as an experience that challenges us now, or that will challenge us later, in a wholly new way. Even in the future with all the changes that are still possible in eucharistic piety, we will never be able simply to forget the knowledge that, in the twelfth century, was given to the Church about the presence of Jesus in the Lord's Supper and under the eucharistic signs, and which she professed officially in the dogma of Trent. That is why eucharistic worship will not simply return to the simplicity it had in the time of the fathers of the Church. In this respect too, the Church, having reached greater maturity, will not simply return to her childhood, even though we cannot say just what this worship will look like in Africa two hundred years from now.

In a Church that only now is slowly turning into a real *world*-Church, the papacy too will experience, in its relation to the worldwide territorial churches, changes that cannot now be foreseen. But it will certainly not return to its beginnings at the time of Cyprian. Because the Church is an ecclesial unity that keeps its identity in history, she carries along from the past into the future, not only her abstract essence but also her history. She does this in many different ways, of course, according to the significance of these historical developments in the past, in ways that we cannot theoretically deduce and thus predict. But because of her own identity in history, and in spite of the fact that her historical achievements and decisions originated in time, her past will never simply disappear.

THE DEVOTION TO THE SACRED HEART
BELONGS TO THE WORSHIP OF THE CHURCH

I am convinced that this is true also of the veneration of the Sacred Heart with an explicit spirituality and a particular worship. It is true that, despite its roots in John's theology of the pierced side as the source of water and Spirit from which the Church is born, and despite the beginnings of an explicit devotion in the Middle Ages, this devotion is an historical event and an historical experience that were given to the Church only in the modern age. Naturally, this spiritual experience has its human-historical limitations that do not always have to remain the same. Christian faith and theological reflection have only slowly understood the proper nature of this spiritual experience, and what is properly meant when we speak of the heart of Jesus. We do not have to hold onto everything that has ever been said in the theology of the devotion to the Sacred Heart, in its efforts to assimilate spiritual experience. Nor are we supposed to hold onto the concrete devotional practices that were very much alive in former times. But when we consider the history of devotion to the Sacred Heart — not superficially, superciliously, or with scorn — and when we see the wealth of spiritual and charismatic experience it contained, when we bear in mind all the Church's official declarations about it, when we remember the liturgical worship of the heart of Jesus in all its grandeur and impressiveness, we should not venture to say that we can simply forget about this devotion as something antiquated. If we were to think and to act that way, we would have to say that we were about to give up something that belongs to the Church's past and therefore something of our own spiritual experience in the Church as well.

We may feel that we *can* easily forget about this past of our Church. In the laziness of our heart we are all too tempted to do so. But this does not prove that we are *allowed* to do so before God and considering our responsibility for the continuity of the Church's history. Such a feeling must rather frighten us. We should face the question whether such a lazy slipping back into a primitive spirituality that wrongly appeals to ancient times, when the Sacred Heart devotion was unknown, is not something that we must overcome in a spirit of hopeful determination. If we do not want to be condemned by our past, we should wonder whether it is possible to expect a renewed understanding of the nature of this devotion and a renewed practice of it. What today seems utterly plausible, all that is everywhere bought and sold, are not always the only things that make us great and holy before God, nor important for the future of the Church. That which is patiently and laboriously learned might also deserve our attention.

THE CHURCH HARBORS
A UNIVERSAL HOPE FOR ALL HUMANITY

A second consideration is in order. Humanity — and humanity in the Church also — is living today in a situation of frightening ambivalence. Humanity is coming out of a modern enlightened optimism, for which the human is naturally good and about to build an earthly paradise of freedom, universal justice, and happiness. In this era of naive optimism, something happened in the Church's consciousness that *looks* like the result or the echo of this bourgeois enlightened optimism, finding in it a favorable climate for growth, although, in the final analysis, it has a quite different cause and justification. Divine revelation, given to the Church in Jesus, makes her *hope* that all human beings not only may be saved but will be saved. True, she will never preach a theoretical doctrine of universal salvation, because, while carefully eschewing theoretical curiosity in eschatology, she will always humbly submit to the fear instilled by the threatening apocalyptic sermons of Jesus. But it seems to me that the Church has learned to have a universal hope for all and to forgo making any theoretical and dogmatically binding statements about the actual occurrence of definitive damnation for a part of humankind.

Thomas Aquinas was of the opinion that we may hope only for ourselves, not for others. Today we hope for ourselves, because we know that we *may*; but we *must* hope for others and we may hope for all. Formerly Christians discussed what percentage of the *massa damnata* (the damned mass) of humanity and of Christians were actually saved. Because of Saint Augustine's doctrine of original sin they considered the failure of human existence through definitive perdition as the normal case, as the outcome of divine predestination, of an unfathomable divine justice. The salvation of a few chosen ones was felt to be a work of God; only in this way could God show that he willed to be not only the God of justice with regard to the many who were doomed but also a God of mercy for the few elect. Today we no longer preach about hell as we used to do, even though in our life and in our preaching we must always realize that we are sinners, who by ourselves are lost, and who do not possess God's incomprehensible grace as something that is at our disposition.

As the Second Vatican Council shows, almost without being aware of it, there exists today a universal hope for the blessed outcome of the whole of history — no *more* than that. But this is a legitimate fruit, granted to the Church today, which, in the long history of her understanding of the faith, has been given to her by Jesus, who was crucified, burdened with the guilt of all humankind, and in this way plunged into the abyss of happiness. And here is the amazing thing which can deeply upset us: with this optimism about salvation gathered in the history of her faith, with this optimism that seemed to be a product of an enlightened world's presumptuous optimism, the Church advances into the future, while maintaining the optimism that she received from God.

But this future which she enters with her courageous hope of universal salvation is, if all the signs are not misleading, a time that is totally different from the past out of which the Church and the world are emerging. Although those who continue to harbor great secular optimism are not forbidden to do so, this dawning time is one in which people are, to a large extent, running into limits they can no longer exceed. It is a time of crisis offering no possible alternatives, a time of resignation, of weariness, sterility, and exhaustion, a time in which individuals become ever more ignorant because they feel increasingly helpless before the enormity of what needs to be known. It is a time in which, despite all the talk of freedom and democracy, individuals are subject to ever more planning, and must be, because otherwise the enormous mass of people could not coexist, because otherwise people would exterminate a great part of the rest of the world by means of nuclear wars, just so that the survivors might have enough space in which to live. We are living in a time in which the anthropological sciences madly endeavor to smash people's illusions, to unmask human beings as the mere product of fortuitous evolution, of the powers of their unconscious, of their drives, and of a society that does not know where it comes from and where it is going. Nature, exploited by humans, threatens them, and they themselves have learned how to bring about the universal suicide of humankind.

It is into such a humanity that the Church enters with Jesus Christ's message of universal salvation. It is because of Christ that we are emboldened to hope that the individual and humankind are advancing irreversibly, singlemindedly, toward eternal salvation in God, when they seem only to be plunging into the dark abyss of death.

The Church keeps this hope, because she wishes to be faithful to the true God and the crucified Jesus. She holds on to it, while being fully aware of the dreadful, seemingly unabating wickedness of world history, which only discovers new and unprecedented ways of spending itself in hopeless guilt. In all this hopelessness for the present and the future, the Church remains the one that harbors universal hope, that even dares to hope more thoroughly than she did in the past.

This universal hope is not an easy painkiller in the wretchedness of our time, but, considered from the human point of view, it is an exorbitant demand. It is a modern form of the folly of the Cross, of hoping against all hope. It is a folly that sets God's wisdom against the world's wisdom, a wisdom in which the world begins to have doubts about itself. It is the courage to live that alone makes us really free; that, without uselessly counting the cost, teaches to let go and to give; that alone can prefer being to having and that can even love the enemy by whom one is killed. True, this hope does not exempt us from thinking about how to make the earth habitable for as many people as possible, from working hard to that effect, fighting for it, even with violence, if we have to.

But this universal hope alone, which the Church herself has only slowly reached as an evident truth, can shed some light in the darkness in which we are drifting, a darkness that we have to bear today and tomorrow, even if we allow ourselves to think that historically such times of darkness have been followed by more luminous periods. And if our thinking nowadays is less individualistic, but more political and collective (or if at least we imagine that it is), the universal hope that the whole of history is not rushing into a final abyss of nothingness and that there cannot be an eternal and definitive rubbish heap for part of this universal history is the final confirmation and the crowning conviction of such a way of thinking and of a political theology.

The universal hope that lives in all individuals and that accompanies them in their inescapable death is for them the form their hope takes today, that hope which, as one of the three theological virtues, saves them and secures their happiness. Who would have the courage today of proudly trusting that their absolute future will be one of fulfillment, if they did not assume the blessed obligation to hope in the same end for all others?

THE HEART AS THE INNERMOST CENTER

But what is the connection between devotion to the Sacred Heart and this frightfully strange situation, in which the Church must proclaim the foolish message of a universal hope for a despairing humanity?

If we wanted to give a really clear answer to this question (we cannot do it here) we would have to say that, despite God's fundamental oneness for which human beings are heading, persons in their religious existence have to do with a great number of religious realities that time and again overwhelm them. If this were not the case, the council would have found it impossible to speak of a hierarchy of truths that is presented to those who believe and that, under the guidance of the Spirit, all persons have to build for themselves and for their own situation. When religious-minded people wish time and again to summarize and organize this huge number of religious realities and to center it around the ultimate mystery of God, they look for basic words, words that in a mysterious way contain infinity. As single words they refer to *everything*. They emerge from the innermost center of one's own existence, where all is still one, and call forth the ultimate unity of all reality. There are many such basic words. Everyone may have his or her own, that tells one everything.

The word "heart" is certainly one of these basic words. It refers to the innermost center where the multiple is still one. So when we say "heart of Jesus" we evoke the innermost core of Jesus Christ, and we say that it is filled with the mystery of God. We say, in a way that frightens us to death while yet making us utterly happy, in a way that contradicts all our experiences of emptiness, futility, and death, that there reigns in this heart the infinite love of God's self-giving. That is what we believe and confess, with all the power of our heart, when we say "heart of Jesus." That is what we confess in the desolation that settles upon us and induces us powerfully to look to the one whose heart was pierced. Many Christians may feel — and it may even be true for them — that "heart of Jesus" is but a verbal duplicate for "Jesus Christ." But those who, in the adventure of their religious existence, are willing to experience more clearly the enormous height and depth, length and breadth of salvation, must remind themselves time and again of the innermost center and the ultimate truth of this great blend of life and death, doom and happiness, laughing and weeping, light and darkness. And then they say, "heart of Jesus." Then they turn toward the heart that was pierced, that loves, that loves us in the darkness of our hopelessness, that is God's very heart and that, without abolishing it, discloses to us God's fundamental mystery.

There is only one place in which, without being destroyed, without falling into despair, we may totally and unconditionally let go of that which is most our own, the salvation which we basically are in the definitiveness of our free decision. It is God whom we experience as mercy. Not as though we were to detach this forgiving and saving mercy from God and from the depths of God's incomprehensibility and sovereignty, and not as though we were to appropriate it as if it were directed by ourselves, but we must surrender to God totally, unconditionally, and without reserve in what we call faith and hope. We can do this only if we commit ourselves to God as to that love in which we must believe, of which we may hope that it is given to us.

This act can be consciously performed only before Jesus Christ, the one who has been crucified and raised from the dead. It is possible only before his heart, his pierced heart, the heart that has known the extreme plight of death and of being forsaken by God, the heart that has surrendered to God's judgment over the world. It is possible only before the heart that, in the ever new and surprising wonder of grace, gives us the unselfish courage to believe in its love as a love granted to each one personally, or, more precisely, the courage to hope for this love in that act of hope which is more than faith, which is already the beginning of love.

We look at the heart of the Lord and the question that is decisive for eternity fills our innermost being, our innermost heart and life: Do you love me? Do you love me in such a way that this love generates a blessed eternity, that it truly, powerfully, and invincibly generates my everlasting life? This question is not answered because the answer would no longer be a secret; we could give it to ourselves. The question enters the mystery that has come near to us in the heart of the Lord. But when it enters this heart, because it is asked with faith, hope, and love, that question is not answered but overpowered by the mystery that is love, by the unquestionable reality of the mystery of God.

God, eternal mystery, immensity without name, blessed abyss, containing everything, contained by nothing, you have uttered your eternal Word in creation and in our being, so that your everlasting mystery might become the unutterable sheltering nearness for us and the very center of the world! We look at this your uttered Word, we look at the one who is the heart of the world, we look at the heart of the Son that we have pierced. All the incomprehensibility that we and our existence are is hidden in this heart. All the anxiety of existence remains in its grip; whatever is lofty and holy returns to this, its origin. There everything finds its true nature and recognizes itself as love. Everything enters the mystery that is blessed love.

It is impossible properly to teach devotion to the Sacred Heart. With confidence in the Church and the Spirit, we must try to approach its mystery. We must eventually, in the luminous and in the dark hours of life, try to pray: "Heart of Jesus, have mercy on me."

We should perhaps try to practice a prayer like the Jesus prayer of the Russian pilgrim. We might venture to use this word like a mantra in Eastern style meditation. But over and above all that, we must experience in life that it is most improbable, most impossible, and so most evident that God, the incomprehensible, truly loves us and that in the heart of Jesus Christ this love has become irrevocable. There first, but, so we dare to hope, there for all.

11

COURAGE FOR DEVOTION
TO MARY

Mariology and devotion to Mary have had a very stormy time during the last fifty years. Let us remember that on November 1, 1950, Pius XII solemnly defined the Assumption of the Blessed Virgin, body and soul, into God's glory. Let us remember the great efforts made during the 1950s to declare Mary the co-redemptrix and mediatrix of all grace. Let us think of the serious discussions about whether the Second Vatican Council should promulgate a separate dogmatic constitution about Mary, or whether a chapter of the Constitution on the Church (*Lumen Gentium*) should expressly treat of Mary and, if it did, what the content of the chapter would be. As a result of this discussion the Constitution on the Church contains, after its seventh chapter on the eschatological nature of the pilgrim Church and its connection with the Church in heaven, an eighth chapter on the Blessed Virgin Mary, Mother of God, and her function in the mystery of Christ and the Church.

However, we cannot ignore the fact that during the same decades, zeal for and emphasis on devotion to Mary have known great changes. Efforts to define a doctrine of mediation of all grace by Mary seem to have faded away since the council. While attributing to Mary a special function within the economy of salvation, the council avoided speaking of any other mediation of grace than that of the one mediator, Jesus Christ. We get the impression that the practice of the rosary has considerably declined. We might notice that the Sodalities of Our Lady are being called "Christian life communities." Prevailing church architecture does not favor the construction of beautiful altars to the Blessed

Mother. May devotions are far from having the importance they used to have in the piety of great numbers of people. Pilgrimages to great Marian shrines have not disappeared; in our age of mass tourism they are even enjoying a revival here and there. But one cannot say that, in the religious life of the average educated Catholic in our rational and enlightened world, devotion to Mary is either intense or explicit.

On the other hand, the council not only presented in the chapter mentioned above a relatively extensive Mariology, it also added a special section on "Devotion to the Blessed Virgin in the Church." The number of writings in theology or spirituality is increasing, which seek to create a new understanding of the dogma of and devotion to Mary and which try "carefully and equally avoid the falsity of exaggeration on the one hand, and the excess of narrow-mindedness on the other" in considering "the unique dignity of the Mother of God" (*Lumen Gentium,* 67). Therefore the theme of devotion to Mary may today again deserve the attention of those who, as Christians, really believe in redemption through Jesus Christ.

AN ANTHROPOLOGICAL APPROACH

When we wish to reflect on the veneration of Mary, we should not deny in Catholic theology and piety the human motivation that undoubtedly influenced the traditional cult of Mary in the past. Why would we disown the human (secular, if you prefer) inspiration for this veneration? It is evident that in the ancient veneration of Mary human reverence for the woman, the mother, the spotless virgin, etc., were at work. Should someone say (as indeed it has often been said) that the veneration of Mary is a continuation of the cult of mother divinities of pre-Christian religions, we should not consider this, if it is rightly understood, an objection to the veneration of Mary. At the most it proves the wonderful fact that in its religiosity Christianity does not omit a single human dimension, that it is not afraid of points of contact, that it does not consider the loftiness of its relation to God through grace to be endangered when Christian existence becomes earthly, carnal, full-blooded, willing to assume whatever is human. If today, when compared with its past, devotion to Mary seems to have become abstract and anemic, then discovering human influences in the ancient cult is a challenge for us today.

How little understanding we have today for all the marvelously human features that used to be alive in devotion to Mary. Is it not a sign of the banality of our modern sensitivity when we see what little interest we show in erecting an image of the great, beautiful, and pure woman and decorating it with flowers? A democratization of society and a legitimate emancipation of women are certainly unavoidable and, in themselves, lawful developments in today's society and culture. But they should not stifle in us the capacity for honoring the majestic image of an exalted human being. They should not smother in us the secular mysticism (so to speak) of the cult of woman, as still presented to us in our time in Paul Claudel's *Satin Slipper*, for instance. The weakness of the veneration of Mary is basically the result of a *human* weakness in us.

CHRISTIAN ROOTS OF THE VENERATION OF MARY

The Christian and truly Catholic veneration of Mary has, of course, deep roots in the Christian message itself. Its decline is ultimately a sign of the decline of our ability to realize in a deeply human and religious way what is properly Christian. It is praiseworthy that excesses of piety and false emphases have been eliminated from piety that often produced the impression that the radical relationship to the incomprehensible God was replaced by a piety that referred only to the powerful reality of the "Immaculate Virgin."

Solidarity with the Deceased

Let me start by asking whether we still possess a genuine relationship with our deceased that derives from the basic tenets of Christianity. Or while as Christians we do not deny that they remain, beyond death, true and real before God, do we give up any living relationship to them? Do we believe in the "communion of saints," the living solidarity of all who are sheltered by and united in God's holy love, whether they are living on earth or have already reached their fulfillment?[1] One of the latest trends in theology starts from the premise that all our Christian convictions, as well as the possibility of speaking theologically, can only be based on our solidarity with those who have been abused in history and with those who are dead. It is held that we give up this solidarity

---

[1]About this see K. Rahner and Johannes B. Metz, "Prayer to the Saints," in *The Courage to Pray*, trans. Sarah O'Brien Twohig (New York: Crossroad, 1981), 29–87.

only at the risk of a banal and inhuman egoism, whereby we reduce
the history of the dead and of those who have been unjustly treated in
history to being the humus on which our pitiable happiness has been
flowering, because we are the ones who came later and so are closer
to the future paradise. But is such solidarity with the deceased a reality
in our religious life? Do the deceased still live for us or have they, so
to speak, totally vanished from our life? Does the city-dweller still feel
a need, like the peasant, to visit the cemetery on Sunday after Mass?
Appealing to the great number of historical monographs and to the
cult of heroes that is manifest in them does not answer our question.
For this hero worship of the saints and of other great people in history
may be very praiseworthy, but it is turned only toward a historical past,
to Napoleon or Bodelschwingh or Charles de Foucauld or Maximilian
Kolbe. It does not imply a relationship to a person who is still alive and
who has reached fulfillment in God.

Living Relation to the Deceased

The Catholic doctrine of the communion of saints, of the unity of the
Church militant and the Church triumphant, of devotion to the saints,
tells us that in our religious life we can and should succeed in developing a strong relationship to living persons who have reached fulfillment,
even when they seem to have moved infinitely far away from us beyond
the gates of death. We may not, of course, use the methods of modern
spiritualists in order to fulfil this duty. They believe that through their
mediums they can establish contact with the deceased. Yet they get in
touch only with persons who have not really overcome the narrowness
and the wretchedness of our life on earth. Christian faith, on the other
hand, in its veneration of the saints and through a living relationship
with all those who have reached fulfillment in God's grace and love, is
looking for persons who have really entered the nameless mystery that
we call God.

Thus we meet the fundamental difficulty that, for us today, seems to
render almost impossible this living relationship to the dead who are
really alive. In earlier times people clearly did not have this difficulty.
However, their greater ease in becoming religiously aware of the living
existence of the deceased does not necessarily speak in their favor. It
may also be explained in part by the fact that they did not sufficiently
realize the incomprehensibility and absolute sovereignty of God. But

the way we feel about all this gives us the impression that the deceased vanish into the namelessness and the unavailability of God, and this precisely to the extent that we believe them to be with God and not merely to have reached some creaturely fulfillment. It is precisely here, however, that Christian faith protests against what looks so plausible to us, namely, that the more God's infinity and incomprehensibility invade our existence, the closer we finite creatures come to nothingness.

Christian faith teaches — even though this message seems to expect too much from our spirit and heart — that the following two things are true at the same time: that God is all in all, and that, nevertheless, precisely when he has really come to us as the Absolute, he causes us to exist and reach fulfillment. Christian faith says that God does not compete with the creature that is distinct from him. Christian faith confesses that God as God can arrive with his infinity and incomprehensibility in the land of our finiteness — God himself near us — without the need for him to become finite, without the need for *us* to perish in the burning absoluteness of his divinity. Hence the radical optimism of Christianity commands us to seek God as God where, according to our pitiful opinion, he cannot be without destroying finiteness. It commands us to look for God among us on earth and not only in heaven.

Veneration of the Saints

It is only from this starting point that the Catholic veneration of the saints can be understood in its ultimate meaning, the praise of God's arrival near humanity. The veneration of the saints affirms human persons, their definitive salvation with God, the definitive consummation of their history on this earth. It is intended for real people who are known to us from their history and recognized as having reached consummation in their history.

But this consummation is ultimately and basically God, who does not create a creaturely reality that consummates persons, but who imparts to persons his own reality and splendor and thus consummates them through himself. That is why the veneration of the saints is something permanent within the most authentic *theo*logy. It is a statement about the history of God who, in fulfillment of the incarnation of his eternal Logos, gives himself to persons and thus both has a history and consummates his own history in this history of the saints. That is why the veneration of the saints means that we find and praise God in his own splendor where he has himself deigned to come. We can understand the veneration of the saints only if we understand in faith that God is not only the one who is infinitely exalted above every created reality and to be adored as such, but that in his grace he has decided to become the innermost reality of his creatures, as a real consequence and completion of the incarnation of the eternal Word. It is true that God and his world do not coincide in simple identity. Yet where the world is consummated and is truly assumed by God as his own reality in the incarnate Son, we may not simply conceive them as being juxtaposed. We find God when we encounter human beings who are filled with grace, saved, and perfected. There the summit of the unity of love of God and love of neighbor is reached. There in the vehemence of the love uniting God and humanity we may almost confuse the two, because in grace the really innermost center of the human is God himself.

It is by starting from such a theology, a theology of God's descent into the world and of God's solidarity with humanity, a true theology of the veneration of saints, that we must understand the veneration of Mary. If it is possible to find God in the person who is loved by God, filled with God's own reality, it is even more true of the holy Virgin, the Mother of Jesus, the one who is blessed among women, and who, according to the words of Scripture, is to be praised by all generations.

MARY'S IMPORTANCE IN THE HISTORY OF SALVATION

However, before we apply to Mary the theology of the veneration of saints, we should also justify and explain it in a quite different way. The veneration of saints does not refer to the abstract idea of humanity in general, but to real persons with their concrete and completed history. True, all the saints have reached consummation. But all of them reached it in their ultimately unique way with their own history, important for themselves and for all others. All of them reached their fulfillment with their own God-given personality, with which they are, without envy, accepted by all the others in the unity of God's love that embraces all of them and that, in this way, grants to each of them their own personal kind of holiness. That is why the personal way in which Mary is important for all in the history of salvation must first be explained before the veneration of Mary may be understood theologically in connection with the veneration of all other saints.

Mary is certainly the humble handmaid of the Lord. We do no damage to her honor if we view her first as a modest young woman, a poor and unimportant woman among many women, in a forsaken corner of the world. We do no damage to her honor if, from the religious and spiritual point of view, we allow her to remain in the circle of pious women among her people and in her time. Yet, when God looks upon the humility of his handmaid, the power of God's grace can work great things in that person, even very great things, without removing her humanity in a miraculous way. This grace induced Mary to allow the incarnation of the eternal God to happen in her, freely, through her faith, in order to share with the world this extreme nearness of God.

She is certainly not a wholly independent partner in the dialogue between God and the world in which the world's salvation is at stake. Her freedom and her free yes are themselves the gracious gift of God's sovereign love, whose only cause is itself. But God's grace itself posits human freedom and the consent of this freedom to the grace of God. God's grace itself brings it about that it has to do with a human partner. That is why the omnipotent predominance of grace is really acknowledged and praised only when it is discerned in the partner whom it faces, because this grace is able to bring forth a free yes to itself.

And thus Mary stands at a place where a humble and unimportant person has, for the salvation of the whole of humankind, freely accepted the enfleshed Grace, first in her faith and then in her womb, for herself and for all of us. The one mediator between God and humanity was able to bring it about that he was freely accepted, that his being freely accepted was one more grace, and that, at the same time, grace would bring forth its own free acceptance. It is at this unique point in salvation history, so important for all times and places of human history, that Mary stands. She is not grace, she is not the one mediator, but she is the free acceptance of grace and of the one mediator, that in the history of salvation occurred once for all of us. In this sense she is really the one who has begotten God, the mother of God, even though, of course, the divinity of her child is not the fruit of her body.

May we call Mary co-redemptrix and mediatrix of all graces, as has been suggested and even said in pontifical declarations of secondary importance? Or should we avoid it in order to prevent misunderstandings and in order not to overshadow the one unique mediation of Jesus Christ? This is not an essential question for theology and faith. Catholic faith acknowledges that Mary has an extraordinary and unique place in the one history of salvation, in which ultimately all persons constitute a common community of salvation. She is the second Eve, the mother of Jesus and thus of all those who believe. Her yes, through which it was done to her according to the Angel's word, is one of the constitutive grounds and dimensions of salvation for Christians, if they really believe in Jesus Christ, their Messiah and Savior, and in the insurpassable nearness of God to him in history, because, although it was this same Jesus who granted this yes to his mother, he himself entered the world on account of it.

ABOUT THE EQUALITY OF MEN AND WOMEN

Nowadays we are quite convinced of the equality and the equal rights of the sexes, unlike ancient anthropology that has continued massively to influence the history of theology, causing a regrettable lack of appreciation of women that we must overcome. That is why, as Christians and as theologians, we are asked how this way of evaluating the sexes, how the equal rights of women must be translated and realized in our theology of salvation history. And, if we are to be honest, this at once brings up a question whose answer is not quite obvious: Why do we have to acknowledge the one mediator as a man, and not as a woman? We will no doubt say that, for his universal and salvific importance, the masculinity of the one mediator is, in the final analysis, unimportant for us and belongs among the contingent particularities which God's eternal Word has to accept in one way or another in wishing to assume our history in a single human nature. Or we will at least entrust this question in obedient resignation to God's sovereign disposition, especially since we ourselves could not be consulted whether we wished to become a human person as a man or as a woman. Our unlimited destiny transcends every sexual difference, while not suppressing it.

In this connection we must also keep in mind that the real human reality of the mediator Jesus Christ also had to be filled with the divine self-communication called grace, which God wants to impart to all human beings, whether men or women. When in this context we consider the unique and irreplaceable position and function of the Holy Virgin, we will no longer be able to say that, from the point of view of theology, we must, in that salvation history that involves all people in solidarity, attribute to woman a function and task that is lower than that of man.

It seems to me that today, on the basis of the anthropology which we accept, every theology faces the question of what rank to attribute to women in salvation history. In Mariology traditional Catholic theology has already upheld the specific nature and the uniqueness of women in general. Now theology should more widely and resolutely than before develop this Marian starting point in the whole of theology and of Christian life.

VENERATION OF THE SAINTS AND VENERATION OF MARY ON THE BASIS OF FINAL SALVATION IN GOD

If we explain the veneration of Mary by means of the theology of the veneration of the saints in general and if we realize through our faith the unique function of Mary in salvation history, it is possible to develop a rationale for this devotion to Mary. The salvation history that underlies the way in which each one of us reaches salvation and human fulfillment has not wholly vanished in the past. It goes on really and definitively in all *those* persons who are already fulfilled in God and have definitively reached their highest reality in God's seemingly silent incomprehensibility. These are the real persons whom the cult of the saints has in mind, finding in them God himself, whose grace has found in them embodiment and consummation. This is true also for Mary, provided our faith does not overlook her unique place in salvation history.

Those who have reached blessed salvation are not abstract uniform models but real persons, whose history on earth has been definitively saved in its uniqueness. We mentioned already that our relationship to them today has become more difficult. It takes all the strength of our faith to overcome the impression that the silent infinity of God into which the deceased have entered has obliterated them, to believe rather that it has confirmed them and made them real for themselves and for us. This power to continue to see individuals in the mysterious reality of God, to trust that God does not let them perish but introduces them as individuals into definitiveness, is already assured for Christians, since they can have such a relationship with the glorified man Jesus. Even in God's incomprehensibility this man may be known and loved. He shows us that God's supreme power transcends every metaphysics of infinity.

CONCRETE VENERATION OF MARY

To what extent do individual Christians succeed in doing this in their religious life? Can they clearly, or only vaguely and darkly, still distinguish, as it were, the individual blessed beings in the supraluminous darkness of God without falsely transforming them into magic-working minor deities? This is a question for the religious history of each individual. It cannot be answered for everyone in general. Jesus says that there are many dwelling places in his Father's house. Everyone does not have every charism which the Holy Spirit may grant to people. It is quite legitimate for individuals modestly to admit that they do not possess a certain charism that they discover and admire in another person, or that they have it only to a very small extent, provided only that they do not, in principle, absolutely reject such a charism if it is offered to them by God's grace in the course of their religious development. This is also true for the veneration of Mary.

It may be present in someone only as a germ, only as good will that is not skeptical or does not feel superior to the veneration which others pay to Mary. We may be good Christians in the Catholic Church, even if we can discover in ourselves little of the deep faith and heartfelt enthusiasm that others feel in venerating the Blessed Mother. It is not always a sign of neurotic sensitivity when married women suspect in many an image of the Virgin Mother a quiet kind of discrimination. Do we not often have to do with a myth about Mary rather than with faith in Mary (V. Schurr)? Undoubtedly we have the right to reject certain forms of the veneration of Mary, as the Second Vatican Council emphasizes, when such forms turn into superstitions or employ practices that contradict the uniqueness of the mediation of Jesus Christ or the free sovereignty of divine grace, or when they hold the absurd opinion that it is easier to be certain of Mary's love than of the infinite mercy and love of the eternal God.

So it is quite legitimate to keep our own religious practice away from a legitimate devotion to Mary. Yet even though this aloofness is allowed, we should not hold it up as a principle. It is better to remain open to a further development in our religious life, in which a more intense and explicit veneration of Mary can also have a place. As often emphasized above, a truly radical Christian relationship to God does not imply that we fade away the closer we come to God and his incomprehensibility.

Moreover, we should not overlook the fact that in the one communion of saints, in the mystical body of Christ, individual Christians have different talents and different duties. Hence the Church as a whole can foster veneration of Mary in a way that is not the way of each individual. The Church as whole has a relationship to Mary, even though the same relationship cannot be expected to the same degree from each individual.

From her beginnings the Church as a whole has honored and praised Mary, as we can see in the Gospels of Luke and of John. About the exact content and meaning of Mary's title as Mother of the Church, which the council avoided and Pope Paul VI adopted all the same,[2] we may think what we will. At any rate the Church as a whole has at all times honored the Blessed Mother, although, of course, with different emphasis at different times in an eventful history. This praise of Mary simply belongs to the idea the Church has of herself. Despite all the dangers and the sinfulness that threaten her, the Church in her ongoing history is the holy community of those who believe not only in an abstract *possibility* of salvation but in its reality. They hold the firm hope and conviction that the power of God's grace actually transforms the possibility of salvation into a reality. That is why acknowledging the victorious arrival of God's power among the dangers that threaten our existence is part of the idea the Church has of herself.

Now how would the Church more clearly and more concretely realize this way of understanding herself, this way of praising God, than by singling out a human being in whom this wonder of God's triumphant grace has operated in all dimensions of this person, and who belongs in this way to the Church? By praising and honoring Mary, the Church welcomes and calls by name that which God has done and continues to do for her until the end of time. The Church fulfills Mary's prophecy that all generations will call her blessed because God has looked graciously upon the lowliness of his handmaid. And as the Church thus praises Mary, she becomes actually, and not just theoretically, aware of her own vocation: that God may become all in all in her and that precisely in this way the blessed perfection of human beings may be achieved.

---

[2]See the apostolic letter *Marialis cultus* (1975) on devotion to Mary.

12

UNDERSTANDING CHRISTMAS

THE MESSAGE OF THE BIRTH

The message of Christmas is first the message of the birth of a man. Jesus' beginning, his birth, must be understood by starting from his *life* and from his death, from the destiny of a man, a very special man, of course. As Christians, we can gain real access to the fact and the meaning of Christmas only by starting from the cross and resurrection of Jesus Christ. We celebrate the birth of the one whom we have discovered, in his death and resurrection, as our redeemer and lord, as God's irrevocable promise of salvation. Only thus can Jesus' birth be radically significant for us, namely, as the beginning of that life and death in which our life received the irrevocable promise of eternal freedom. Christmas may remain the lovely feast of a gracious child, but we would not be able to grasp its meaning if we did not understand it as the beginning of a life that, by traveling through the depths of human experience, leads us to the blessed fulfillment hidden in the incomprehensible mystery of God.

Without suppressing our freedom the knowledge and will of God contain and carry forward the whole of human life. Through his own will God disposes of the beginning of life and leads it to its end and completion. Since a life and its completion reveal what its beginning already contained, life and its completion disclose the beginning as it was willed and destined by God for this very concrete end. That is why Christmas is for Jesus, as it is for us, the beginning of death.

Death suffuses the whole length and breadth of our life; it is not simply something that happens at the end and that does not yet concern us.

In our everyday life, therefore, if we live in a sober but not dull fashion, and if we always try to accept our death, then we may celebrate Christmas in a very sober way.

Christmas is really the beginning of that consummation in which Jesus unreservedly and without clinging to anything but God let himself fall into the incomprehensibility of God as his own consummation, a consummation which he himself did not control. Christmas is the beginning of the man who, like us, would have to die in an act that is the most profound act of his faith and obedience.

When, full of faith, we stand before the crib of the newly born child, we must see that here begins the downfall that is called death and that alone saves us, because its emptiness is filled with the nameless incomprehensibility of God. That incomprehensibility alone answers all the questions that come up in our life in the guise of thousands of partial questions. It answers them because it transcends them. Of course, we are speaking here of death as it is saved by God, filled with God, of death that for us means the end of our existence and for God means God's dawning in what we call resurrection. Christmas is the start of this redeemed death, and it can really be understood only from this point of view.

The light of Christmas and the song of the angels, as they praise God and announce to human beings their ultimate reconciliation through the grace of God, must fall into the abyss of death. Otherwise they are neither seen nor heard. Christmas is not a cheerful feast, to make us forget for a while the mystery of our destiny. It should be celebrated where we are living, in the looming shadow of our death, because the birth of Jesus was the beginning of his death.

THE CENTRAL DIFFICULTY

We must now consider the principal difficulty that we meet when we celebrate Christmas, a difficulty that we meet even if, from lack of interest, indifference, or boredom, we do not simply capitulate to what has become routine. This general difficulty is rather complex. It has two main aspects: the remoteness in time of the event and its contingent historicity make it difficult for us to understand Christmas as the foundation of the salvation of our whole existence.

REMOTENESS IN TIME

The remoteness of Christmas in time frightens us; it happened so terribly long ago. Like other events out of a distance past, Christmas too seems to demand too much from us. As human beings we cannot help wondering whether history in general can tell us anything, whether we are people who can still react with grief or pride to any event of our history, whether decisions made by our forebears have the power of binding us, whether we are endowed with a historical memory.

If we are honest we will have to admit that in the average person today the sense of history is underdeveloped. The knowledge of general immutable laws of nature and the planning for a future that has not yet come to be are the main concern of modern consciousness and produce forgetting of the past that is often inhuman.

To the extent that people neglect history they become inhuman and disoriented. Their life should be the creative conquest of an unknown future. But the future will always turn out to be the completion of the beginning, the product of a history that started long before the tiny light of our individual consciousness began to shine.

Christmas is a question addressed to us. It asks whether we are persons without a memory, in the proper sense of the word, living only for the everyday bustle of the present and unable to build a future because we have no past, or whether our mind and heart can stand the living tension within ourselves that introduced the past into the present and carries it into an everlasting future. If we find it difficult to celebrate Christmas, the reason might be that, having no history, we have allowed the roots of our existence to die away in whole or in part, the roots that reach back into the past, into the beginning, to find there the fullness of the future. If Christmas is a strain for us, there is no harm in that. It may be the strain that unavoidably accompanies that return into the past which means a true return to being truly human.

A SINGLE EVENT IN HISTORY
WITH A UNIVERSAL SIGNIFICANCE?

Next we consider that difficulty of faith in Christmas that is supposed to be the hardest and the most specific. It has been known ever since the time of the Enlightenment and it remains worth considering. Is it possible that a unique event, localized in time and space, would be decisive for the total salvation of the whole person and of all of humanity; that an historical truth would have universal meaning for human existence; that a single point in history would decide the whole of history, a history that we know today is a history of perhaps millions of years? Is it possible that the whole chain of history, which in its origin and in its end is lost in the unknown, would not only be carried by the Lord of history who lives outside of it in eternity, but that it would also be suspended from a single line of the chain?

For three hundred years theology and philosophy, and secretly even the preaching of the gospel, have struggled with this problem. The faith of Christians may clearly refer to this one event, "Jesus Christ," within time and history, as to the Lord and key of this whole history, and never falter in that respect. But this does not imply that efforts to understand this fact of our faith are finished, or that all Christian theologies have reached the same conclusion. In order better to understand this central difficulty we must go way back and start from the central point of Christology itself.

THE DESCENT OF THE WORD OF GOD
INTO THE WORLD

With the amazing boldness of John and of Paul, especially in the letter to the Colossians and in the hymn to Christ in the letter to the Philippians, we can start with the descent of the divine Logos of God into the world. "And the Word was made flesh." This implies that God has not only created a world distinct from himself, which he encompasses and directs without being affected by it, but that he wishes to communicate himself with his divine splendor, to insinuate himself into the very heart of the world, as its innermost dynamism and definitive goal. Hence we confess that this penetration of God into the world has irrevocably happened in Jesus, with the result that Jesus, as one who was from the start of his existence definitively and irrevocably accepted, is the definitive, historically tangible self-promise of God to his world.

In this way we let God, apparently straight from above, enter the world for its salvation only at the point "Jesus." However, we cannot forget that this apparently unique event, being historical in a historical world, was actually prepared for by a prehistory, and that this history of the world, as a preparation for the arrival of the divine Logos would not really have been his prehistory if it had not been filled and borne by the working of the Holy Spirit of God, who, from the beginning of history, was already the innermost dynamism of the world.

And thus this invasion from above of the self-communicating God into his world may be equally well understood as the irruption of the Holy Spirit of God from the innermost center of history into the tangibility of this history. In this way God confers upon his work, including humanity's free history, definitiveness and irreversibility.

JESUS, THE BEGINNING OF THE REALIZATION OF ALL HUMAN HOPE

The important point in our study of Christmas is the following: when we meet the historical Jesus as the unity of human question and divine answer in his life, death, and resurrection, when we accept this life as the measure and strength of our own life, then we are at a point from which Christmas may be understood. Christmas is the start of that life, the birth that is able to initiate such a life.

What does it properly mean when we say: The eternal Word, in which the eternal God, called the Father, expressed himself from all eternity for himself, while being with himself, has become man, he who is the ground directing everything, positing all things in their diversity and keeping them together, the foundation of this inconceivably immense world of matter, life, and spirit, which we know today is still becoming? Is this God not at once too near and yet too remote from all things, so that we might think of him, almost as in Greek mythology, as if he were someone walking around on the small forlorn planet that we call our earth? We say "And the Word was made flesh," and we say, "The man Jesus from the start was so radically accepted by God and remained so to the end, that because of him we may also hope to be accepted by God." And, if we understand them well, these two statements say the same thing.

In Jesus the human question and God's answer have become one, unconfounded and undivided. In him God and humanity are one without suppressing the other. In Jesus God as the unutterable mystery has totally and irrevocably expressed himself as Word; in him the Word is present as spoken to all of us, as the God of nearness, inexpressible intimacy, and forgiveness.

THE CHILD — BORN LIKE US

So this is how we stand before the crib of Jesus; the stable and the cattle in it do not surprise us. Things still look the same today where we were born, even if it happens in the sterile elegance of a modern obstetrical ward. There, in that crib, someone starts to be a human being. He has not decided to do this; he has not been consulted. His whole existence has been imposed on him with the inexorability of the will of another — of God — so inexorably that every question, every conceivable protest, comes too late.

This child fares like us: it is there without having been consulted. But there is a difference between the child and us. We are tempted to experience this inexorable necessity to *be*, the fact that we cannot step out of our existence, as a stifling constraint, just like the terrible fact that it is impossible for us not to be. Because this child is a true man, indeed the man who, when the time came, went down into the depths of his humanity in a Godforsaken death, this child has undoubtedly also gone through the dreadful experience of being unable not to exist. However (and there he may differ from us, who philistines that we are, never quite know whether, we do not deep down in ourselves hate this necessity) this child accepted this experience as the experience of the effect of love. The inexorability of his being born without being consulted was for him but the blessed inexorability of love, the marvel of being chosen, the obviousness of being, that must answer for itself in the presence of nothingness.

The child possessed this terrible, seemingly destructive knowledge: I am once more encompassed by a love that is a gift and the result of my own free response. I am allowed to be, I want to be, and accept the necessity of my being, as the product of an infinite love that has posited me in a sovereignty that is answerable to none, only in order to give itself boldly away to what it has posited. That is the fundamental act of this child, that he had to carry on throughout his life, until he used it also to illuminate the dark abyss of death.

ACCEPTING OUR EXISTENCE

We are standing before the crib of this child, and we ask ourselves whether we too manage to accept the existence imposed on us. Do we accept it? The fact that we actually exist is not yet a proof that we have really accepted our existence, as it was, as it is, and as it will unexpectedly turn out to be for us. We have certainly not yet accepted it wholeheartedly in all its dimensions. It always remains with us an open question, a question which we do not as a rule even admit: that is, whether we love or hate the one who has imposed our existence on us, whether we lovingly accept that existence as the marvel of love or reject it in secret protest.

The child in the crib had to start his life under Caesar Augustus, at that very moment, no sooner, no later. At that moment the wheel of his time started to turn, the moments started to run, one after the other, each one only once, all of them in an inexorable course that, without stopping, headed for the end of time. In that child, eternity assumed time, for that child and so for the whole world, encompassing it from beginning to end, carrying each one of its moments. Otherwise our time would really be what it seems to be to us: a fleeting time, in which moment by moment our life dwindles away. But where through faith, hope, and love our time turns into the time of this child, becomes a continuation of his life in ours, there death has died in our earthly life, and we live the time whose end is the beginning of eternal reality.

We are standing before the crib. There, in that stable, starts the earthly life in which God expressed himself, even though this expression seems to be as frightfully ordinary as in every human life. There, in that stable, starts the self-uttering of God. The stage of this divine drama seems to be pitifully narrow and small, with a few worn props where not much can be shown. The place is narrow and remains narrow, exactly like our existence.

Yet in this child God succeeds in squeezing his infinity into a small existence. That God may be wholly everywhere may seem relatively obvious to a metaphysical mind, but that he might give himself away, with his infinity, to the puny existence that we are is vouched for only by the child in the crib on Christmas day. Our existence may seem to us as narrow as a crib in a stable, tedious, not smelling too good, suffocating. We would hardly have the courage to hope that we would ever get out of it, if God had not entered into this child in this stable, and thus made obsolete the terrible question of how the eternal creature might ever get out of its narrowness.

SAVED AND LIBERATED BY THE CHILD

We are standing before the crib. The frightful narrowness of our existence may squeeze our heart — so much so that we believe we have lost the breath we need to hope that we might escape. Alas, we are so tired, resigned without admitting it, so that even the word of unending hope seems to make us more irritated and overtaxed. The night seems to become even darker when we begin to speak of the dawning day. Yet we are standing before the crib. It is no easy pretence but — since we ourselves say it with the last strength of our heart — it is the truth, that this child also hopes for us, when our hope seems to die, when we feel that we can only save ourselves by fleeing into the humdrum of everyday where we do not have to believe, hope, and love, and where therefore we do not feel threatened by despair.

But the child has come. And just as we were not asked whether we wanted to exist, neither are we asked whether we want to be saved and liberated. We are saved and liberated by that child. God's grace will undoubtedly induce us to accept this salvation. For this acceptance too, the last action of our life, is one more grace. Paul also said it: God who is faithful has called us, and will bring it about in us.

We are placed before the crib. We will not succeed in running away from it. Christmas has occurred in the night of our existence.

GOD IS NEAR US

Those who in the quiet of peaceful recollection, of docile resignation, in the silent Christmas of their own heart, let the press of things, of people, of desires fall back, which would otherwise obstruct their view of infinity, those who for a while at least extinguish the earthly lights that prevent them from seeing the stars in the sky, only those who, in a silent night of their heart, allow themselves to be called by the ineffable, wordless nearness of God speaking through its own silence, if we have the right ears for it, only they celebrate Christmas as it should be celebrated, if it is not to degenerate into a mere worldly holiday. We should feel as we do on a clear winter night, when we walk under the starry sky: far away the lights of human nearness and the security of home are still calling us. But above us stretches the sky, and we feel the silent night, which may at times impress us as uncanny and frightening, like the quiet nearness of the infinite mystery of our existence that is at once sheltering love and wide expanse.

The eternal future has entered our time. Its brightness is still dazzling, so that we believe it to be night. But it is a blessed night, a night that is already warmed and illuminated, a beautiful night, cozy and sheltering, because of the eternal day that it carries in its dark womb. It is silent night, holy night. But it is so for us only if we allow the stillness of that night to enter our inner person, then in our heart too "all is calm." And that is not difficult. For such a loneliness and stillness are not heavy. Its only heaviness is that which belongs to all sublime things that are both simple and great.

Yes, we are lonely. There exists in our heart an inner land, where we are alone, to which nobody finds the way except God. This innermost unreachable chamber in our heart exists. The question is whether we, in a foolishly guilty way, avoid it, because nobody else and nothing of what is familiar to us on earth can enter into it with us. Let us enter there ever so quietly! Let us shut the door behind us! Let us listen to the ineffable melody that fills the silence of that night. Here the silent and lonely soul sings for the God of her heart her finest and most personal song. And she may be sure that God hears it. For this song no longer has to seek the beloved God beyond the stars in that inaccessible light where he dwells and where no one can see him. Because it is Christmas, because the Word was made flesh, God is near, and the faintest word in the quiet chamber of our heart, the word of love, reaches his ear and his heart.

We must be quiet and not fear the night, else we will hear nothing. For the ultimate message is uttered only in the night's stillness ever since, through the gracious arrival of the Word into the night of our life, Christmas' silent night, holy night came down among us.

13

THE THEOLOGY OF THE RELIGIOUS MEANING OF IMAGES

A s I try to write a few things about this topic, I must start by saying that I do not claim to possess the competence that belongs to an expert in the philosophy or history of art, whether sacred or secular. I understand little about these things. I do not even believe that I belong among those who have more than an average background in these fields. In my theological and "philosophical" considerations (if they can be called such) statements will be blended somewhat. I feel entitled to do this because I believe that the "philosophical" statements are either sufficiently supported by the theological assertions or they meaningfully complement them.

CHRISTIAN ANTHROPOLOGY

I would like first to present a few considerations about the insuperable pluralism in empirical human experience. First, for a Christian anthropology persons are beings of an a posteriori, historical, and sensory experience. This holds also for that dimension of their existence in which they face God in their religion. Until recent years repeated efforts were made to devise a metaphysical anthropology that postulated for human beings a specific source of religious knowledge, which would not depend at all on sensory or historical experience. These efforts derived generally from the conviction that only through such a source of knowledge could religion be possible as a relationship to the absolute and personal God.

We do not have to consider in more detail how this source of knowledge was explained, whether as a mystical experience that is within one's reach, or in the sense of ontologism, or as the operation of a religious organ that is more or less independent of other cognitive powers. Ordinary Christian anthropology is convinced that in human knowledge two levels must be distinguished: sense knowledge, that is, one having a strictly material component, and spiritual conceptual knowledge, that is, one reaching out to being as such. However, against all kinds of ontologism, against all attempts to safeguard religious knowledge by detaching it from other kinds of knowledge, traditional Christian anthropology has always clearly insisted that sense knowledge and spiritual knowledge constitute a unity, that all spiritual knowledge, however sublime it may be, is initiated and filled with content by sense experience. Thomas Aquinas, for instance, emphasizes expressly in his metaphysics of knowledge that even the most spiritual, most "transcendental," most sublime concept can be reached by human beings on this earth only through a *"conversio ad phantasmata,"* that is (in Kantian language) that every concept without sense intuition is empty, that is, nonexistent. This statement applies also to religious knowledge. That knowledge too is necessarily reached by an intuition that depends on sensory, and therefore also historical experience.

RELIGIOUS EXPERIENCE — SENSE INTUITION

It is, of course, not our task here to show, against a large segment of modern philosophy, why, even when we admit that metaphysical knowledge depends on sense experience, a real knowledge of God is possible, although this God is infinitely exalted above all that can be grasped with the senses. Although this task may be very difficult, we must presuppose that it can be carried out. The only thing that concerns us here is that every religious experience has its origin in sense experience and exists only by referring — ever so implicitly — to some sense intuition. There exist in religious language very concrete concepts, representations, and images, and beside them a language that, as we say, sounds abstract, imageless, purely conceptual. But, in the final analysis, even in the religious domain, concepts and words can only be understood if and insofar as they contain a sensory moment. Once more it is not possible to show here in detail, by means of examples, how such a sensory element is present in all religious operations that contain a conscious component or are simply states of consciousness. The livelier these religious operations are, the clearer is the sensory component. This is evident especially in Catholic piety. Central to it is the preaching of the Word, whose concepts also are always carried by representations that enter into consciousness through sense experience and that are present in the concepts even when, to ordinary people, the latter seem to be wholly abstract and devoid of imagery. Moreover in this piety there are also sacramental signs, bodily attitudes for prayer, pilgrimages, songs, vestments, incense, and a thousand other things, through which human sensory corporality is involved in religious activity.

RELIGIOUS ACTIVITIES INVOLVE THE BODY, REFER TO THE NAMELESS GOD

Meanwhile there will always exist a certain antagonism between this corporality of religious activities and their transcendental reference to the nameless God, whom, as we are told in John 1:18, nobody has ever seen. Catholic doctrine and devotion too speak of a mystical ascent to contemplation, which is experienced as being without images, without object, as being engulfed in the incomprehensibility of God. They emphasize that we will one day contemplate God directly, without the help of any created concepts or images. Nevertheless, by emphasizing the resurrection of the flesh, the lasting incarnation of the eternal Logos, Christianity remains the religion that can conceive of human fulfillment only as the consummation of the whole human being, in which that being, although transformed in a way that we do not understand, reaches its consummation with all the dimensions of its reality in their unity, hence not by shedding some dimensions that would belong to it only in this life. For Christianity, human beings take with them, in their consummation, albeit in a way that we can neither conceive nor imagine, their whole reality, hence also their body, their senses, their history. We must reject the idea stemming from the Enlightenment, according to which the "immortal soul" would already be such that, without a radical transformation but simply by shedding the body as a merely provisional instrument, it might enter the realm of final fulfillment.

SENSE POWERS — A COMPLEX REALITY

All of this, although indicated very roughly, is here presupposed. What concerns us here, as we continue to reflect on it, is that what Christian philosophical and theological anthropology generally calls corporality, more exactly the human sense level, is a very complex reality. Despite the unity of the human subject it consists truly of many and ultimately incommensurable powers. Let me mention now that it is only when we understand this clearly that we will be able really to understand the meaning of images in religion.

What do we mean when we speak of the plurality of sense experience as ultimately incommensurable? Let us start very simply. Everyone has heard of the five senses. We do not have to examine here whether there really are five senses or more, whether sense perception as a whole should be subdivided and arranged in another and better way, how the plurality of sense powers has slowly developed during the evolution of animal life. In any case, there is a plurality of sense experiences. We hear, we see, we touch, we feel the movements of our body from within; we smell, we taste, we feel pain and we experience bodily well-being. We cannot suppress this plurality of sense experiences; we cannot, as we experience them in space and time through our bodily nature, reduce this plurality to a unity. True, we may combine them under the concept and word *sensorium* as the a posteriori power of experiencing things in space and time. We may even abstractly, through concepts, think that there might still exist other such powers, for instance, the power of seeing ultra violet light or others that are supposed to exist in bats, and so on. Biochemistry can certainly discover and describe common features in all these different senses and thus also explain the possibility of a differentiation that happened during evolution.

INCOMMENSURABLE PLURALITY
OF SENSE EXPERIENCES

It is undeniable that there exists a plurality of sense experiences that cannot be reduced to each other. Seeing and hearing are not the same. It is true that we can, through our power of abstract concepts, through words and ideas, describe seeing and hearing together in their diversity as well as in their abstract similarity. But from such a description a person who has never seen would understand about seeing about as much as an individual born blind to whom we try to explain what seeing is. The same is true for the other sense experiences. They are in themselves incommensurable with each other; they remain such in the unity of the experiencing subject, even if, as spiritual, that subject can reflect on these experiences with concepts. By mentioning this incommensurability of sense experiences we are not denying the unity of the experiencing subject, through which these sense experiences communicate with each other and thus bring about a unity of this plurality. Nor do we claim that every one of these sense powers and dimensions occupies the same rank and is equally important for the subject.

What is implied in the thesis of an incommensurable plurality of the sense powers and experiences is that, where one is totally (insofar as this is possible at all) self-aware and self-present, all these various sense faculties must enter into action together. In other words, to be completely human, persons must produce a work of art for which all their powers collaborate. This may be beyond their reach. Because of their immersion in time it is possible that they can fully realize themselves, even on the sense level, only partially and in successive attempts. At any rate, every human sense power has an essential importance and cannot be replaced or repressed by another one. We are and we should be persons in whom the many incommensurable dimensions of our *sensorium* enter into activity.

THE EYES OF FAITH —
THE ETERNAL LOGOS AS GOD'S ETERNAL IMAGE

What we have said applies also to human sense powers insofar as they are an essential element of the human capacity for religion. For Christianity, as one of the principal religions, this is evident with regard to the word, to hearing. In a positive (but, as we intend to explain it here, not exclusive) sense Luther is right when he says: the ears are the organ of the Christian. Paul is right when he says: faith comes from hearing. But if persons are fully themselves only when all their sense powers work together, if these powers are incommensurable, if the complete person and complete Christian are identical, then Christianity can be present in persons fully and completely only if it has entered them through all the gates of their senses, and not merely through their ears, through the word.

It is not true that the divine reality which must penetrate into human beings can enter their existence fully and completely through the single gate of the ears, of hearing. This statement does not imply that all these sensory gates are equally wide and important for God's self-communication to humanity. So we are not rejecting what Luther said or, more importantly, what a lengthy Christian tradition holds, namely, that revelation and God's gracious self-communication happen fundamentally through the word and through the hearing of the message conveyed by words.

However, Christian language speaks also of the eyes of faith, the eternal Logos is conceived not only as God's self-utterance but also as God's eternal image. Eternal happiness is presented primarily as a seeing of the triune God face to face, not as a hearing. So, in principle, we may not deny that sight is a power that cannot be replaced by other sources of experience within human sense faculties, that sight also belongs to the sensory foundation of religious knowledge.

We cannot here, in a philosophical and theological epistemology, explain in more detail how reality perceived by the senses is a starting point and a moment of religious experience and knowledge. That would lead us too far. Therefore what we said above about the function of sight, which can be replaced by no other sensory power, not even by hearing, is at first still a very vague and obscure formal statement, which does not bring us much light. But it might perhaps serve as a basis for a few considerations about religious images, which we will presently submit.

WHY RELIGIOUS IMAGES ARE IMPORTANT IN CHRISTIANITY

Religious images have always had a great importance in Christianity. The production, the appreciation, even the veneration of religious images is one of the features that distinguish Christianity and its piety from the piety of the Old Testament, with its prohibition of images, and from Islam, hence from the two other great monotheistic world religions. The fact that these two other monotheistic religions reject religious images, at least in principle, is also time and again a new incentive for rejecting religious images in Christianity as well. Well known are the rejection of images in the East, between 730 and 843; a similar Carolingian opposition to images at the end of the eighth century; the rejection of images by Karlstadt, Zwingli and Calvin; and the iconoclasm in Zurich, France, and the Low Countries in the second half of the sixteenth century.

Upon closer examination, the Orthodox and the Roman-Catholic defense of images derives from very different mentalities and arguments. In the East (if we may put it so briefly and simplistically) the veneration of images is supported by the mystical feeling of an "incarnational" identity between the image and its object (Christ, the saints, God). In the West a more rational feeling prevails; images are legitimate in the religious domain. Compared with the importance of the word they are a kind of *biblia pauperum* (poor people's Bible), which makes the story and the doctrine that have been explained more vivid for those who cannot read.

OUR OWN STARTING POINT

These two basic ways of understanding religious images are of course generally combined in practice and in the theory that tries to interpret it. They led to the complicated theories (from John Damascene to Thomas Aquinas to Bellarmine) that justified in more detail the veneration and cult of images and that, within the domain of piety too, are still today, even in the Catholic Church, very different in different countries and popular mentalities. I do not have to insist here on these questions, which are generally treated in the theology of the veneration of the saints. I will rather try, by using my own starting point, to submit a few considerations about religious images. At first, no attention will be paid to the distinction between properly religious icons that enjoy a cultic veneration (in places of pilgrimage, etc.) and religious images in general.

THEOLOGY OF RELIGIOUS SEEING

Our starting point leads us to say that because they can be seen religious images have a religious significance that cannot be replaced by the word. Religious images are in principle more than simply a poor people's Bible, a way of illustrating, for pedagogical reasons, the religious realities that can be conveyed wholly to people only through the word. Even though, within a religion based on a historical and social revelation, we must attribute to the word an irreplaceable and fundamental importance, the viewing of images is not a mere illustration of the spoken word, but it has its own religious significance. We may naturally speak of this significance, interpret it, and thus once more explain the image by means of words. Yet these words are no substitute for the viewing in itself and as a religious activity. The fact that theology speaks of this specific and irreplaceable significance of religious viewing not at all or very rarely, and practically only in passing, is not an argument against this assertion. Theology does not say more about religious dance either. In the doctrine of the sacraments, after having spoken abstractly of the sacramental matter, it speaks only of the "form," the word, of the sacrament. And one has the impression that the "matter" of the sacraments (washing, anointing, imposition of hands) is only a more or less arbitrarily prescribed ceremony, which could just as well have been replaced by another.

REACHING GOD WITH THE EARTH

In connection with this basic thesis, if we ask how this irreplaceable function of viewing images is to be conceived in the total religious act, we should first emphasize again that we are speaking here of a fundamental and irreducible moment of the total religious act. Now this moment can be rendered intelligible only by performing it, not by talking about it. Here analogically we may apply the old adage: use images, artists, no words! If this basic thesis is correct, the modern attempts to meditate with images may be recommended, even though, as mentioned above, it remains a difficult question to reconcile contemplation without any object with the significance of meditating with images. This question is connected with a question that refers to Christianity as a whole, which, in its efforts to arrive at the absolute God, intends to take along the earth as a whole, the glorified earth. It is only if we accept this basic thesis that it is possible ultimately to understand the Ignatian method of meditation, for example, in which contemplation has an important role, one which requires frequent practice and in which the "application of the senses" is to be considered not the lowest but a most sublime level of meditation.

EVENTS OF SALVATION HISTORY
MUST ALSO BE CONTEMPLATED

But once more: how shall we more precisely conceive of the function of seeing, as compared with that of hearing, as an irreplaceable moment in the total religious act? We might start by saying: insofar as religious images represent events of salvation history that may be grasped by the senses, this question presents no special problem. Such images provide the experience of visible historical events. In this way the problem is moved further, transformed into the question how the first historical and visible experience of salvation history could have a religious significance. This is a question that we cannot examine any further. But we can say: one irreplaceable way of getting to know a person is to see and not just to hear that person; a portrait cannot be totally replaced by a biography. The same is true of salvation-historical events. They must also be seen, and seen in an image, if we are not actually present to see them.

VIEWING A PROPERLY RELIGIOUS PHENOMENON

But still we have not totally grasped the proper nature of images and of seeing as a properly religious phenomenon. A religious reality is truly such only when it helps us to refer directly to the absolute God. It stands to reason that such a direct reference of an innerworldly reality to the true and sovereign God is conceivable only in connection with what we Christians call grace, whether or not we are aware of this grace when referring to God. We do not have to spend more time on this problem, nor on other presuppositions of an innerworldly reality's mediating function with regard to God.

RELIGIOUS IMAGE—
ITS MEDIATING FUNCTION TO THE ABSOLUTE GOD

An important point for us here is the following: if religious images may exist, it must be possible for them to have such a mediating function with regard to the absolute God. Such a function should not belong exclusively to the word. This assumption is implicitly present in our basic thesis, which holds that all peak experiences of every *sense* domain, and not only those of the sense of hearing, may be the basis and element of a religious act. We must grant, of course, that such a function is more immediately and easily understandable in the case of words than in that of images, insofar as words contain essentially a moment of negation, enabling them at once to transcend beyond the finite object toward the absolute God.

At first it may seem as though viewing stops at the finite object which is immediately seen, making it thus impossible to transcend it toward the absolute God. But we may reject this and say: every experience of an object, even though the object is always a single and finite one, is carried by an a priori pre-apprehension of the whole breadth of the formal object of the sense power. It is more than the grasping of the concrete single object that is being known. This is not true for hearing alone. It is not true only for the spirit as such with its unlimited transcendentality. It is true that the senses and the spirit differ from each other by the fact that the latter has an unlimited formal object, an unlimited a priori pre-apprehension, whereas this is not true for the senses. Yet, even so, every act of the sense powers as such implies some experience of transcendence. Thus every time we hear a certain sound we also hear the stillness that surrounds it and constitutes the space in which a single sound may be heard.

SEEING TOO IMPLIES A SENSORY EXPERIENCE OF TRANSCENDENCE

Such an experience of transcendence, although a limited one, is also necessarily given in the act of seeing. Every time we see an object, we look, as it were, beyond it, into the expanse of all that may be seen. We see something as well determined because, in this seeing, we are also aware of the unseen fullness of what may be seen. We can experience the limits and the proper nature of what we directly see only because our glance goes beyond this limit into the expanse of what might be seen, without being seen. Hence in seeing too, and not only in hearing, there is a kind of sensory experience of transcendence, that serves as foundation and mediation in referring the sense-endowed spiritual subject to God.

RELIGIOUS IMAGES
WITHOUT IMMEDIATE RELIGIOUS THEMES

If this is so it follows, rather surprisingly, that even an image that does not have a specifically religious theme can be a religious image, when viewing it helps to bring about, through a sensory experience of transcendence (if we may call it so), that properly religious experience of transcendence. This consequence, which chooses sides in a strongly disputed question from an angle that is perhaps otherwise not explicitly mentioned, should not surprise the theologian too much. A naive theology will spontaneously think or silently presuppose that only explicitly religious acts (of prayer, of expressed love of God, of explicit observation of a moral norm *as* a command of God) will bring about a salutary relation to God. But, theologically speaking, that is false. Moral acts may be conducive to salvation; by God's grace they may be finalized toward God's immediacy, without any objectively represented or verbalized reference to God. Salutary acts do not always and necessarily have to be accompanied by a "good intention." The totality of a free subject's way of life is always and undeniably a yes or a no to God, even when this subject is not aware of it or does not put it into words. Hence the statement that viewing an image that has no explicitly religious object may be the experience of a freely accepted transcendence toward God, may be a religious act, and that, in this sense, the image may have a religious significance, is not as surprising for the theologian as it may seem at first.

IMAGES THAT POINT TO SALVATION HISTORY

This does not deny the necessity of specifically religious images for Christians. In their piety, Christians have always to keep in mind their faith in a special salvation history, which can be narrated and visualized, as part of the whole of secular history. So they cannot express and visualize their religiosity only by means of abstract paintings without using, for instance, the crucifix and other explicitly religious images. This is especially true for the Church as a community that is constituted by professing the same faith in words used and understood by all its members. It needs images that are basically understood by all and that refer explicitly to the history of salvation that all believe in and confess. On the other hand, as we have said, this does not exclude the possibility of images that may be religious, although their object is not directly and clearly such.

IMAGE AND WORD
HAVE COMPLEMENTARY FUNCTIONS

So when we affirm the special and irreplaceable religious significance of images, we do not deny (to say it once again and more explicitly) that images need a verbal explanation, both to be recognized as expressly Christian by those who see them, and in order that, as the religious images of a Christian community, they may perform a social function in the Church. There exists naturally no visible reality from which alone its Christian significance might be gathered. That this image of the crucified Jesus Christ refers to the historical savior cannot be gathered just from seeing it, although the religious significance of this image of the crucified Lord is not totally explained by the words used to interpret it. That is why images that serve as Christian images for a community particularly require a verbal explanation. Such an explanation is given also when it is presented with conventional signs and symbols. In this way word and image have complementary functions and work together in constituting the religious act. It is, of course, not possible to expatiate here on this statement by pointing to other sense experiences that could be added to this word-image unity in the religious act. Such are spatial features provided by architecture; experiences of movement provided by liturgical gestures, walking in pilgrimages, or religious dance; olfactory experiences deriving from incense; experiences of touching or of tasting in sacramental activities. All the sense powers may, in their mutually irreducible experiences, and in countless different ways and combinations, enter into the religious act.

THE COLLECTIVE FUNCTION OF THE CULTIC IMAGE

One more remark based on what has been said above must still be added about the properly cultic image, the icon, insofar as it is more than an ordinary religious image with a content taken from salvation history. As a rule, the proper character of a cultic image, in the strict sense, is gathered from the fact that it is actually an object of veneration, and it enjoys some kind of official approbation. Hence the main question for the theological interpretation of the cultic image is how veneration of such a cultic image may be justified and how this veneration should more precisely be interpreted. Is it being paid in some way to the image itself, or does the veneration, as it were, through and beyond the image, aim only at the person who is represented? And is it possible to show that the different interpretations of this veneration of an image do not cancel each other out?

Our previous considerations allow us to say: an image is cultic if the image is always considered religious in the experience of a great number of Christians, and if this collective meaning is known and acknowledged. The cultic image is "venerated" because it has for many people a lasting religious meaning. From this point of view, it is an additional and secondary question whether, and in what sense, this image is "venerated." In whatever way this veneration may be described more precisely, it is based on the image's collective function as a religious image, the viewing of which has become an essential element of the religious act. On account of this function such an image may be highly esteemed and put above other religious images. In that sense it may itself be "venerated." We do not have to insist on the fact that the veneration belongs only to the reality represented by the image.

14

ART AGAINST THE HORIZON
OF THEOLOGY AND PIETY

We must perhaps first inquire precisely what art is. It is already difficult to decide whether the different arts — sculpture, painting, music, poetry — may really be subsumed under the one concept "art." In connection with our discussion, I would like to defer consideration of the arts that operate with human words. For such *Wortkunst* ("word-art"), as we say in German, is, of its very nature, quite similar to theology, which expresses itself also by means of words. If we consider only those arts that do not use words — architecture, sculpture, painting, music — we may start by saying that all these arts are also ways in which people express themselves, in some way return to themselves. And thus the question arises again whether self-expression in the arts that do not use words is of the same level and importance as in the arts that do use words.

Musicians will certainly claim that their music is not a lower kind of human self-expression, but a special and irreplaceable one, which cannot be replaced even by words and by the arts that use words. The same might be said about painting and sculpture. Standing before a Rembrandt painting, we may, of course, try to translate by means of words what this painting expresses. But even though it is possible to translate from one art into another one, we will eventually conclude that sculpture, painting, and music (let us not speak of architecture, because it is more utilitarian) may be considered autonomous ways of human self-expression that cannot be adequately translated into words.

162

ART — ACTIVE ELEMENT OF THEOLOGY

If we admit that it is impossible to reduce all the arts to the art of words, the question comes up: what is the precise relation between theology and *these* arts? Insofar as in all the arts, and in theology as well, persons express themselves, although in different ways, these different arts and theology are mutually related. But the situation is more complicated than it would appear to be. If theology is the conscious self-expression of persons about themselves from the point of view of divine revelation, we might submit the thesis that the most perfect kind of theology would be the one that appropriates these arts as an integral part of itself. We might then argue that the self-expression contained in a Rembrandt painting or in a Bruckner symphony is so strongly inspired and borne by divine revelation, by grace, and by the self-communication of God that it tells us, in a way that cannot be translated adequately in a verbal theology, what persons really are in the sight of God. If, from the start, we do not identify theology with a theology that uses words, but understand it as the total human self-expression, insofar as it is backed up by God's self-communication, religious phenomena in the arts themselves would be constituent elements of an adequate theology.

Practically speaking, this is rarely being done. Yet, when listening to a Bach oratorio, why would we not have the impression that, not only through its text but also through its music, we are in a very special way brought into a relationship with divine revelation about humanity? Why would we not believe that this too is theology? Of course, if we arbitrarily define theology as being identical with the theology that uses words, we cannot say this. But the question comes up then whether, by thus reducing all theology to a theology that uses words, we do not unfairly degrade the dignity and the special nature of these other arts as well as the fact that God uses them for divine purposes.

A ROAD TO THE ORIGINAL EXPERIENCE

If we come back to the distinction made above, and separate art that uses words from the other arts and think only of lyric, dramatic, and epic art, this kind of art should presumably be characterized, from the theological standpoint, by the fact that in different ways and by what is peculiar to it, it succeeds in making people aware of their original religious experience. When I say for instance, "We must love God," I have said something very profound in a simple statement, but in the shallow dullness of life I have not really brought it home. However, when I read a lyrical poem in the style of John of the Cross or a novel by Julian Green, through which, to be sure, the immediate genuine religious experience cannot be conveyed (because that is quite impossible), but my own religious experience may be evoked, then this religious work of literature has a function which an explicit, purely conceptual and rational theology cannot perform.

There are theologians in the stricter sense — I am thinking of Augustine and Thomas Aquinas with his eucharistic hymns — in whom religious experience and explicit conceptualization are closely connected. But this is rather exceptional and something that is hard to find in modern theology, at the most perhaps in a sermon by Newman. Hans Urs van Balthasar said once that our modern times lack a *kniende Theologie* (a theology on its knees). We might also say that our times also lack a poetic theology. That is a real lack. But we must be prudent. There is also a theology that, holding its breath, as it were, patiently and rightly undertakes long conceptual explorations from which we cannot expect immediate religious or mystical experiences. We have to leave it to individual theologians to decide to what extent they appeal or do not appeal to religious experience in their theology. But we must admit that it is a consequence as well as a defect of a theology that is rationalistic and proceeds only "scientifically" that the poetic touch is lacking. Nowadays we demand from theology something which, although not new, has been neglected during the last few centuries: theology must somehow be "mystagogical," that is, it should not merely speak about objects in abstract concepts, but it must encourage people really to experience that which is expressed in such concepts. To that extent we might understand poetic theology as one method of a mystagogical theology.

DIFFICULTY OF A NEW SYMBOLIZATION

We say generally that a poet speaks in images and metaphors. The possibility of such religious language is ultimately based on the analogy of being, meaning that all realities have an inner connection, refer to each other, are in some way related, and can in the final analysis be understood only when we transcend them, as individual things, in the direction of the whole of reality. This *analogia entis* enables poets to understand a certain human experience as mysteriously pointing to God. They can present human love in its mysteriousness as an analogous reference to God's love. Faithfulness, responsibility, resignation to the mystery of life, et cetera are, even when they are mentioned in a context that is not explicitly religious, references to that of which theology expressly speaks.

I am not certain that there is today so much less Christian religious literature of a poetic or artistic kind. It is possible that the symbols used today by real poets have changed and can therefore not be correctly understood by traditionally pious people, although their authors are basically treating religious topics by means of unfamiliar symbols. This question should be carefully examined.

The whole of Christian theology should, in the right sense of the word, be "subjective." It cannot speak of objects that are situated beyond the spiritual, personal, free human reality. We cannot make a theological statement about a ladybug. That is why, a priori, no object studied by the positive sciences falls within the domain of theology. So we might say that theology starts only where it becomes really subjective. This does not mean that theology can say anything at all, that it can swear that black is white.

Christian theology must be subjective because it speaks of faith, hope, and love, of our personal relationship to God. It must be subjective because, in the final analysis, it describes and evokes directly or indirectly these personal spiritual relationships of persons with God, because it introduces them mystagogically into those relationships. In other words: theology, even as theology of revelation, is precisely that which transmits God's invitation to human subjectivity. Where theology no longer manages to do that, where, in the wrong sense of the word, theology becomes objective, it is no longer a good theology, but a bad one.

THE ETERNAL IN HISTORICAL PECULIARITY

Analogy makes it possible to understand a given reality as a secret revelation of a higher, different, more comprehensive reality. Whatever is expressed in art is a product of that human transcendentality by which, as spiritual and free beings, we strive for the totality of all reality. It is only because from the start we are beings that transcend every limit, that can never stop, that are always reaching for the incomprehensible mystery; it is only because we are transcendental beings that art and theology can really exist.

Another question is why and how this human transcendence in art is expressed in a certain historical way. Genuine art is the result of a well determined historical event of human transcendentality. That is why art can and must always be historical. There exists a real history of art. Artists do not always say the same thing.

Of their very nature artists are discoverers of a concrete situation in which persons concretely realize their transcendental being in a new way, one that differs from former ways. This does not entail an opposition between historicity and transcendence, but their necessary mutual relationship. Real artists undoubtedly announce what is eternal in truth, love, and eternal yearning. But they are artists and not concept-mongering rationalists. They announce what is eternal in a unique manner, in which their historical peculiarity and their longing for eternity are combined in a unity that constitutes the essence of the work of art. I may understand Dürer's hare as the most concrete aspect of a well-determined insignificant human experience, but when I look at it with the eyes of an artist, I am beholding, if I may say so the infinity and incomprehensibility of God.

THE WHOLE PERSON LISTENS

The difficulty is that the eye as an optical instrument or the ear as an acoustical instrument cannot, as such, perceive God. To claim the opposite would be nonsense. In the Middle Ages the question was raised whether the human senses are used in heaven in the contemplation of God, and the answer was negative. But when something exceptionally intense is seen or heard, is it not possible for the whole person, with all one's powers, to have a very powerful religious experience? In other words, might it happen that, when the whole person is absorbed in seeing or hearing, a religious experience takes place? Let us, for instance, take the German song, "Dear moon, how quietly you glide," a trite song that has nothing to do with religion. They say that the melody of that song is the same as one we used for the *Tantum Ergo Sacramentum*. It follows that an acoustical phenomenon — depending on the human context in which it takes place — may be religious or not. If hearing is not the work of the ears alone, but of the whole person, an acoustical phenomenon is religious or not depending on the disposition and the concrete situation of the person listening. The religious quality of this melody depends simply on this: is the melody evaluated only in an acoustical context, or is the overall human situation also taken into account? In the latter case even acoustics are different — not in themselves, but because of the situation.

The statement "God is everywhere with his grace" does not mean that every reality has the same relation to me or to God. God is not present in the same way in a physico-chemical reaction occurring in my stomach as when I practice faithfulness, love, or responsibility on behalf of others. Likewise, the problem of art with regard to religion is a difficult one. I may say, for instance, that the paintings of Impressionism are not religious because basically they try only to reproduce the color impressions of one's immediate surroundings. If this is their only purpose and result, we will probably have to say that they are not religious art. And we must, without hesitation, say that there may exist art that is not religious. It does not have to be anti-religious. But it moves in a dimension of humanity where the relationship to God is not yet present.

But it is quite another question when I put the painting of an Impressionist of the early twentieth century in a wider context, a more human one, which would also bring up the question of its religiosity. This might allow us to speak of the anonymous piety even of an Impressionistic picture. Especially since a religious painting is not simply identical with one that represents an explicitly religious object.

When I paint the crib with Jesus, Mary, and Joseph, using aureoles to show from the outset what is being represented, I have, objectively speaking, a religious picture. It may, in fact, not be very religious, because it is unable to evoke in those who see it a genuine and deep religious reaction. There exists what we call religious *Kitsch*. We might perhaps say that basically the pictures in the nineteenth century of the Holy Family were painted with the best intentions by pious people, but nevertheless, they were not truly religious paintings, because they do not affect us deeply enough to elicit religious feelings. On the other hand, it is quite possible that a Rembrandt painting, which is not intended as religious, moves people so deeply, bringing up the question of life's ultimate meaning, that it is, strictly speaking, a religious painting.

BEING HOLY AND HUMAN

We are touching here a real problem. We might defend the thesis that real saints are those who have developed all their human potentialities. When people are fully attuned to life, have wholly developed their power of seeing and hearing, their experience is at once identical with their religious attitude. One of the reasons why we may say this is that in heaven one is obviously not only very pious but also absolutely human, enjoying the full development of all one's human capabilities. That is one side.

However, if we proceed empirically, we may easily reach an opposite opinion. Are there not people who are really genuine saints, who love God and their neighbor in a radically unselfish way, and who, nevertheless, have hardly developed any artistic capabilities, who in matters of art are real lowbrows, capable only of rudimentary reactions? On the other hand, there are those who have developed an extraordinary artistic sensibility without being saints. We probably have once more to distinguish here between innate and freely accepted religious possibilities.

Thus a case might be made for asserting that Goethe had developed his humanity to such a breadth and depth that, if he had started to love God, he would have done it with the whole fullness and intensity of his humanity, therefore in a much greater, wider, freer, more differentiated way than a nice pious saint. Nonetheless, possibly Goethe might, in fact, not have done this, might not have used these possibilities sufficiently to actualize his developed humanity in the service of God, whereas the lesser, more modest possibilities of a nice humble saint may have been better utilized. Here we touch upon the old problem: to what extent does holiness mean psychic health? This too is a difficult question. Wasn't St. Margaret Mary Alacoque, as many Catholic psychotherapists say today, a very neurotic person? Wasn't St. Alphonsus Liguori, the founder of the Redemptorists, in his old age both a real saint and a neurotic one? All these questions might be transposed into the following one: what is the relation between artistic talent and holiness?

15

AGAINST THE WITCH HYSTERIA

WHAT CAN FRIEDRICH SPEE TELL US TODAY?

When a modern Jesuit of the older generation considers the life of Friedrich Spee (1591–1635), he may notice how the way a man like Spee lived in the Society of Jesus has survived until today: two years of novitiate, three years of philosophy, a few years of activity in the education of young men, four years of theology, and then (often soon thereafter) tertianship. And then the normal activity, which, then as today, was generally quite diversified: pastoral work, teaching of philosophy and theology, writing, and so on. Thus a Jesuit today (if we overlook the latest changes) could have the impression that, both then and now, life was much the same in the order.

This may give rise to some surprise, to some joy too, that a program of life adopted by an order could be maintained and remain viable for such a long time. One might also wonder whether many of these old customs have not become outdated, or whether many of today's novelties have not been too easily adopted.

But (you will excuse me for saying this) it is a beautiful thing to live centuries later in the same order as a man like Spee, and to notice how great was the basic conception of Ignatius Loyola who, impelled by a mystical experience of God, tried for God's sake to work in the service of others serving and building up the Church, and who was thus capable of transmitting a charism that is still active centuries later.

IMITATING THE CRUCIFIED ONE:
DYING IN ORDER TO LIVE

But when a Jesuit of today considers Spee's life, something else occurs to him. Ignatius Loyola wished to see his followers imitate the crucified Jesus. They had to understand that one had to die with Christ in order to live with him, as is written in the Second Letter to Timothy (2:11). That was realized in a frightful way in Spee's life, but it is generally overlooked, when the greatness of this man is praised in the history of humanitarianism and of poetry. The very fact that Spee led the ordinary life of a Jesuit shows his courage in faith and hope, which enabled him to lead with many others a regulated life that was quite dull and ordinary. He was put to all sorts of tasks without being consulted; he lived according to the will of his superiors, in a restless age, in many places, with many occupations, which generally, he did not choose himself. His special difficulties with the order will be mentioned later.

But there was much more. He lived during the fearsome Thirty Years War, amid dreadful epidemics and in immediate contact with the stake at which poor women, after much torture, were burned alive as witches. He was firmly convinced, in mind and heart, that these women were innocent. How bitter a life, yet how ordinary! Moreover, the word of Jesus about the grain of wheat that must die was fulfilled in his life. Many of his hymns passed anonymously into the Church's repertoire. Two of his books came out only after his death. His *Cautio criminalis* had to come out without his name;[1] his moral theology disappeared anonymously into that of his successor H. Busenbaum, whose work reached a couple of hundred editions by the end of the eighteenth century. Spee always had to start all over again and never really saw the full results of his work and of his unselfish service. His death was undoubtedly the completion of an unselfish love for people of all kinds, but to die in a pestilential epidemic is a pitiful thing, when one has to die at the early age of 44.

Nowadays together with Leibniz, Brentano, Ricarda Huch and other important witnesses we sing the praises of Spee. But we should not forget how socially narrow, how ordinary, and how bitter was this man's life. And that is why I believe that this life, almost more through its normalcy than through its grandeur, asks us whether we can cope with our life today; whether (like Spee before the witches' stake) we can believe

---

[1]Friedrich Spee von Langenfeld, *Sämtliche Schriften*, 3 vols. (Munich, 1968); idem, *Cautio criminalis oder rechtliches Bedenken wegen der Hexenprozesse* (Munich, 1982).

in God in a time of the Holocaust and still dare to hope for humanity; whether, even amid the constraints of our society and beyond all protests against its inhumanity, we still understand our life as an imitation of the crucified Jesus and feel able to grasp, even now, ultimate freedom in God; whether we can hold out to the end despite our frightful anxiety amid ominous dangers; whether (as Böll says in praise of Spee) although wholly disconsolate, we reject both cheap consolation and despondency.

Even though the blessed ecstasy of the pious child in Spee may seem far away from us, this Christian's brave common sense amid life's bitterness might continue to be a reminder.

A FEARLESS FIGHTER
AGAINST THE INHUMANITY OF HIS TIME

When we start to acknowledge and praise Spee's greatness as a poet, this praise is generally introduced with the remark that nowadays we can no longer do much with his spiritual bucolic poetry, with his bridal mysticism and his mystique of the wounds of Jesus, and with his talk about "sweet Jesus." We are even tempted to add that for us such ways of speaking about religion have become utterly insufferable. Now it is quite true that every epoch has a right to its own religiosity and that our piety and that of Spee are not and should not be of the same kind. But, prompted by the peculiar nature of Spee's religious lyricism, if we read it not only as poetry but also as a religious witness, we should also be willing to face the question whether the reason why Spee's piety has become so strange to us that we are unable to share it is because our own piety has become lukewarm. After all, although he enjoyed mystical familiarity with God and Jesus, he was not naive or timid or inclined to flee from reality into sentimentality. Rather, he fought fearlessly against the inhumanity of his time, against stupidity and superstition, against envy and a frightful sadism that was on the rampage at all levels of society. He publicly exposed the untruthfulness and cruelty of the penal system of his time. He visited prisons. He rescued and nursed the wounded, and he shared the death pangs of the poor women who were to be burned alive. For him the experience of God's nearness in ecstatic love was translated into looking for the poor and the sick in the city, buying a basket of white bread for the sick in the hospitals, paying for poor students' schoolbooks.

OUT OF AN UNCONDITIONAL, WORSHIPFUL
LOVE OF GOD

Spee shows us that his spiritual bucolic poetry probably had a different meaning from what we gather today from his verses. He asks us whether our love for neighbor and our commitment to justice in the world are not, despite all our noisy slogans, so pitiful and so prone to drown time and again in our narrowminded selfishness, because we do not love God with our whole heart, as evidenced by the prosaic scantiness of today's piety. According to a modern historian of literature, Spee's prose and poetry "combine strength and sweetness, inner musicality and festive exuberance in perfectly constructed writing." These are not only literary qualities in Spee's work that we can still appreciate and enjoy today, they emerge from a most intimate experience of God that enabled him to overcome all anxiety and to enjoy the sweet intimacy of an unconditional worshipful love for God in Jesus Christ. It is a Protestant prejudice that induced Ricarda Huch to believe that the young Spee had entered the cloister so that he would not have to see the sufferings of so many people. He joined the order so that he might be sent to the missions, where he would certainly have been unable to avoid encountering the world's suffering. Nor did he foster any illusions about it, since in that time missionaries had to envisage the possibility of real martyrdom.

The intimacy of his experience of God and the will to help people bear their sufferings were for him always inseparably united, even as in the gospels the commandment of love for neighbor and of love for God form a unity. That is why the intimacy of his rapturous love for God, which affects us as truly baroque, should not simply be shrugged off as the style of life of a time that is passé. It should rather make us face the question whether we ourselves really love our neighbor in deed and in truth, or whether we imagine that such an unselfish love of others does not require an ardent love of God.

MASS HYSTERIA — FORMERLY, YESTERDAY, AND TODAY

Spee has been generally admired for the undaunted courage with which, in his *Cautio criminalis*, he spoke up for the victims of witchhunts. He did so with all the sagacity of a mind trained in scholastic philosophy and theology, and also with the full power of a heart that loved others and shared their plight. Even today his *Cautio criminalis* is a work that may still captivate our mind and our heart. It contains maxims that have not yet become self-evident. For instance, Spee wrote: "Christ's command in Matthew chapter 13 said: When there is danger that the wheat may be uprooted, one must not destroy the weeds." Even today this maxim does not appear obvious to us, although it is based on the gospel. Penologists especially might let Spee invite them to have a good look at the way people are punished in prisons, so that they may see what in fact they are sponsoring with the penal norms that are in force.

There is another point, however, where the *Cautio criminalis* challenges us today. True, the frightful mass hysteria of Spee's time and of long thereafter has disappeared. But even if the obsession with witches as it existed then is a thing of the past, it demonstrates that even so-called Christian countries, at all social levels, may become victims of mass hysteria. People might keep a good conscience and defend this hysteria in the name of reason or the gospel, as something that is evident, not subject to discussion, something that only people who are not quite normal could call into doubt.

Are we so sure that today these kinds of hysteria do not exist among us? Has the mass hysteria of National Socialism disappeared so long ago and so completely into the past that we can now imagine ourselves free of such mass psychoses, which may exist even among intelligent people and popular leaders, without anyone noticing or admitting it? Is the arms race all over the world, at costs that allow millions of people to starve and die, not such a mass psychosis? Should other maxims of certain lifestyles, which present themselves as obvious, not be unmasked by a "political theology" and shown to be norms suggested by mass hysteria? Is it not a fact that in all our present social organizations similar false ideas, considered to be self-evident, are at work, as they were in Spee's time? Do we have enough men and women who, prompted by a sound mind and the selfless love of their heart and guided by the basic truth of the gospel, spot these erroneous ideas, expose and combat them with all their strength, even if they are opposed and mocked as naive idealists or cranks, even if people tell them they are choosing pious utopias that a clearheaded realist cannot share? Should we, who cannot at least a priori let false opinions go unnoticed, not try to be more prudent and kinder to contemporary prophets in the style of Spee? Are there not still today church dignitaries who react to warning voices like that of Spee, as they did to Spee, in the frightfully naive conviction that nobody could seriously deny that numerous witches really existed? Do we today have enough courageous people who criticize the false plausibilities with which we live quite comfortably, without wanting to be disturbed?

True, there are quite a few gospel norms that are defended by church authorities against prevailing opinions. We must admit this, although it is sometimes difficult totally to get rid of the suspicion that these Christian norms are so strongly defended by the Church because they are supported by what was plausible in the past. But are there not norms that should be defended against a present lifestyle, considered sanctioned by the past, norms that most church authorities ignore or defend too faintheartedly and too weakly? Should not many *Cautiones criminales* be written against the madness of our times, and for which we wait in vain? Nor would it be a bad idea if such a *Cautio* were written for a change not by the highest authorities, but first by some humble and unimportant priest or lay person, as was done by Spee.

BETWEEN THE VOICE OF CONSCIENCE AND RELIGIOUS OBEDIENCE

A Jesuit of today might be allowed to say a few things about Spee's relation to his order. Spee wanted to be a Jesuit, to remain a Jesuit, and he was one until his death. Today too we ought to respect this unconditional decision of this great man, if we want to do him justice. Many peculiarities of his life in the order, which may surprise an outsider, are, viewed from within the order, more or less ordinary harmless events. In an order made up of men, each man has his own ways and convictions, which he cannot simply turn off in community life.

In a religious order, when a man's request to be sent to the missions is turned down, when that man is sent to work in many different places, at many different occupations, when it happens that he is discharged from some function, when he cannot always live in perfect harmony with his superiors, all of this is for a true Jesuit, as Spee was, a matter of course, something that is unavoidable, that he has to expect in the order, even though he does not like it, and with which he tries to cope with common sense. In this respect many things in Spee's life are not surprising for those who are familiar with the way Jesuits live. However, when he spoke out against the witch hysteria, a situation did occur in Spee's life that cannot simply be considered a matter of course for one who lives in a religious order.

Apparently, Spee really wrote the *Cautio criminalis* hoping that it would be read by others and aware that, by so doing, he ran the risk of entering into conflict with his superiors and his vow of obedience. However, if we understand religious obedience correctly, we may not claim that one offends against the spirit of one's order by assuming such a risk if, in doing so, one is not looking out for oneself, for one's own opinion, fame, "self-realization," or convenience, but wants to obey the voice of conscience and an unselfish love for neighbor. Jesuit obedience does not at all mean that a Jesuit is forbidden to assume personal responsibility, to take initiatives that have not already been approved from above. The opposite is true; both belong basically to this obedience as understood in this order. Therefore Spee could write his *Cautio criminalis* without a previous order or permission of his superiors.

It is a question for historians whether Spee himself secretly arranged the first and second editions of his *Cautio* in order to bypass the order's censorship or whether he really knew nothing about it and the *Cautio* was printed without his knowledge and permission. But even should the first supposition be correct, we must not accuse Spee of having offended against his vow of obedience and the spirit of his order in this particular case. Every moral theologian will admit that, in the concreteness of a human life, situations may occur in which two distinct demands present themselves in such a way that they cannot be satisfied harmoniously at the same time, but that only one or the other can be carried out.

Ignatius Loyola deems it possible that a superior may, in good faith and clear conscience, give a Jesuit an order that the latter cannot, in conscience, not consider a sin, and therefore would refuse to obey. That is why we may admit in principle that Spee might have considered the task of speaking up against the witch hysteria so unconditionally binding on his conscience that an eventual order of his superiors in the opposite sense could not impose any real obligation on him. He would then have had to accept all the consequences of this decision of conscience, consequences which his superiors, on account of their own conscience, deemed necessary. Such bitter situations often occur in human and Christian life. In a religious order, they may occur as a dilemma between a decision of conscience, responsibly taken before God, and the command of a religious superior, even when the latter is fully credited with good will.

God's providence saw to it that in fact Spee did not have to face an ultimate conflict between his legitimate mission and his obedience as a Jesuit. It is useless to rack one's brain about how Spee should or would have acted, if he had been confronted with an absolute dilemma: either to obey his superiors' orders or to give up the *Cautio criminalis* and its publication. I for one consider it a comforting fact that in Spee's case such a clear dilemma was avoided until his death. Indeed his provincial superior in Cologne, Goswin Nickel, who kindly and gently defended Spee against the general of the order at the time, later became general superior himself. Conflicts such as the one Spee confronted may still arise in the Church, even with the best intentions of both parties. This is one more reason why Spee's life could be an important example for priests and lay persons in the Church. His life shows that an artificially contrived harmony among all members of the Church would in fact amount to a graveyard peace, and is by no means an ideal to be sought in all circumstances.

EXAMPLE FOR BOTH HIGH AND LOW

In his life Spee was not only the courageous author of the *Cautio criminalis* and the tender author of poetry, he was an ordinary priest, active in schools, in young people's sodalities, in jails, in village pulpits, and in chairs of theology, which in his time did not bestow a special distinction on those who occupied them. Thus Spee is not only a patron and model for courageous critics of the mentality of their time, not only a great figure in German literature, but also a model for the ordinary workers in God's vineyard who, without expecting much gratitude and fame, bear the heat and burden of the day. If the widow's mite in God's poorbox is more highly appreciated than the fat alms of the wealthy, something similar may apply to the everyday work of an average parish priest compared to the spectacular deeds of exalted leaders in the world and in the Church. In a strange way Spee belongs among both the great ones and the little ones in the Church and in the world. He was by nature intent only on the ideal of a good and pious life in his order. But it happened that in that life great possibilities were presented to him and much was expected from him. In the valiant love of his heart he answered the call.

A SAINT?

Some have wondered why Spee has not been canonized by the Church. As far as we can judge, he would have deserved it, as does also Wilhelm

Eberschweiler, who is buried in the same church as Spee and who represents a quite different type of Jesuit. But there is no need for every saintly person to be officially declared holy. We may try to imitate them and pray that they intercede for us before God, even if they are not expressly mentioned in the missal of the Church.

PART FOUR

Sacraments

16

FAITH AND SACRAMENT

When we remember how Paul and, in fact, the whole New Testament emphasize the unique and fundamental importance of faith for our salvation, we may be somewhat surprised that faith and sacrament are mentioned in the same breath. This seems to imply that they are equally important. Faith means our total personal dedication, as free subjects, to God in response to God's self-manifesting and self-communicating revelation. It does not seem possible that, compared with faith, any other reality in our lives could have the same salvific significance.

Indeed Christians are convinced that salvation even without sacraments is possible, whereas no salvation is possible without real faith. And since the Second Vatican Council it is impossible to admit that in many cases a more fundamental moral attitude could replace real theological faith. This position makes it very difficult to find an answer to the question of how a genuine faith in response to a real revelation is possible for the incalculable multitude of people who have not been reached by the historically revealed message of the Old and the New Testament. Compared to faith, sacrament seems to play only a secondary role, if any at all.

On the other hand, Catholic Christianity at least, almost naively, considers it self-evident that infants, when baptized, experience the basic event of salvation. It claims (although this is rightly being called into question today) that children who die unbaptized are not saved but are consigned to limbo. When, on reaching the age of reason, baptized children make a conscious act of faith, this faith is almost considered as just a secondary actualization of the habit of faith received in baptism. Belonging to the Church is considered an effect of baptism alone, so that it is deemed impossible for those who are not baptized to belong to the Church, even when they openly declare that they are convinced of the Christian message. However, as a result of a theology of the catechumenate, the exact limits of the Church have again become somewhat imprecise.

All this goes to show that the real relationship between faith and sacrament is not as clear and obvious as may seem to follow from traditional theology, which tends, somewhat too positively, to juxtapose the different doctrines of the faith. Of course (let me say this at once and in a very imprecise way) behind the difficulty of the relationship between faith and sacrament lurks the difficulty of determining and clearly expressing the exact relationship between existence and essence (in the modern sense of these words), between persons as free subjects and persons as "nature," between persons as unique individuals and persons as generic beings, between persons who cannot adequately objectify their true self-realization and persons who necessarily reach this self-realization as bodily, social, and historical beings, and in history, and in this way alone take full possession of themselves. All these and other dialectical relationships of diversity and mutuality make up the background of the dialectical unity and diversity of faith and sacrament. But here we cannot expressly study the background of our topic. We will start immediately from faith and sacrament in order to shed some light on their mutual relationship.

Faith comes from hearing says theology with Paul and with a history of revelation that reaches back into the Old Testament. Faith is the answer to the hearing of God's self-revelation. By starting from this point we might (at least so it seems) make rapid progress in our study. Faith is based on a revelation, which is understood as one that has been spoken in history. In Christianity that revelation, which has been heard in history, is of an eschatological nature, because it is unsurpassable and irreversible, because it is the sovereign and victorious pledge to the world of God's innermost reality.

That is why the word that proclaims the eschatological and, as far as it is concerned, victorious self-promise of God has an exhibitive character, which means that what it says is not merely a word about God, but a word of God who promises himself, hence necessarily it is also a conferring of grace. God speaks and he is heard because, by communicating himself to the messenger and to the hearer, he contributes to this conferring of grace by means of his own reality. Thus the revealed word has an historical and exhibitive character; it produces grace, and in this sense it works "ex opere operato," as a sacrament. That is why a sacrament in the traditional sense is but the most intensive instance of God's revealing word, insofar as it is addressed to individuals, in a peak moment of their life of faith, by the proper and ultimate messenger of this revealed word, that is, by the Church.

Let me mention by the way that, in the final analysis, as we face the historical difficulties of sacramental theology, we will be able to vindicate the traditional and binding doctrine of the nature of the sacraments, of their differentiation and their number, only by using the above starting point. Moreover, and once more by the way, from the exegetical point of view and quite unlike the situation at the time of the Reformation, today the difficulty of vindicating the sacramentality of most sacraments is not greater than it is for baptism and the Lord's Supper, so that ecumenical agreement in the doctrine of sacraments is possibly easier.

In the eschatological stage of our faith it is through the very nature of this faith that the sacramental character of faith itself, hence the sacraments also, may be rendered intelligible. The sacraments are presented as the high points of the history of revelation and of our faith. They are not presented as additions to faith. In this way may our binary title "Faith and Sacrament," be read correctly and it is relatively simple to answer the basic question that we have brought up. There is no need to explain in more detail or more exactly what we have only briefly mentioned.

FAITH AND REVELATION

But we must speak of a difficulty that could be brought up against this basic conception of faith as the foundation of the sacraments. More or less consciously, in many ways, in the most diverse theological contexts, and under the most different labels, this difficulty has always been at work. In the time of the Fathers people had already given thought to the possibility of salvation for pagans, or at least for catechumens. But for all practical purposes, until way into the nineteenth century, even almost up to the Second Vatican Council, the possibility of salvation was said to exist only for those who in some explicit way had entered into contact with the revelation of the Old and the New Testament. Some authors used hypotheses that sounded very mythological; some of them substituted other realities for revelation or for theological faith in revelation;

others, with a humanitarian optimism, simply allowed the majority of humankind to reach salvation without any faith at all in revelation.

Today, after Vatican II, the theological situation in this question has become more difficult. On the other hand, according to the council's decree on the missions, one can no longer admit a possibility of salvation without supernatural faith in revelation in the strict sense of the word. On the other hand, considering the universal optimism of the council about salvation, which does not exclude even guiltless atheists and polytheistic pagans, we must admit that faith in revelation, inspired by grace, is a universal possibility even for those who are not reached by the revelation of the Old and New Testament, as they are understood traditionally as well as in the council's Constitution on Divine Revelation, which, after the so-called primordial revelation, blithely skips a few million years and lets the history of revelation continue with Abraham and Moses.

The following explanation is one to fill this gap. The supernatural grace of salvation that is offered to all (without necessarily becoming conscious or verbalized) provides the spiritual free subject with a new formal object, because through it the subject strives for God's immediacy. This new formal object realizes fundamentally the idea of a genuine personal and free self-revelation of God. And thus the free acceptance by a subjectivity that is aiming for the immediacy of God truly means theological faith in the proper sense of the word. I accept this interpretation, and I do not see it we can defend the doctrine that the true faith is universally, always and everywhere, offered to human beings without it. At the council the magisterium did not have to defend it because it is not its function to construct theological theories. But in theology, when we try to vindicate Christianity, we may not content ourselves with saying simply that God will find some way to lead to a faith in revelation those who are cut off from every historical revelation.

However, if we solve the problem of the universal possibility of faith for all human beings in this or some similar way, we meet the difficulty that claims our attention in this paper. It is possible to render intelligible the universal possibility of faith, and thus the universality of a revelation that reaches all only by approaching the question "transcendentally" (if I may be allowed to use this way of speaking). By claiming that this possibility of faith is already given by the proffer of supernatural salvific grace wherever spirit and freedom exist, we are saying that, through the always offered grace of God, spirit and freedom are being directed toward God's immediacy. If we establish the universal possibility of faith in this way, "transcendentally," by appealing to the grace that is everywhere and always proffered and that, despite its universality, remains gratuitous and freely given, faith seems to be possible. However, both faith and revelation seem to lose their historical and their fully sacramental character. The way we have suggested for defending the universality of faith seems to rob faith of its relation (as explained above) to sacrament (to the sacramentality of the exhibitive word of grace, to the Church as the sacrament of salvation). This is obviously a fundamental problem for Christianity.

HISTORY AND GRACE

Christianity is an historical religion, in which revelation itself (and not only the human theological reflection on it) happens historically. And the same Christianity intends to be the universal religion, destined for all, required for salvation even by those who lived before Christianity started. Christianity wants to be both universal and sacramental, and if we consider these two concepts more attentively and do not indulge in primitive pragmatism, these concepts seem difficult to reconcile. The problem does not consist in the fact that faith is possible even without sacrament in the traditional sense of that word. The fact that faith and the grace of faith may exist, without (collectively or individually) its full historical development in the sacrament of faith, in baptism (and in the other sacraments of the Church), is admitted by all and is not a special problem for those who can think of grace as an existential of historical humanity.

But this does not yet explain how this grace (established transcendentally) always and everywhere possesses a sacramental character in the broadest sense of the word, an incarnational character that ultimately refers to the Church. That grace must always and everywhere, at least initially, be historical, incarnational, and sacramental (which does not mean: mediated by a real sacrament of the Church). Are these conditions fulfilled simply by the fact that it is the grace of historical human beings, who mediate their transcendental essence (in the domain of nature or of grace) always and everywhere by means of historical activities, and never without them? It is true that human beings never possess their spiritual nature as intellect and freedom in abstract purity, but only as concrete historical beings. They do not live their transcendentality apart from their history (as in some pure mysticism, for instance), but in and through their history. It is in history and not outside of it that we experience for the first time what spirit and freedom is. This applies also therefore to that transcendental, existential endowment of human beings that we call grace, in which through his self-communication God has become the inner principle of the creature's striving for God's immediacy.

The primordial revelation in paradise seems to be an old mythological idea that we are no longer able to accept. Moreover, in a realistic history of religion, it is difficult to imagine how such a revelation would have been developed and transmitted in later times. However, if we understand the primordial revelation of paradise as the primordial historical mediation of God's self-revelation that is always provided by grace, a historical mediation at the very beginnings, which belongs to the nature of a human being who has received grace (even though, of course, we cannot imagine that mediation and we may think of it as very primitive and barely conscious), then primordial revelation loses its mythological appearance. It becomes self-evident for those who can think that wherever there is spirit and freedom, hence human beings even in their most primitive guise, these beings are already, although quite unconsciously, striving for God's immediacy under the influence of grace, and they have accepted themselves as what they are. This may rightly be called "faith as the acceptance of God's self-revelation" because human spiritual transcendence has been radicalized toward God's immediacy.

GRACE AND REVELATION

Our problem is solved if we accept two things: first, if we construe grace transcendentally as a revelation of God and admit that it is always transmitted to spirit and freedom through historical concreteness. Secondly, if we understand this historical transmission of the grace of revelation to human spirit and freedom as historical revelation. The latter point may sound bold and unusual; it may produce the impression that we downgrade the history of revelation to the level of the general history of freedom that goes on always and everywhere. But in reality, history and the history of revelation are not simply identical, but the history of revelation is coextensive with history as such. This cannot be denied by a Christian who admits that salvation may occur always and everywhere in history and that this salvation must always and everywhere be salvation produced by faith. What we add here to this conviction of Christianity today is only the assertion that the indispensable categorial and historical mediation of the grace of faith may occur everywhere in human life. Hence it occurs where "only" the voice of moral conscience is being heard and where this apparently merely "natural" message is nevertheless the transcendental proffer of grace, the self-revelation of God, thus constituting what we necessarily call the historical revelation of God. Theologically speaking we cannot require more.

Whoever, on the one hand, with Vatican II, considers as necessary for salvation a genuine faith in divine revelation, which is more than what the old terminology called natural revelation, and who, on the other hand, says that nevertheless the guiltless atheist finds salvation, cannot demand more for the salvific faith of this guiltless atheist (who remains an atheist) than the grace of a radicalization and orientation of his moral activity toward God's immediacy (which includes God's self-revelation) and the historical mediation of the free acceptance of the subjectivity that has thus been raised by grace. This mediation, despite its seemingly natural character, transforms the moral decision, elevated by grace, into an historical revelation.

This position implies of course that, on account of the unity of human history, every moment in it includes an objective reference to the totality of this history, hence also to its summits, among which belongs that which, in the traditional sense of the word, we call the explicit history of revelation with its highest summit in Jesus Christ. It also implies that it belongs to the nature of freedom to accept, when making absolute decisions, those implications of reality of which we cannot become expressly aware in a free decision. If we accept these presuppositions (and nothing seems to make this absolutely impossible), we may understand all real faith as referring to its origin in the historical event of revelation. This applies also to that grace which we must consider as universally given because of the universal infralapsarian salvific will of God. On this point, we wondered, because of its transcendence, how it was possible to discover in it any incarnational character.

True, every grace that makes for faith and salvation is rooted in human transcendence. But, since that grace is necessarily mediated historically, and because of the unity of human history, in which every moment is related to the whole and influenced by all other moments, we may say that this grace is to a sufficient degree incarnational, historically mediated, and in this sense a sacramental grace. We do not even have to deny the sacramentality of a grace that is not immediately mediated through an historically visible relationship to the revelation of the Old or of the New Testament.

Those who require more than what we considered necessary, but also sufficient, for the sacramental character of all grace that leads to salvation must wonder how they will handle the following dilemma: either one excludes too many human beings from a concrete possibility of salvation, which we believe today to be excluded only by personal guilt and by nothing else (not even by original sin); or one grants to many persons a possibility of salvation that bears no relation to Christian revelation and to God's grace founded on Jesus Christ. It may require some arduous theological thinking to reconcile the universality of Christian salvation with the historicity of revelation and of Christianity. It is only when we succeed in doing this, only when we show that *every* divine grace, in which God communicates himself to humanity, has an inner dynamism pushing it to become historically and irreversibly manifest in Jesus Christ, in the Church, and in the sacraments, that the binary expression "Faith and Sacrament" may be understood as a real unity of two realities that condition and require each other. Only then does the expression "Faith and Sacrament" have a real theological importance.

For today's proclamation of Christian faith it is of decisive importance that the connection among the individual mysteries of the faith be established by theology as accurately as possible and proclaimed in the Christian message. When the realities of faith are merely enumerated one after the other, as so many ideas happening to occur in God's mind, they become hard to believe. That is why we should explain that the one and entire self-communication of God to the one and entire world in its one history itself has a history. God's self-communication has a history not in the sense that this coming of grace into history occurs only here and there amid other natural and secular events, but in the sense that this universal and permanent descent of grace into the world has a history, has gradually become manifest, and that it is God's will that in the history of creaturely freedom it may reach its eschatological definitiveness. Where the universal and permanent descent of grace into the world reaches the historical stage of irreversibility, there is the Church, there are the sacraments.

17

QUESTIONS ON THE THEOLOGY OF SACRAMENTS

I f we wish to understand sacraments, we must first keep in mind that everywhere in human life, and not only in the religious domain, there are gestures that express something, signify something, but, in addition, that also really *bring about* that which they signify. This is not obvious; there are many gestures that do not bring about what they signify. When I telephone to somebody and tell him that we are having a thunderstorm, that storm is not affected at all by my message. But when somebody consciously and spitefully slaps another person in the face, such a slap expresses the offender's contempt and hatred. But the expressions of these feelings sometimes produces an increase of this contempt and hatred in the offender, and it may make them insurmountable. Persons who are in love certainly give each other kisses that are not only an expression of love but also the concrete activation of this love, so that it would not be the same love if it were not expressed in this way.

EXPRESSION AND EFFECT

There are gestures that bring about what they express. If this is true for human life in general, we may apply it to the properly religious domain: God, Jesus, and the Church — the three of them considered, as it were, as *one* acting subject — make a sign or a gesture that expresses not only that the person to whom it is addressed has a loving relationship to God but that also brings about this relationship. There are certainly

189

many such gestures in the religious domain. When a father blesses his child, when a mother traces the sign of the cross on her child's forehead, when somebody kneels or kisses a crucifix, these are all religious gestures and signs of an inner human happening, and to some extent at least they effect that which they express. Where the Church addresses such a gesture to a person, in a solemn and official way, we have to do, in this gesture of the Church, with what we call a sacrament. When the Church admits a baby into the community, when she lets a person share the Lord's Supper, her bond of unity, when during a serious illness she comforts people by imposing her hand, which tells them in a dark hour of their life that, despite all, God is merciful to them — in such gestures decisive situations are marked with holy signs, and such gestures effect what they signify.

DERIVING FROM JESUS

In a long history of reflection on her faith the Church has become aware that she has seven such fundamental gestures for individual Christians, which through God's power effect what they signify. These seven fundamental signs or gestures, possessing this power, are called sacraments. Such a "gesture" will generally consist of an action and the words that go with it. It may also consist only of words. The Church is aware that these gestures and signs have been given to her in virtue of the authority of Jesus.

How can these holy gestures of the Church be traced back to Jesus? That is a rather difficult theological question. It is at once clear from the New Testament that Jesus instituted the Eucharist. And we may refer to Matthew 28, where Jesus gives the command to baptize his followers. However, we might bring up a difficultly against this point: does this injunction to baptize, as mentioned there, really go back to the historical Jesus? The trinitarian formula used in baptism and mentioned in this text cannot so easily be considered as having been used by Jesus.

However, even if we cannot trace the sacraments back to Jesus in this way, by appealing to the words by which he would have instituted them, this does not by any means deny or cast doubt on the real connection between the Church's individual sacraments and Jesus. First, it is not necessary that every single sacrament be traced back to Jesus in exactly the same way. The Council of Trent teaches explicitly that the individual sacraments differ considerably from one another in their nature and significance. It is also possible to apply this teaching to the way in which the individual sacraments were instituted by Jesus. It is not impossible, it is even probable, when we consider the way in which the sacraments grew in the early Church, that for serious reasons, using the power given to her, the Church, so to speak, divided a sacrament. Thus the early Church was convinced that baptism not only forgave sins, made the person a member of the Church, but also imparted the Holy Spirit in a very special way to the neophyte. It is easy to see how baptism with water and the imparting of the Holy Spirit through the laying on of hands, which immediately followed, have been separated and thus represent two sacraments for the later reflection of the Church.

However, the decisive point in this question of the origin of the sacraments is the following one: he who was crucified and rose from the dead is the last, unsurpassable, definitive, and victorious pledge through which God communicated himself definitively to the world. He is, as we might say in our terminology, the sign of God's grace whereby that which the sign means and intends to say is irrevocably given to the world.

THE PERMANENT ACCEPTANCE

If this permanent and definitive pledge addressed to the whole world and to the whole of human history is really to stay with the world, it can do so only as accepted, therefore as really believed, by persons throughout all times to come. God's pledge to the world, a pledge called Jesus Christ, must be and remain the pledge that is accepted and believed. The permanent presence of this divine pledge in Jesus Christ is called Church, the community of those who believe, who not only accept something that Jesus said but who, with their faith, help to constitute through all times the permanence in the world of the divine pledge in Jesus. We must not hesitate to say this in other words, as the Second Vatican Council did: the Church is the irrevocable sacrament of the salvation of the world that perdures in the world. The Church is the great and unique gesture of God and the accepting gesture of humankind, in which divine love, reconciliation, and the self-communication of God are forever manifested and imparted.

Now when the Church diversifies, as it were, this word which she herself is and utters it in the individual histories of persons at the decisive points of their existence, such a tangible instance of the sacrament that is called Church has, with regard to individuals, the very characteristics that belong to the nature of the Church. It is the active word of the Church, a word which imparts what it says, a word that is infallibly effective by itself. When the Church addresses this word to a certain person, a word in which she, as it were, diversifies and embodies herself, this word must be accepted by the faith of the person who receives it. Failing this, it is and remains inoperative.

This victorious, definitive, irrevocable significance of the Church's word in the sacramental signs is also called the effectiveness of the sacraments of and by themselves: in Latin *opus operatum*. This by no means denies or obscures the fact that what God on his side tells people unconditionally in the word of the Church can reach them only in faith, hope, and charity. But it is God's word, and it is either a person's happiness or, if received without faith, their judgment, as Paul expressly says about the Eucharist.

HISTORY IS NOT FINISHED

The way in which the Church promises to individuals her innermost being as the presence of God's victorious grace has itself, in the course of two millennia, had a varied history. The rite of baptism has not always been the same. It is necessarily different for babies and for adults. The way in which the Eucharist was received has changed at different times: in the manner of celebrating the Lord's Supper, in the kind of bread, in the question of whether only the bread or also the chalice would be received by the faithful, in the secondary question of communion received on the tongue or in the hand. The same happened for the other sacraments. The conditions under which the Church allows the word of lasting love between two human beings to have the value of a sacrament have changed and have been changing until the present day. For the most diverse reasons (among them social ones) the frequency of the anointing of the sick has varied considerably at different times. The same is true for confirmation. In the Eastern churches it continues to be conferred immediately after baptism. In the West many years of religious education separate baptism and confirmation.

The sacrament of reconciliation has had an enormously eventful history. And it does not look as if this history has yet reached a praxis that will forever remain unchanged. For many and justified reasons, deriving from the concrete social and historical situation, the indispensable priestly function, which, in the final analysis, is *one* in the Church, had to be divided into different partial functions. Very early the functions of priests, bishops, and deacons had already become different, and accordingly the concrete rites under which the corresponding powers were conferred have been shaped differently. Thus until the pontificate of Pius XII it was not absolutely certain in the West whether the laying on of hands was the decisive rite, or whether the validity of priestly ordination required that the bishop hand over paten and chalice to the candidate for the priesthood. Such developments are not definitively excluded for the future. It is, for instance, quite conceivable that in fact the Church performs a holy rite, hence a gesture of God that confers grace, without knowing expressly and certainly that this is a sacramental rite. In the Middle Ages Saint Thomas said that episcopal consecration was not a sacrament. It was performed at that time almost in the same way as today, but it was not clear to the Church of that period that this gesture carried the dignity of a real sacrament of Jesus Christ. Today, in the Second Vatican Council, the Church has expressly affirmed the sacramentality of episcopal consecration. She has, so to speak, made progress in her reflection.

We might think today that other functions, too, that are entrusted to different people in the Church might share the sacramentality of the transmission of functions in the Church, although the Church is not yet clearly aware of it. I do not believe that it would be heretical to claim that the official, solemn, and permanent appointment of a pastoral assistant might share the sacramentality of the transmission of functions in the Church, since Saint Thomas claimed that this was the case for the function of acolyte in the Church. This is not a terribly important question. But it shows that in the Catholic theology of sacraments all questions have not yet been elucidated. And new questions may come up that have a serious religious significance.

A GREATER LATITUDE

We already said above that the reception of such a sign and gesture of the Church, which confers what it signifies, is meaningful and morally justified only when it takes place in a way that corresponds to this gesture. The mere receiving of the eucharistic bread by those who do not have the right moral disposition, who routinely accompany the others to the altar, is absurd and immoral. Paul already demanded that those who attend the Lord's Supper first examine themselves to find out whether they have the right disposition and really discern the eucharistic bread from other bread. This requires not only that they have a certain, even if rudimentary, knowledge of the Eucharist; they must also have the right fundamental moral attitude.

As for the so-called "disposition," that is, that which is presupposed in soul and body for the true and fruitful reception of Holy Communion, the Church teaches that those who objectively and subjectively are aware of serious guilt, which they have not yet erased in the sacrament of reconciliation, should receive the Eucharist only after having been sacramentally absolved. This applies to normal situations. Exceptionally, an inner return to God in sincere contrition for sins committed may be sufficient.

However, the question of when and in what circumstances we have to do with objectively and subjectively serious guilt (not yet sacramentally remitted) is a difficult one and not easy to answer. In previous decades average Christians had the impression that, when they missed Sunday Mass out of laziness they had committed a serious sin, which they had to erase through confession before they could receive communion again. Today there may be many good Christians who are convinced that such a missing of Sunday Mass does not constitute before God, at least subjectively, a serious offense that must be blotted out sacramentally before a new reception of communion.

Because these questions cannot clearly be answered by the Church, they leave a very great latitude to individual Christians with regard to the question: may they or may they not allow themselves to receive Holy Communion without previous confession? We cannot deny that during the past few decades certain changes have occurred with respect to these questions. It is praiseworthy and quite unlike the praxis of former times that nowadays an ordinary Christian is convinced that, as a rule, attending the Eucharist implies also that one personally receives communion. However, this also entails the danger that Christians may admit a certain laxity of which we cannot approve.

18

BAPTISM AND THE RENEWAL OF BAPTISM

The Church understands baptism as the sacramental entrance into the Church and thus into the fullness of Christian life. That is why we really understand baptism only to the extent that we understand Christianity and the Church. So if we wish to render baptism understandable, we must in fact speak of Christianity and of the Church herself. Since it is, of course, impossible to explain sufficiently, in a short paper, what Christianity means in the Church, what we will say about baptism is necessarily fragmentary, not more than a rather arbitrary selection among things that should be said about baptism.

According to Christian doctrine baptism, as we read in the New Testament, is the sacrament of faith and justification. Hence it imparts that life which God gives us through his self-communication, or indwelling, or sealing with the Holy Spirit, in order to make us capable of eternal life in immediate unity and community with God. So, when we wish to explain baptism, we should in fact speak of God, his eternal life, his self-communication to us through the grace of the Holy Spirit. But that would no longer be the doctrine about one single sacrament or active sign of grace, but the doctrine about Christian humanity in general.

That is why for our considerations we will use another approach, which may help us better and more clearly to handle the main difficulty concerning baptism which today troubles quite a number of people even in the Church. They ask why baptism, and even baptism of infants, exists, when we know, or at least hope, that God leads to eternal salvation every person of good will, hence also non-Christians, "heathens," and even atheists (if they obey the voice of conscience). Before trying to answer this difficulty, a few preliminary remarks are in order.

DISPOSITION AND GESTURE

Persons are one yet manifold. Their unity is the unity of many things that are distinct but still constitute a unity. These differences condition each other in this unity and neither difference nor unity can reach its own perfection without the other. We have put this very abstractly. But what we mean is universally observable in human life. For example, the love of one person for another, considered as an inner disposition, differs from a glance, a gesture, a caress, and so on. Yet the inner disposition of love can often fully develop only if it is also expressed and "embodied" in such a bodily gesture. The inner solidarity of several people is something in their disposition. Yet it often becomes wholly itself only when these people share a common meal.

In such cases and in countless others there is in people an interior and an interior. They differ from each other, yet they belong together. The interior reaches its perfection wholly and clearly only when it manifests and embodies itself in the exterior. Occasionally the exterior may deceive (as in a Judas-kiss) when the exterior, which should be actualized and manifested by it, is not really present. But when people perform the exterior action sincerely and readily, that action may bring about the interior disposition. Thus many people have suddenly and intimately understood the meaning of prayer simply by kneeling down. Love itself may increase as innermost reality simply through the fact that one person treats another person with love. We will suppose that these remarks have been understood and accepted. The question remains what they may mean for an understanding of baptism.

IRREVOCABLE OFFER

Let us quietly and confidently start from this certitude: God loves all human beings, having called them by their name. At the moment of calling them into existence, God has already, in free love, inserted himself with all his reality in each person as innermost strength and as final end. God offers himself to all persons and to their freedom as their goal and, at the same time, as their innermost strength and their dynamism toward that goal, even though human freedom may reject that offer that is always given and always irrevocable. This is possible because human beings are undeniably spiritual beings, who nevertheless may freely, in an animal way, contradict their inalienable being. Seen from God's side, this ever-present offer of divine life exists, whether we know it or not, because God has willed the whole of humankind for the sake of the Word-made-flesh, because the whole of humanity has been adopted by God in Jesus, in the one who was crucified and raised from among the dead. That is why God's innermost offer of grace, from which no human being is ever excluded, is also essentially "Christian."

Now this innermost presence of grace in each person wants to embody itself in all the dimensions of humanity and to become manifest as a divine and "Christian" reality. It is intended for the individual as irreplaceably individual and as member of the whole of humanity. Of course, this inner presence of grace in persons can also exist without the appropriate outer embodiment and manifestation. Christian faith has always known this: it speaks of baptism of desire as justifying, that is, as endowing persons with divine life, even before they are baptized with water. It speaks of perfect contrition through which persons, even before receiving the sacrament of reconciliation, freely accept the divine life that is always proffered to them.

Yet this does not mean that the embodiment and manifestation of divine grace through the sacrament (baptism or sacrament of reconciliation) is something that is up to individuals. For, of its very nature, this divine life in the grace of the Holy Spirit wants to embody itself, to become visible in the social domain of believers, called the Church. Those who freely and guiltily resist this tendency of divine life to become visible in a bodily and social way not only reject this embodiment as such but also the very offer of grace. It is as though we said in our heart that we love a person with whom we live while refusing to render that person a necessary service through which this inner love should be experienced. Refusing to render the service is tantamount to denying the inner love, even though love and service are not the same thing. This applies also to baptism.

If someone knows nothing about baptism or is unable to receive it, divine life nevertheless lives, in the innermost heart of this person, as proffered or as freely accepted divine life. As accepted, even if not in some expressly conscious way, the person welcomes this divine offer in what we call faith, hope, and love. These virtues may be present, even in a wholly unconscious way, in unselfish acts of love for neighbor and in other decisions through which one gets involved in the divine life.

BODY OF GRACE

However, when people are living in a situation where the bodily and social manifestation of divine life, called baptism, is possible, they cannot say that they desire divine life while rejecting its bodily manifestation. That would be as if someone refused a concrete act of love while, at the same time, affirming one's love. Or, as if a person refused to grow because it is said that even as an embryo one is already a human being and, for that reason, the person forgoes further development. Baptism is the concrete becoming-visible of the divine life, insofar as this life is also a Christian and therefore an ecclesial life. Because this embodiment of the divine life is also an ecclesial reality, it is not up to individuals in what way they will shape this bodily expression of divine life. They must shape it in *the way* that is prescribed to them by this ecclesial community. And this way is precisely baptism with water and the invocation of the triune God. When somebody wants to state a juridically effective intention to bequeath an estate to a freely chosen heir, his intention, in order to be effective, must be stated in a will that is valid according to the laws of society. Something similar is true for baptism with water.

We must still give some thought to two questions that follow from what precedes and that present some difficulties. The first question derives from the way in which we have approached the problem: sacramental causality with regard to grace seems to be less intelligible than it would be if we simply thought of the sacramental activity as the cause of grace, without first seeing baptism as manifestation and so as sign of the inner conferring of grace. The second difficulty that we must consider refers to the baptism of children.

ACTION OF GOD HIMSELF

Up to now we have seen baptism as the historical and social manifestation of divine grace, of God's coming into our innermost being and God's offering of self to our freedom as the power of faith, hope, and love directed toward God. Seen in this way baptism seems only to be the disclosure of a reality that is also given without it. However, the doctrine of the Church speaks of an efficient causality of the sacraments, which is also applied to baptism with regard to grace. Can these two statements be reconciled? Or can we say that the character of baptism as a sign disclosing grace on the one hand and the efficient causality of baptism on the other mutually condition each other, so that we may affirm baptism as the cause of grace *because* it is the sign of grace? It stands to reason that, if we are to speak this way, we cannot make use of an arbitrary concept of cause, but we must have a correct and meaningful notion of the causality that is at work here. Even traditional textbook theology draws our attention to this point when it states that in baptism God is the real and the only creative cause of divine grace, that baptism may be conceived only as an "instrumental cause." Theologians offer the most diverse theories to explain this instrumental causality of the sacraments.

One cannot reject a priori our approach to an understanding of baptism, which started from the fact that baptism is a sign, for the following reason. When adults are baptized they must, in order to receive the sacrament worthily, bring to baptism faith, hope, and charity. The usual expectation is that this charity is love of God for God's own sake. It must be "perfect love," as distinguished from the love that is implied in "imperfect contrition," that is, contrition caused by fear. When these conditions are fulfilled, the common doctrine of the Church and of theologians holds that these adults come to baptism already "justified"; they have already accepted the divine life offered to them; they are, through the indwelling of the Holy Spirit, children of God. In such a case at least those who are baptized already possess what baptism is supposed to give them, the grace of justification.

Theologians try to avoid this difficulty by saying that the baptism of persons who are already justified causes an increase of this grace of justification and gives them besides something which they do not yet possess, namely, the "baptismal character" and social and juridical incorporation in the visible Church. This explanation seems to be rather artificial, but we cannot insist on this point.

In order to proceed, let us start from a consideration that was presented at the beginning. What happens when someone sincerely loves another person and, although for one reason or another he or she may not find it easy, addresses the decisive word of love to this other person? This word is a declaration and a decision about one's love. Yet this love is realized in its full intensity and definitiveness *through* this word; the love would not be the same if it did not express itself in its disclosure and so translate *itself* into reality. To that extent we may consider this word, the sign of this love, as being also its cause, because this love renders itself real through the disclosure that is, at the same time, distinct from it.

Let us apply this to the baptism of those who are already justified. They bring to their baptism the grace of God that has already freely been accepted. But through the ceremony of baptism this very grace wants to make itself visible historically (in time and space, in the body) and socially (in the Church). And by becoming visible in this way it becomes present also in the bodily and social dimensions of the baptized person. Baptism is an effect of grace in such a way that through it this grace itself assumes full reality. And to that extent baptism is also the cause of grace. (The explanation mentioned above, is correct in itself: that baptism "increases sanctifying grace" in the person who is already justified before being baptized. Only it understands this "increase" almost as a quantitative addition, not as a self-realization of the same grace that is fully realized on account of the sacramental sign.) When we look at it this way, we understand what we mean when we say that the sacrament, *as* sign of grace, is the cause of grace. If we understand things correctly, sacramental sign and sacramental cause do not occur next to each other, but in each other.

THE BAPTISM OF CHILDREN

Finally we must present a few considerations about the baptism of children, which for so many centuries was taken for granted in the Church. Today it has again come under attack because (as some say) there is no mention of it in the New Testament and it contradicts the personal character of becoming a Christian. The Church nevertheless clings inexorably to the fundamental correctness and meaningfulness of the baptism of children, although we may not affirm with the same assurance the obligation of baptizing children.

Why is the baptism of children meaningful? Why should it not be rejected by parents who say that becoming a Christian and a member of the Church should be left to the free decision of the child, that the child should therefore not be baptized before it is of age? First, that which baptism reveals visibly and socially is not something optional, something about which people may decide as they please. For God's love, through which God becomes the innermost dynamism of human beings and of their history, is irrevocably and always prior to a personal free decision. God asks us whether or not we are willing to accept the challenging love of God, whether it is to turn, through our free decision, into our salvation or our judgment. We are necessarily being invited — whatever our answer to the invitation — and baptism discloses this irrevocable "being-invited" by the holy love of God. When we are born, we may accept or we may hate our existence, but we cannot get rid of it. Human freedom is always and unquestionably a reaction to something that we have not chosen; it is not merely creative in an empty space. So if in baptism that which a human person really is becomes manifest — namely the creature loved by God, destined to receive divine life — then freedom does not suffer any injustice, because, with regard to God and the world, it is always a responsive freedom that never has the first word.

Should someone object that baptism not only manifests the inescapable relationship between human persons and God, but that it also makes them members of a visible Church, something which they ought to be allowed to choose freely, we would answer: in her real nature the Church understands herself as the historical and social manifestation of the fact that all persons are called by God. That is why the Church feels that belonging to it is a natural "becoming-visible" of the standing invitation addressed to everyone by God. We may admit, without going into detail, that in earlier times the Church concluded from this fact that the baptized belong in the Church, a conclusion that is questionable. She also concluded that she had the right to use compulsion against baptized people, a right which, as she understands herself, she did not have with regard to the nonbaptized. But the Church no longer draws such a conclusion, because she admits that both the baptized and the nonbaptized enjoy the same freedom of conscience. Thus the difficulty deriving from church membership no longer exists. Baptism is the obvious manifestation of the fact that every human being should belong to the Church. As such it is not an anticipation of a decision that depends only on human freedom.

But something else deserves our attention with respect to the baptism of children. In our region of the world it is overlooked because here baptisms of children are frequent and baptisms of adults unusual. If baptism is the effective becoming-visible of God's love for human beings, bestowing upon them not some created good but God's very being, it is of its very nature an invitation to accept this love. That is why we can say that the baptism of children reaches its real meaning and completion when eventually they accept in faith, hope, and love this love of God which is offered to them. The baptism of children reaches its full meaning and purpose only in adults.

The decisive question is not whether, through the love and fidelity of their ordinary Christian life, they accept God's self-donation offered to them when they were children or whether, time and again, explicitly in Christian freedom, they ratify the baptism they received as children. The ultimate and decisive acceptance of baptism in personal freedom takes place throughout the length and breadth of human and Christian life. Yet it is certainly good and helpful to revive explicitly, with faith and confidence, the memory of the baptism received at the start of life.

That which the liturgy presents to each Christian during the Easter Vigil in the renewal of the baptismal vows might also take place independently of the official liturgy in the life of every Christian. They look back upon their life, knowing that from the start they have been accompanied by God's power and love and that, in his providence, God has lovingly disposed that this love should be manifest to them, in a bodily and explicit way, by means of their baptism at the beginning of their life. Christians may time and again render the event of their baptism present and accept it. When we read in 2 Timothy 1:6f., "Hence I remind you to rekindle the gift of God that is within you through the laying on of hands; for God did not give us a spirit of timidity but a spirit of power and love and self-control," all Christians can take this word, which was originally said about the conferring of a church function, and apply it to their own baptism. In it they received the divine Spirit of love and they have the duty to keep this divine fire burning. We should also, in the privacy of our room, renew our baptismal vows.

RENEWAL OF BAPTISM

To help us understand what is meant by renewal of baptism, we should first remember that a Christian's life of grace is a real *life*. It develops, grows, and increases during a life lived in free Christian responsibility. There is a life and expansion of grace wherever people freely direct their life toward God, hence also in the seeming banality of everyday life. Now this growing and maturing life is, of course, the life and growth of the grace that is received with sacramental tangibility in baptism. So it is a life and increase and ripening of baptismal grace. When we are honest, when we work hard and unselfishly in the service of our neighbor, when we are courageous and control our moods, when we remain cheerful, even when it is far from easy, but especially when we make the great and heavy decisions of life in a Christian way, we also come nearer to God (even though we do not always explicitly think of God), and the grace of our baptism keeps growing. In order to avoid expressions that are too simplistic and quantitative, we might better say: baptismal grace is more and more assimilated, becomes more deeply rooted in the center of a human existence.

All of this is properly already a renewal of baptism, even when we do not expressly think of the fact that we are baptized Christians; baptismal grace lives and grows in the whole length and breadth of Christian life. Yet in daily life we might also once in a while tell ourselves explicitly, "You have been baptized. The Holy Spirit lives and wants to operate in the innermost core of your being. God has called you by your name, sanctifying and divinizing you. God wishes this divine life to grow strong in your life, all the way down to the smallest details. It is not enough for you to be sealed with the Holy Spirit; you must also bring forth the fruits of the Spirit, which according to Paul are love, joy, peace, patience, goodness, fidelity, meekness and self-control." When we try in this way explicitly to remember our baptismal grace and expressly urge ourselves to live out of its spirit and power, we explicitly renew our baptism. If we seriously mean it and we honestly try to do what we prompt ourselves to do, baptismal grace really increases, it acquires increasing influence in our life, and we become what we were in the seed planted at baptism: Christians.

The words "renewal of baptism" should also remind us of the renewal of baptism that is celebrated in common by a Christian community in liturgical solemnity during the Easter Vigil. Over and beyond what was mentioned above, such a feast can call our attention to two main points: in such a renewal of baptism we also renew our rejection of the dark powers of evil that are always trying to take over our life. We are reminded therefore that a renewal of baptism, whether or not it is made explicitly in everyday life, also has to include the fight against evil in and around ourselves, in individual life and in society. We are also reminded that the grace of our baptism can stay alive and active in us only if we are always ready to deny ourselves certain pleasures, if we have the courage to say a Christian no. The renewal of baptism in a Christian community reminds us also that the life and growth of baptismal grace is not an individualistic event, but that we can ultimately bring our Christian existence to maturity only in common prayer, love, and solidarity in grace, even as the different members of a body or the branches of a vine can reach their full development only in union with the whole of which they are a member or a branch.

19

THE STATUS OF THE SACRAMENT OF RECONCILIATION

Recently a new development has occurred in the sacrament of reconciliation that deserves to be examined.[1] For many centuries (since the early Middle Ages) the practice of this sacrament had hardly changed. Catholics had the impression that they were obliged to confess their sins at least once a year to their parish priest. And besides this the so-called confession of devotion was taken for granted by pious Catholics, who confessed minor sins in the sacrament of reconciliation more than once a year, or even as often as they received Holy Communion.

Today the sacrament of reconciliation is going through a critical stage. To put it in a few words, people go less frequently to confession, in many cases the sacrament is not received at all by Catholics who consider themselves devout Christians and who most likely receive Holy Communion every time they attend Mass. We wish to give some thought to the way one might pass judgment on such a crisis.

It is, of course, not true that every new development in the Church must be evaluated positively. There are undoubtedly developments of longer or shorter duration that are less desirable, that might even have to be resisted and suppressed. Because such a thing is quite possible in the Church, the question arises how the present state of the sacrament of reconciliation should be evaluated. This question must be asked, but the answer is not immediately clear. To answer it, we must first say something about another question, namely, what obligation divine law

[1]On this see also K. Rahner, "Vom Geheimnis menschlicher Schuld und göttlicher Vergebung," in *Geist und Leben* 55 (1982): 39–54.

imposes and does not impose on Christians with regard to individual sacramental confession.

CONFESSION AND SERIOUS SIN

The answer to the question about the obligation of divine law is that Catholics are obliged to receive the sacrament of reconciliation if, and only if, they have committed a sin that is subjectively and objectively grave. We will not inquire here how quickly they have to fulfill this obligation. This may be considered a secondary question, which we do not have to take up here. Actually this question has been answered by a commandment of the Church issued by the Fourth Lateran Council, which obliges a Catholic who has committed a sin that is objectively and subjectively grave to fulfill this obligation of the divine law within a year.

But we have to give some more attention to the general principle that we have mentioned above. According to the doctrine of the Council of Trent, it is difficult to question the obligation of Catholics who have committed a serious sin to erase their guilt by receiving the sacrament of reconciliation in individual confession, although even here a few theologians would have questions to ask. In such a case, neither purely subjective contrition with a private prayer for forgiveness nor a so-called penitential service is sufficient. Let us then take as our starting point that in such a case there exists the obligation of an "auricular" confession, an obligation imposed by divine law, which follows both from the nature of a person's relation to the Church and from the nature of the Church herself and of the sacrament of reconciliation within the Church. Hence it is not within the Church's power to abolish this obligation.

However, with such a principle the concrete practical question facing us is not yet answered. For when we admit this principle and want to translate it into practice, the question unavoidably arises about when such an objectively and subjectively grave sin exists. It is obvious that there are sins which do not belong to this category, which therefore a Christian does not have to confess. In catechism jargon we usually call them venial sins, as opposed to so-called grave or mortal sins. In other words, the question comes up now how to distinguish these two kinds of sins, which are essentially different. We are speaking not only of the *objective* difference between a grave and a venial sin, for instance, the objective difference between a murder and a voluntary inattention or distraction during prayer, or a voluntary but slight unkindness with regard to another person.

That there exists such an objective difference is a doctrine of the Church, which was clearly stated by the Council of Trent. But when we speak of an obligation to confess, we have to consider not only an objective distinction between grave and venial sins (only the former having to be confessed) but also the question of the person's subjective guilt. Certainly a person may violate an obligation that is, of its very nature, objectively grave in such a way that in God's eyes this person is not really guilty. It is wrong to poison somebody. But if, through some negligence, a pharmacist makes a mistake in preparing a prescription, and the client dies as a result, we may speak of an objectively grave offense. Yet subjectively, the error does not in the proper sense render the pharmacist absolutely guilty before God, that between God and this person there would occur an absolute, albeit remediable, separation.

So this principle, that we must have grave sins forgiven by means of an individual sacramental confession, must be understood for sins that are both objectively *and* subjectively grave. In the case of a sin that is objectively grave, but not really experienced as such by the person in question, there is, according to the doctrine of the Council of Trent, no absolute duty, obliging under pain of another grave sin, to make use of individual sacramental confession.

SUBJECTIVELY AND OBJECTIVELY GRAVE SIN

For many centuries — at least from the early Middle Ages until the present time — religious education in the Church more or less neglected this fundamental distinction between a sin that is both subjectively and objectively grave and one that is grave *only* objectively speaking. Ordinary Catholics in the sacramental confession that they made at least once a year, or even more often, simply confessed whatever the usual moral teaching called objectively grave. Not much thought had been given to the question whether the traditional evaluation of a sin by moral theologians was truly certain, or only a more or less reasonable but not absolutely certain opinion of theologians.

The obligation of Catholics, if not legitimately prevented, to attend Sunday Mass was called a grave obligation by theologians. Whoever did not fulfil it had committed a grave sin. Not much attention has been paid to the fact that in many cases the question came up whether an objective transgression of this commandment of the Church was also subjectively a grave sin. Catholics simply confessed: "I have missed Sunday Mass so many times, although I would have been able to attend it, since I was not sick or in some other way legitimately prevented." And they have considered this the concrete performance of their obligation to confess serious sins.

Quite recently, for a number of reasons, there has been much discussion about what constitutes not only objectively serious sin but also one that is subjectively serious as well. First, even moral theologians now admit that, in a great number of cases, notwithstanding traditional moral teaching, things that were formerly considered to be serious obligations or objectively grave sins are really not such. It is difficult to affirm today that every voluntary omission of a single Sunday Mass plunges Catholics into the same utter enmity with God that they would have incurred if they had treacherously murdered another person.

When we speak of sin today, we will make more distinctions and, in many cases, be more lenient with regard to *objective* gravity. We will also rightly and without any moral laxity say that, in many cases, there is no subjectively grave guilt. Many people do not in fact possess that power of moral discernment by which every objectively serious conflict with the divine will is felt to be so grave that they tell themselves: "If I do this anyway I say a really radical no to God and to God's will."

We know more clearly today than ever before that a great number of people have little power of discernment with regard to the urgency of a moral duty. That ability is often weaker than would be desirable. But it is weak. We know from modern psychology how often we may admit a lower degree of responsibility, not only in criminal cases but also in everyday life. Moreover, we also have the impression, rightly, that people who are poor, weak, living in a difficult environment will not so easily and so often enter into such a conflict with the divine will that this conflict (if not settled through contrition) would have to be punished with eternal damnation by God's holy justice. We may even — and once more not without good reason — be of the opinion that a really subjectively serious sin, one that deserves eternal damnation, is not something that will occur very often and very easily in the life of a decent Christian. In this respect we are more optimistic, and why would we not have the right to be?

We do not have too high an opinion of the moral quality of the average Christian. We know that they are weak and strongly influenced by a public opinion that may be very un-Christian. Because of their background, their lack of education, and the ups and downs of life, they may have a relatively obtuse and primitive moral sense. We cannot be very enthusiastic about the moral standards of most people today.

But at the same time, as Christians, we cannot rightly claim that people today are, as a rule, so wicked in the very core of their free will, that they address an absolute no to God, which is but the reverse side of eternal perdition. Basically we are more optimistic than Saint Augustine, who considered humanity a *massa damnata* out of which only a few were saved through the exceptional grace of God.

DECREASE IN THE FREQUENCY OF CONFESSION

However, while on the question of the existence of subjectively grave guilt we take a more cautious position than formerly, and while we have a right to have an optimistic opinion of human beings in spite of their primitive moral sense, the question of when and how often a Catholic is strictly obliged to receive the sacrament of reconciliation is much more difficult. In its pastoral activity the Church has not tried very hard to make the faithful aware of the difference between objectively grave and subjectively grave guilt, nor has it elaborated this doctrine. But according to the Church's official teaching it is undoubtedly true that only when the faithful have a sufficient moral (albeit not absolute) certitude that their sin is also subjectively grave are they obliged by divine law to go to confession. And if today, as explained above, we judge for good reasons that subjectively grave sins do not occur often or naturally in the life of an ordinary Christian, we have a right to say that the existence of a divine command to receive the sacrament of reconciliation does not occur as frequently as the formal pastoral doctrine practically and tacitly assumed.

We might, of course, say much more about what I explained above. We might speak of the problem of the difference between venial and grave sin, a question that is not as simple as I have presented it above and as it is also assumed to be in our ordinary moral theology. We might inquire how, in the practice of Christian life, we might, with a certain moral certitude, reach a reasonable conclusion that in this case we have to do only with a subjectively venial sin, and in another case with a subjectively grave sin, and so on.

But here and now we cannot further discuss all these very important questions. We can only observe that, if we interpret more accurately the obligation to confess, we will find it not so strange and inconsistent that people go less frequently to confession. Is this decline in the frequency of confession desirable or deplorable? Should it be stopped and reversed by means of prudent pastoral education? This is another question, about which we will have to say something later on. However, should someone ask whether the decreasing number of confessions is a clear proof that a great number of Catholics ignore the obligation to go to confession when they have committed a subjectively serious sin, we would answer this question negatively. The purely numerical decrease in the number of confessions does not allow us to conclude with certitude that today's Catholics transgress an important divine command. This might be said only if, on the one hand, people rarely went to confession and, on the other hand, if really subjectively grave sins occurred not rarely, but frequently. But since the latter statement cannot be made with certainty, and since we may certainly hope that such sins which render human beings worthy of eternal damnation do not, at least in a normal Christian life, occur frequently, or even at all, we may not, from the lower frequency of confessions, conclude with certainty that Catholics do not in fact comply with an obligation to confess that is objectively binding for them.

True, there are also Catholics who infringe such an obligation, while committing really serious sins, sins that are both objectively and subjectively grave. When a mother, who might very well have another child, who economically and personally would be quite capable of it, who is not living in cramped external conditions, but who merely out of laziness or for other shabby reasons, accepts an abortion, there is a real possibility that we are dealing not only with an objectively but also with a subjectively serious transgression of the fifth commandment.

But even if this is granted, it is not yet certain that subjectively serious guilt occurs so frequently in the life of the ordinary Christian that we may conclude, because of the infringement of the obligation to confess, that there exists a frightful and massive dechristianization. The praxis of the Church in pastoral activity, in sermons, in promoting the use of the confessional, and in catechetical instruction in the schools should not try to bring back a more frequent use of the sacrament by using false and invalid arguments, or by concealing principles that apply objectively in this matter and that we have mentioned above. Even a very devout Christian, on the authority of God's command, might say even at Easter: "I am not going to confession, and I am not thereby infringing the Church's commandment, because thanks to God's grace I know that I am not guilty of any subjectively grave sin; therefore even at Easter there is no obligation for me to receive this sacrament."

I used to know a pious old lady who, possibly on account of a strange set of psychological reasons, was simply unable to enter the confessional and there to whisper something in the priest's ear. And she was a devout, prayerful woman, who would never hurt anybody and who loved God with her whole heart. We should tell her: If you have these subjective inhibitions against confession, you do not have to confess, even at Easter. That is perfectly all right, in full agreement with the doctrine of the Church and her commandments.

However, the considerations outlined above do not solve the problem. If only that which we have said up to now were important and taken into account, we might say that the present falling off in the frequency of confession is legitimate and nothing but the fulfillment of the divine precept that only really serious sins have to be confessed. We are rightly convinced that such sins are not all too frequent, or at least that there is no proof that they are very frequent within the Church. Therefore, we might conclude, if today confessions are so scarce, this is nothing but the obvious application of the dogma which the Church proclaimed at the Council of Trent. However, things are not quite that simple.

CONFESSION — NOT PUT OFF UNTIL DEATH

To proceed further we must first submit a general consideration. There are necessarily in the Church many important things that are not immediately covered by a divine order, by the church institution itself. There are, for example, religious orders in the Church. The fact that a Franciscan, a Jesuit, a Benedictine order, and so on exists may not be considered a divine command strictly obliging on the Church. Yet there must exist in the Church the kind of life that flourishes in religious orders, that is organized and protected by them. We might say that the divine instructions about the Church and its life are, as it were, something like the skeleton of a living organism. Yet much more than bones are needed in the organism. There must be flesh, there must be metabolism, and so on. Something similar is true in the Church. There are religious orders, there are certain devotions, there are certain developments in theology, there are theological schools, there are special ways of leading a Christian life. All of these aspects of Christian life are present in the Church not simply as the result of a divine obligation.

Almost paradoxically we might say: The Church is obliged by God to include realities, activities, signs of life that in themselves are not imposed by God. Whoever would claim that whatever expresses the life of the Church, of Christianity, needs a divine authentication *juris divini* would state something that is absolutely false and would — however strange this may sound — suppress the real life of the Church. In order to be fully alive the Church must include activities and lifestyles that cannot themselves immediately appeal to a divine authorization and that nevertheless belong more or less necessarily to the full life of the Church.

Something similar applies to frequent confession. The first evidence we might bring up is the simple fact noticed even by a few of the church fathers that, if only very serious sins were confessed, this obligation would in fact cancel itself out or be put off until the individual's death. If, for instance, it was certain that all the people waiting at the confessional had committed very grave sins — perjuring themselves, breaking their marriage vows in a really terrible way, and so on — it would be obvious that these people would not be waiting at the confessional, because, in that way they publicly accuse themselves of very grave sins. We cannot expect this from people.

This simple reason would already allow us to say that, if only grave sins were confessed because they have to be confessed, none would be confessed at all. From the pastoral point of view, it is clear that the Church will see to it that the sacrament of reconciliation is received also by those who are not obliged to receive it on account of a really grave sin. The ancient Church in fact experimentally demonstrates this. In the beginning only very grave sins were confessed. The result was that Christians often postponed confession until their deathbed.

From the point of view of divine law it would be hard to demonstrate that such a postponement of confession of serious sins until the time of death is explicitly contrary to God's law. But everyone understands that a truly active Christian life, which supposes that one takes sin very seriously and that one is firmly resolved to be at peace with God, would be destroyed more or less by such a practice.

So from this point of view, the Church is right in her desire that the sacrament of reconciliation be used more often than is absolutely commanded. And ancient practice thoroughly convinced her that she may naturally use her powers of forgiving not only for grave sins, in the strict sense of the word, but also for other offenses and sins. Jesus' statement in John 20:23, that when the Church forgives sins, she does so before

God, does not make any a priori distinction between sins. That is why it would be foolish to claim that the Church can only forgive very serious sins and cannot use for other sins the full power of forgiving given her by Jesus.

Moreover, there are still many other reasons that render frequent confessions of devotion meaningful. We cannot fully present and develop them here, because this would lead us too much into a theology of sin, into a theology of the life of a Christian between grace and sin, into a complete theology of the Church and of her nature as the sacrament of forgiveness in general. That is not possible here. We will only briefly mention a few points.

SACRAMENTAL AND EXISTENTIELL FORGIVENESS

First, for many centuries Christians have had the impression that their sins were more certainly and clearly forgiven when they submitted them to the sacramental judgment of the Church and heard God's forgiving word expressly from the mouth of the Church. If we are honest and use sober theological reflection, this conviction is not so obvious, for it is obviously true that, apart from grave sins, such sins can also be forgiven by God if we are truly sorry for them and refrain from them. Without such an inner disposition, which basically already brings about the forgiveness of such sins, the sacrament of reconciliation too would not have any effect. For those who only admit their imperfections and sins without at the same time being sincerely sorry and resolved to avoid them, sacramental confession is perfectly meaningless and useless. It was obvious to Saint Thomas Aquinas that whoever receives the sacrament of reconciliation must normally come to it in a state of mind that by itself, before reception of the sacrament, already brings about the forgiveness of the sins for which one is truly sorry. From this point of view it is not so obvious why ordinary Christians feel that they may have more confidence in the remission of their sins when they receive sacramental absolution.

It would be better not to separate this inner — we might say existentiell[2] — process of grace, justification, and forgiveness from the sacramental, ecclesial, bodily signifying process in the sacrament. It stands to reason, for instance, that if unbaptized adults believe, hope, and love before being baptized and turn with an inner heart-felt decision toward

---

[2] *Existentiell* might also be rendered "personally felt." — Translator.

the God of love, forgiveness, and grace, they are already justified *before* their baptism. Yet nobody will say: Therefore these adults, who are justified by their subjective acts, should forgo baptism. According to the principle stated above, baptism would be unnecessary, since its purpose is to render persons justified, and since these persons, before their baptism, are already justified, in the state of grace, bound to God in love through grace, and so on. This example, taken from another sacrament, from the most fundamental sacrament, shows that we should not consider the inner process and its outer sacramental embodiment to be two processes lying next to each other without any connection. They must be viewed as an inner unity. The sacramental sign must be the ecclesial incarnation of that which happens in the innermost center of a person's existence.

SACRAMENTAL ACTIVITY AS EMBODIMENT

In other domains too it is true that we almost necessarily translate through bodily expressions the inner sentiments of our heart. We do not simply love each other, we embrace each other, kiss each other, and perhaps caress each other. We do not in inner secret loathing turn away from some outrage, we clench our fists. We do not merely adore God in the innermost core of our heart, we kneel down before God. In short, our innermost religious life in our relation to God spontaneously has the tendency to embody itself.

For the baptized sinner the fullest ecclesial embodiment of our turning away from guilt, of our turning back to God, is the Church's sacrament of reconciliation. There we not only hear mysteriously, intangibly, with the ears of faith, in the core of our heart, God's gentle word of forgiveness, we also hear with our bodily ears: "Your sins are forgiven." In God's place, commissioned by the Church, the priest causes the Church to make perceptible the intimate spiritual process, which — such is the nature of bodily humanity — has a congenital desire to be embodied.

Of course, this embodiment has many different degrees. When I like somebody I may shake hands with him, pat his back, I may perhaps also embrace him. And two people who love each other, who are really in love with each other, as a married couple, will express this innermost communion of their hearts not only by shaking hands or kissing each other, but in a much more intimate way. This embodiment of the most intimate subjective processes runs the whole gamut of intensities. Thus people may really pray in the Lord's prayer, "forgive us our trespasses," while having the genuine and true awareness, based on their faith, that God forgives them their sins. But they may also express this embodiment of their contrition, their hope of forgiveness, and their confidence in God in a much clearer and more solid way, precisely by having recourse to the sacrament of reconciliation. And even from the purely human point of view, independently of the Church's teaching on sacramental activity, such an expression of a human attitude rooted in our bodily nature not only expresses this inner attitude, but reciprocally it strengthens and deepens it.

When, for instance, two persons who love each other in true communion have in some way offended each other, it may happen — as is often the case in everyday life — that this is settled simply by carrying on as before without mentioning it further. Each party thinks, as it were, "Let bygones be bygones, let's forget it." But it may also happen that such an inner readiness to forgive becomes more radical, more genuine, more determined, if they express their forgiveness to each other. Pascal knew that a gesture expressing humility is not only the expression but also the cause of inner humility. There have been many people who have, as it were, finally had the courage to capitulate in love and hope before God only *after* kneeling down and not before.

In other words, the sacramental embodiment of contrition and forgiveness between God and humanity serves not only to express the fact of forgiveness in a human incarnational way, it also has the purpose of arousing that inner attitude of which it is a sign and an expression. This is the remarkable thing in human beings, that the body shapes the soul and the soul shapes the body. The inner and outer life are intimately connected, hence that *mutual* relation between that which in our body expresses our feelings and that which induces them.

SOCIAL DIMENSION OF SIN AND FORGIVENESS

Many more considerations might, of course, be presented, but we cannot take them up here. For instance, the fact that practically, in all minor or major offenses and mistakes, we not only go astray as individuals, but we also assume a social debt. That too, among many other points, should be more carefully considered. Taking up again a conviction that seemed obvious in the ancient and medieval Church until Luther, the Second Vatican Council taught that ecclesial forgiveness of sins also means our reconciliation with the *Church*. The sinner offends not only God but also, more or less intensely, the Body of Christ. And this offense inflicted on the Body of Christ is forgiven when one turns back to God with sorrow. It is therefore natural that this peace with the Church be embodied in and sealed by an act of the Church.

Much more might be said about this question that refers more to the usefulness of confession for one's supernatural growth, but we cannot do so here. It is a fact that most people clearly and deliberately face their sinfulness only when these sins are acknowledged and forgiven in the sacrament of reconciliation. Christians who lead a really Christian life must, of course, attach great importance to the petition for forgiveness of their sins in the Our Father. They should likewise take part in the confession of sins at the beginning of the eucharistic celebration, even though this is not in the strictest sense a sacramental action. They should occasionally attend a penitential service. Every night, in their evening prayers they should ask God's pardon for their sins, and so on. But individual sacramental confession, even though not imposed by divine law, is a concrete action that helps ordinary Christians to live up to this inner disposition which makes them constantly turn away from sin and turn back to God. The more searching examination of conscience, the possibility of making, on the occasion of such a sacramental confession, what the French call a *revision de vie*, all these and many other advantages are given with sacramental confession, advantages that Christian should not scorn and by which they may be induced to make use of sacramental confession when they are not strictly obliged to do so.

FREQUENCY OF CONFESSION

The question of the frequency of confession can probably be answered only on an individual basis. It depends on so many things: on the possibility or the practical impossibility of going frequently to confession, on the individual disposition of each person, and on the kind of life each one has to lead and in which more or less serious and numerous occasions of sin may occur. These and other factors make it difficult to suggest a general norm for the frequency of devotional confession. So we will not try to do it. But we will say that we surely may be excused from sacramental confession if, on looking back over a short span of our life, we can say, with some reason, that nothing has happened of which we might seriously repent.

Of course, we may be sorry for more things than the ordinary Christian might consider. There is unkindness, indifference with regard to one's duties, lack of interest for one's environment, lack of care for one's neighbor, for whom one is perhaps responsible. There are such things that spread over a whole life almost unnoticeably. Thus a serious examination of conscience may make it eventually more possible for us seriously to repent and to change than we would suspect in our everyday unfeeling mood. On the other hand, as we said, nobody should feel obliged or bound to go to confession who can really say: "Here and now I really have nothing to repent. My daily life has proceeded so normally, albeit in a rather bourgeois way, that I cannot feel it right now as the proper object of a sacramental accusation."

When we look at both parts of our reflections a few more remarks seem called for. They are, to my knowledge, rarely mentioned or suggested in usual pastoral practice. If lay people (I am speaking of them here) are inclined to receive the sacrament more frequently, even though they are convinced that, strictly speaking, they do not need sacramental absolution, they should make a wise choice of confessor. It stands to reason that, although all elements of a sacramental procedure must be present in every confession — examination of conscience, contrition, confession of sin, absolution — in a confession of devotion the emphasis shifts more to the subjective life of the penitent than is the case in the absolution given for a serious sin. In other words, frequent confession merely out of routine, in which practically nothing happens for the subject's inner life, makes no sense as a sacramental activity.

The possibility of taking such a confession of devotion seriously also depends on which confessor one chooses. Ever since the Middle Ages the Church has tried more and more to put a great selection of confessors at the disposal of lay people. While the Fourth Lateran Council still prescribed that the yearly confession be made to the local pastor, the Church in canon law, made it more possible and pastorally feasible to choose a confessor freely. In a confession of devotion as we understand it today, quite correctly to my mind, it is evident that a mere sacramental absolution does not, in this case, make much sense. That is why the inner attitude of the penitent is of decisive importance, and such an attitude may be strongly influenced by a suitable confessor. There have been and there still are, of course, pastors who see in the greatest possible number of absolutions on Saturdays a triumph for their pastoral activity. There used to be Christians, for instance in convents where this was possible, who asked for absolution everyday in the sacrament of reconciliation.

Such practices that make no real sense for the life of the soul should be dropped. Ultimately the number of times we receive a sacrament does not matter. And that is why it is also important to choose the right kind of confessor for the correctly understood confession of devotion.

It is really not evident that every priest who has the liturgical and sacramental power of giving absolution is for this reason alone a suitable confessor. We should not exaggerate the effects of a sacrament. I believe that in the pious practice of the last few centuries there have frequently been confessions that were practically invalid. The accusation referred very often to sins which people really, in their heart, did not wish to give up. It followed that there was no real contrition; therefore the absolution was useless and ineffective. This may very often have happened in good faith, yet it is not to be recommended.

A good confessor should occasionally be ready for a serious conversation during confession. He should have an ear for things that have perhaps not been completely stated in the accusation, not in order to discover sins which the penitent would have forgotten or withheld — as happened with Don Bosco — but to discover real difficulties in the penitent's psychic life and to help him or her to the extent of his abilities. The confessor does not have to be a real psychotherapist in the sacrament. He has before him a penitent who is looking for forgiveness from God and the Church, not for psychotherapeutic advice. This may be quite true, yet the priest should not be an absolution-machine, because this makes no sense and is of no use. It contradicts the nature of a sacrament, in which, according to the doctrine of Saint Thomas, the person's inner personal collaboration is an inner element of sacramental activity and not merely a preparation for it. How can one find such a confessor? How should one speak to him in confession so that he may really be of help? The answers to these questions differ according to the penitent's different situations, and we cannot give any precise answers and directives.

LIST OF SOURCES

ANXIETY AND CHRISTIAN TRUST
IN THEOLOGICAL PERSPECTIVE
Published in *Christlicher Glaube in moderner Gesellschaft*, vol. 9 (Freiburg i Br., 1981), pp. 86–98. This is the second part of an article, "Angst und christliches Vertrauen," of which M. Boss wrote the first part.

NUCLEAR WEAPONS AND THE CHRISTIAN
Written with T. Cremer, published in *Atomrüstung–christlich zu verantworten?*, edited by A. Battke (Dusseldorf, 1982), pp. 98–115.

PLEA FOR A NAMELESS VIRTUE
Published in *Mut zur Tugend: Von der Fähigkeit, menschlicher zu leben* (Festschrift for R. Scherer), edited by K. Rahner and B. Welte (Freiburg, 1980), pp. 11–18. Main title of essay: "Die Spannung austragen zwischen Leben und Denken."

INTELLECTUAL PATIENCE WITH OURSELVES
Lecture delivered on 13 May 1982 in Tübingen upon bestowal of the Dr. Leopold Lucas Prize; previously unpublished.

A BASIC THEOLOGICAL AND ANTHROPOLOGICAL
UNDERSTANDING OF OLD AGE
Published in *Nochmals glauben lernen: Sinn und Chancen des Alters*, edited by M. Schmid and W. Kirchschläger (Innsbruck, 1982), pp. 9–21. Main title of essay: "Lebensstationen im 20. Jahrhundert."

AUTHORITY
Published in *Christlicher Glaube in moderner Gesellschaft*, vol. 14 (Freiburg i. Br., 1982), pp. 5–36.

THE SITUATION OF THE SOCIETY OF JESUS SINCE ITS DIFFICULTIES WITH THE VATICAN
Lecture on 14 April 1982 in Freising at a symposium of the South German Province of the Society of Jesus; previously unpublished.

DIMENSIONS OF MARTYRDOM
Published in *Concilium* 18 (1983) 174–76.

EUCHARISTIC WORSHIP
Published in *Geist und Leben* 54 (1981) 188–91.

DEVOTION TO THE SACRED HEART TODAY
Published in *Korrespondenzblatt des Canisianums* 116 (1/1982/83) 2–8.

COURAGE FOR DEVOTION TO MARY
Published in *Geist und Leben* 56 (1983) 163–73. In part identical to "Die Gemeinschaft der Heiligen und die Heiligenverehrung," in *Die Heiligen heute ehren: Eine theologisch-pastorale Handreichnung*, edited by W. Beinert (Freiburg, 1983), pp. 233–42.

UNDERSTANDING CHRISTMAS
Published as the Foreword to *"Fürchtet euch nicht": Das Weihnachtsgeschehen in Zeugnissen der abendländischen Kultur*, edited by K. Gröning (Munich, 1983), pp. 11–19, largely derived from K. Rahner, *Die Gabe der Weihnacht* (Freiburg i. Br., 1980), and K. Rahner, *Gott ist Mensch geworden* (Freiburg i. Br., 1975).

THE THEOLOGY OF THE RELIGIOUS MEANING OF IMAGES
Lecture of 10 November 1983 in Munich; published in the biannual publication of the German Society for Christian Art, Munich (5/1983) 2–8.

ART AGAINST THE HORIZON OF THEOLOGY AND PIETY
Published in *Entschluß* 37 (1/1982) 4–7, under the title "Nicht jeder Künstler ist ein Heiliger: Zur Theologie der Kunst."

AGAINST THE WITCH HYSTERIA
Published in *Geist und Leben* 56 (1983) 284–91; also in *Friedrich Spee im Licht der Wissenschaften*, edited by A. Arens (Trier, 1984).

FAITH AND SACRAMENT
Published in *Fides Sacramenti: Sacramentum Fidei* (Festschrift for P. Smulders), edited by H. J. Auf der Mauer et al. (Assen, 1981), pp. 245–52, under the title "Kleine theologische Reflexion über die gegenseitige Beziehung von Glaube und Sakrament."

QUESTIONS ON THE THEOLOGY OF SACRAMENTS
Published in *Entschluß* 38 (11/1983) 6, 8–9. Main title of essay: "Das endgültige und siegreiche Zusagewort für die Welt."

BAPTISM AND THE RENEWAL OF BAPTISM
Published in *Entschluß* 37 (9/10/1982) 6–11. Main title of essay: "Das göttliche Feuer in sich lebendig halten."

THE STATUS OF THE SACRAMENT OF RECONCILIATION
Published in *Entschluß* 35 (9/10/1980) 4–12. Main title of essay: "Warum man trotzdem beichten soll."

Index

INDEX

Anxiety
  concerning salvation, 6
  existential, reason for, 7–8
  experienced only in synthesis
    with fear, 5
Anxiety and fear
  necessary distinctions be-
    tween, 5–6
  peace with God that ex-
    cludes, 6
  theological connection be-
    tween, 3–6
Apostolate of the Society of
    Jesus, 102
Art
  and theology, 163
  theology and the transcen-
    dent, 165–66
Authority
  basic elements concern-
    ing the appointment of
    bearers of, 71–72
  coercive power and, 74–76,
    82–83
  concrete manifestation of,
    68–69
  dignity of, 74
  general concept of, 61–68
  individual and collective
    bearers of, 70
  intrinsic nature of, 68–76

  necessity of, 76
  and order of precedence
    among bearers of, 74
  reality of, 69
  traditional, reasons for in
    church, 85

Baptism
  action of God himself,
    198–200
  of children, 200–202
  renewal of, 195–204
Burden of proof, powerful and,
    31–32

Central Committee of German
    Catholics, and armaments
    reduction, 25
Christian anthropology, 149–
    50
Christian trust, existential
    fundamentals of, 8–9
Christmas
  central difficulty of, 141
  descent of word of God into
    world, 143–44
  God's nearness, 147–48
  message of birth, 140–44
  remoteness in time, 142
  saved and liberated by the
    child, 147

THEOLOGICAL INVESTIGATIONS

ALSO BY
KARL RAHNER